SOUL
NATCHING

THE WAR FOR SOULS

STEVEN TREADWELL

ISBN: 979-8-88640-998-7 (sc)
ISBN: 979-8-88640-999-4 (hc)
ISBN: 979-8-89031-200-6 (e)

Because of the dynamic nature of the Internet, any web addresses or links contained in this book may have changed since publication and may no longer be valid. The views expressed in this work are solely those of the author and do not necessarily reflect the views of the publisher, and the publisher hereby disclaims any responsibility for them.

 THE EWINGS
PUBLISHING

One Galleria Blvd., Suite 1900, Metairie, LA 70001
1-888-421-2397

CONTENTS

PREFACE

America wake-up! Snap out of it! This is not a test! America has been mentally kidnapped and you have a need to come inside this book and take a look at your mind and you will be surprised what you are going to find. "True lies" are being told. Truth is the supreme reality of all existence and is beyond the reach of the mind. It may be true that the devil was kicked out of heaven because he got confused and spread confusion like a disease to a third of the angels in heaven. John 17:17 says, "Sanctify them through thy truth, thy Word is truth. Truth is the fact of reality.

A lie is the way things are situated or arranged to give a false impression, motives lay hidden. Abortion is a "True Lie" when a woman who is pregnant goes into a dark room and delete the baby that she is pregnant with as though it never happened. In order to delete something it has to first be there. A "True Lie" is a lie that becomes true when told or spoken by the Supreme Court or those in authority. They are leaders. No! Misleaders!

Isaiah 3:12, "As for My people children are their oppressors, and women rule over them! Moneylenders oppress my people and their creditors cheat them. Kids are unjustly inflicting hardship on society in a manner that is not morally just or fair. As women get into more leadership positions in a time when evil men and seducers will grow worse and worse.

The new generation of today is weighing heavily on the mind and the heart, and spirits of their parents and government causing depression and discomfort. The problem begins in the home and it then come from your home into the streets. My people your leaders are misleading you from the White House to the Church House into our homes.

Your American Idols on T V reflect "True Lies" on the T V screen as they magnify people who are no more than 4 feet tall and make them look to you as a super hero or irresistible. When a lie is magnified in your sight over and over again it becomes enticing to you because this all you see. A lens brought light to a fixed focal point makes a pretty man or woman. It is the sharpest man or woman because they are the only one you see right now. Keep moving and there is someone even prettier sharper right up the road.

A "True Lie" is when a man or woman believes they are of the opposite sex and begin to act in their mind as such. When American citizen vote for a lie and it becomes law will make it a "True Lie. The lie becomes true when our government made it law, but it is still a lie if it goes against the unadulterated, uncompromising, unchanging word of Jehovah God. A True Lie is when couples separate or devoice and their spouse is still living. The scriptures say, that they are bound or in prison with that person as long as he or she lives. Romans 7:2, 1 Corinthians 7:39. They must remain single in 1 Corinthians 7:10-17.

American Legal System has begun to validate Satan's agenda and fulfil the Bible prophecy in the book of Revelations. Come on in this book and check out your mind. These laws run from God who has all of humankind answers. The Lord God is listening to humankind defiance as they worship idols. The kingdoms of the earth must know that you alone are God. This is not a test.

Jehovah is the God of heaven and earth. Jehovah says in 2 Kings 19:27 LB, "I know everything about you. I know all your plans and where you are going next; and I also know the evil things you have said about me. And because of your arrogance against me I am going to put a hook in your nose and a bridle in your mouth and turn you back on the road by which you came".

These laws of direction of application made right wrong and illegal legal through the pressures of necessity. The passing of these laws causes Satan's agenda to intensify and mature by artificially accelerating the normal process of human kind through electronics. God's agenda is thrown out as a base runner in baseball in a forced play.

The American Heritage College Dictionary defines kidnapping as to seize and detain unlawfully, usually for a ransom, to snatch or seize. The laws of America has begun to snatch and nab the minds of its citizens aided by television, electronics and Tech giants by saying right is wrong and wrong is right. Those who do not agree with this tactic is being kidnapped mentally and terrorized because it goes against their beliefs.

Television and the laws of this great nation has become a force by planting seeds in the mind to renew the minds of its citizens about what to believe. This is an intense effort to brainwash its citizens to comply when they would normally disagree. Satan works thru women in America that go from country to country spreading the disease of homosexuality and abortion. They spread open rebellion and disobedience against God their creator. Many wars that you see are because of their fight to be free to go to hell. Misery loves company.

The different appetites in our government are a sudden inspiration placed in the brains of our society that controls us as a brain wave which regulate laws that control life. This small group has become the seat of our consciousness, our memory, emotion, intellectual abilities even your entire mind. Our government has us on the edge of rethinking our consciousness. This means they control your intellectual power, your intelligence, and your soul, which are your mind, will and emotions. The laws passed have become our primary director or planner as of an organization.

Satan is the father of lies and he has his agents out in full force to accomplish his mission. Passing laws like no prayer in schools, legalization of pot, even same-sex marriages (Alternate life styles), are steps of brainwashing. Wars have broken out on the borders of America to make sure that America gets its cut of the drugs coming in the country.

Satan's first step is to take away your fellowship with Jehovah our God. Satan knows that without God you can do nothing to defeat him. God wants both the king or president and its people to worship him. Not to replace it with the god of this world and begin to teach you that wrong is right and right is outdated by making you proud to be all wrong.

The American Heritage College Dictionary defines brainwashing as an intensive, forcible indoctrination aimed at replacing a person's basic convictions with an alternate set of beliefs. The application of this concentrated means of persuasion in order to develop a specific belief or motivation is a form of Mental Kidnapping and children have become the ransom.

This is why we have religion that is a social cultural system of designated behaviors and practices, morals, world views, and text along with sanctified places, and prophecies from the Holy Bible. This book has the message from God that was communicated to the prophets of the Holy Bible. Man was made in the image of God. This is the book that shows all of mankind how to return to their creator because of the fall of Adam and Eve in the Garden of Eden.

Adam was like God from the day of his creation. God created man and woman and blessed them, and called them man from the beginning (Genesis 5:1-2). America has too many appetites and has made too many choices contrary to the Word of Jehovah our God. These choices and appetites look like good ground but they are only Sinking Sand (Quick Sands). This is the time to worship the Lord with true enthusiasm and for us to not turn our back on him in any way.

CHAPTER 1

THE ENEMY OF THE SOUL

Those who believe in Jesus Christ have become God's voice here on the earth by guarding the ways of justice in a very imperfect world. When we do this God will cause us to dwell securely in the land. Revelation 12:12 after Satan was kicked out of heaven and the heavens rejoiced, but "Woe to the inhabiters of the earth and of the sea! "for the devil is come down unto you, having great wrath, because he knoweth that he hath but a short time."

Rebellion is the enemy of the soul and we must be strong in the Lord and in the power of his might, not yours. Keep doing things through Christ which strengthens you. Mark 8:36 "For what shall it profit a man, if he shall gain the whole world and lose his own soul." America does not have to worry about China, Russia, or any other country when it comes to war. A struggle came to humankind in the Garden of Eden after couple #1 rebelled with pride against God when Adam and Eve's mind was turned away from God by rationalizing in their mind.

God's true worshippers acknowledge the truth that follows godliness. Titus 1:2-3 says, "In hope of eternal life, which God, that cannot lie, promised before the world began; (Vs.3), "But in due times manifested his word thru preaching, which is committed unto me according to the commandment of God our Saviour. The most dangerous place on earth to be is in the pulpit. God want his ministers to warn the wicked about their sins.

Ezekiel 3:17-18 warns any that hold the truth of God, "Son of man, I have made thee a watchman unto the house of Israel: therefore hear the word at my mouth, and give them warning from me. (Vs.18), "When I say unto the wicked, Thou shalt surely die; and thou givest him not warning, nor speakest to warn the wicked from his wicked way, to save his life; the same wicked man shall die in his iniquity; but his blood will I require at thine hand." God tells us that all souls are mine in Ezekiel 18:4. The church is supposed to be collecting the souls that are his. The church organizations should be in the soul business. Every man or woman has to die for their own sins. The righteousness of the righteous shall be upon him and the wickedness of the wicked shall be upon him. God wants you to Repent and be sorry for your sins. Hebrews 4:1 says, Let us therefore fear, lest, a promise being left us of entering into his rest, any of you should seem to come short of it.

There is not a man, woman or group that I want to go to hell with and nothing I want to go to hell for. God want us to obey his voice and show a difference between thee holy and the profane. In the book of Ezekiel 22:30 speaks about the conspiracy of the prophets like raven wolves to destroy souls to get dishonest gain. They lie on God when he has not spoken. "And I sought for a man among them that should make up the hedge, and stand in the gap before me for the land, that I should destroy it: but I found none." Sin is the strength of sinners.

Chapter 33: tells the watchman if he sounds the warning and the people don't heed the warning their blood shall be upon their own head. But if you blow not the trumpet to warn the people their blood shall be upon your head. We should be getting rid of the seeds of evil doers. Those who trust in his own righteousness and commit iniquity, all his righteousness shall not be remembered.

Once saved always saved is a lie from the pits of hell. For his iniquity that he has committed he shall die for it, but if you warn him and he repent and turn from his sin and do that which is right his sins shall be forgiven and he shall surely live. Some think that when they get saved that they have a right to sin. The Holy Scriptures says, "God forbid, To whom you yield yourselves servants to obey his servant ye are to whom you obey, Whether sin unto death or obedience unto righteousness. If you die in your sins to hell you go. If you die living on that Holy Highway or the narrow road without spot or blemish you have a good chance for heaven.

The world is taking God for granted as it breathes his fresh air. The willingness to disobey God has become common to mankind and willful sinning shows no fear of God. Most men think that they can do what that want with their bodies. Adam only sinned once and now look at the condition of the world today. There was a void or opening in the hearts of men and women that was filled with Satan and sin. The lie told by Satan is that God is holding out on you, and you can do anything you want with your body. The lie is for those who live fleshly lives. Those in the flesh cannot please God. Romans 8:9 tells us that you are not your own and "Now if any man have not the Spirit of Christ, he is none of his."

Men and women are tattooing and branding themselves into a mental prison and a world of selfishness. Adam and Eve only sinned one time and God's creation is now saying, I can do whatever I want with my body. This is the world's attitude of disobedience towards God. Me, myself and I, are the selfish words that got Satan snatched and thrown out of heaven like a lightning bolt and his sinful merchandise brought the flood in Noah's day. All souls except Noah and his family were snatched from the face of the earth.

When Adam and Eve sinned they changed masters and their life became unstable. Their spiritual journey was threatened because death came upon all mankind and a curse upon the earth. Our world has gone beyond shame listening to the discourse of selfish people. When Adam and Eve were questioned by God because of their sin they played the blame game by using the merchandise of Satan who is the accuser of the brethren. Satan blamed God to Eve that God was holding out on her.

This is the world's belief that God is holding out on them. Adam blamed Eve and Eve blamed the serpent. There are a lot of leaders and pastors who are flipping the script against the word of God. "Except the Lord build the house they labor in vain that build it." They are giving into temptation, lust, money and power so they unloosen their Halo. They say that their "Halo" is pinching them and it is too tight. This makes them compromise their salvation.

As the world re-imagine itself the question that I want to ask you is who is on the Lord's side? Let this mind be in you that was also in Christ Jesus. We need to put on the mind of Christ and hold the thoughts, feelings and purposes of his heart. We have choices to make in our everyday life and we must choose all day long to obey God or listen to the lies of the Devil. There are too many people angry about their situation and feel like God is holding out on them.

Verily, Verily means to pay attention. We must keep our focus on God and his word. Let's pay attention to the family separation of Mexicans from Mexico that says, "They did not cross the Borders, but the Border crossed them." Lord God gave us a mind to be holy. Holiness is the wisdom of God and the instruction from God. Holiness is the basic instructions before leaving earth. The book of Hebrew 12:14 warns us to, "Follow peace with all men and holiness, without which no man shall see the Lord." Remember that it is never wrong to do the right thing.

We must also have God's spirit so we can in Jude 1:20, "But ye beloved, building up yourselves on your most holy faith, praying in the Holy Spirit." God is tired of a lying stiff-necked people that in Jeremiah 9:3, "And they bend their tongues like their bow for lies: but they are not valiant for the truth upon earth; for they proceed from evil to evil, and they know not me, saith the Lord." God said in Isaiah 35:8, "And a highway shall be there, and a way, and it shall be called the way of holiness; the unclean shall not pass over it; but it shall be for those: the wayfaring men, though fools, shall err therein."

Our world thinks serving God is fun and games. The church is now functioning under past down traditions of men and leaders that are afraid to undo the lies that they have been taught in the church about Jesus Christ. Jesus Christ is the head of the church. Jesus said upon this rock I build my church. "For though ye have ten thousand instructors in Christ, yet have ye not many fathers: for in Christ Jesus I have begotten you through the gospel" 1Corinthians 4:15.

Jehovah's church is supposed to speak the same things. 2 Corinthians 4:13 says, "We having the same spirit of faith, according as it is written, I believed, and therefore have I spoken; we also believe and therefore speak." Most churches read from the same Holy Scriptures but it never occurred to them why they are not speaking the same thing. 1 Corinthians 1:10 tells us, "Now I beseech you, brethren, by the name of our Lord Jesus Christ, that ye all speak the same thing, and that there be no divisions among you; but that ye be perfectly joined together in the same mind and in the same judgement."

The church that Jesus Christ is the head of should speak and obey the same Holy Scriptures that Jesus taught his Apostles. Some churches want to ignore the teaching of Paul because he was a man, but Jesus also was in the flesh when he taught. God used men all through the bible to run errands for him telling what he said. We should do this because Colossians 3:17 says, "And whatsoever ye do in word or deed, do all in the name of the Lord Jesus, giving thanks to God and the Father by him." Adam and Eve give us the best lesson that we can learn about rationalizing in our minds. We even have China experimenting on men to see can a man get pregnant. Satan seems to always find a body to work through to pervert what God has already done.

God said in Jeremiah 30:5-6, "For thus saith the Lord; "We have heard a voice of trembling, of fear, and not of peace. (Vs.6), "Ask ye now, and see whether a man doth travail with child? Wherefore do I see every man with his hands on his loins, as a woman in travail, and all faces are turned unto paleness? Men need to be aware that Satan is using our society to take away their manhood. Designers are making men clothes feminine and tighter to go along with their bangs, pony tails and ear rings that some men are wearing as style and fashion. Scientist are making designer men and women. I heard three women talking with my own ears about a new born baby boy. The mother said to two other women in the room that he is going be my little girl.

Mothers have the task of nurturing little children first and the child's destiny is in their hands. It's sad but it is true that the Left movement is in full force trying to change God's original plan for men and women. Men are under heavy attack because he was made in the image of God. Satan hates God and he hates God's children. This is a misrepresentation of faith in parenting and churches because families and churches have the lead to nurture the family. God is talking to us in Isaiah 62:11-12 that the Lord hath proclaim unto us to be a holy people. "Behold, the Lord hath proclaimed unto the end of the world, Say ye to the daughter of Zion, Behold, thy salvation cometh; behold, his reward is with him, and his work before him."

Preachers should be preaching Jesus Christ and him crucified. When Jesus Christ comes back what do you expect? (Vs.12), "And they shall call them, "The holy people, The redeemed of the Lord: and thou shall be called; Sought out, A city not forsaken." Holiness was here before the world was formed because it is from a holy God who made the heavens and the earth. Isaiah 63:15 explains, "Look down from heaven, and behold from thy habitation of thy holiness and of thy glory: where is thy zeal and thy strength, the sounding of thy bowels and of thy mercies toward me? are they restrained? Isaiah 63:18, "The people of thy holiness have possessed it but a little while: our adversaries have trodden down the sanctuary." "Holiness is God's design for his creation. When he made man in his image he wanted mankind to be holy because he is holy.

Most of the world has its own war within itself and every male and female is fighting its own individual internal war. I am full of matter. I listen to everybody else now let God's word speak thru me. I don't need a flattering title to agree with Jehovah my God. Our world is living in darkness. "Then said Solomon, The Lord hath said that he would dwell in thick darkness" 11 Chronicles 6:1. Jesus brought a sword to this war for souls that cut and divide the holy from the profane. We must stand firm in the spirit of God centering in on the Gospel's work.

Your enemies could be that of your own household. "The Battle for Souls" will show you how this great nation is destroying itself internally from the Whitehouse, to the pulpit, all the way into the everyday homes. There are many anti-christ already in the world and they are deceiving God's very elect thru elections because of Christians that are fighting against God's word. These elections are searching the hearts of those who call themselves a child of God. Men and women with degrees are rationalizing themselves right into hell. The fight for their rights is against the righteousness of God that Christ Jesus paid for at the cross. He did not die for the world to become a world of abomination.

They fight God because they have family members and friends who are homosexuals and friends having abortions. These Christians choose their family members and friends over God when they vote at the poles and this make the antichrist fool God's very elect in elections. They err by fighting God for the rights to do whatever they want with their mind, body and soul. Friendship with the world is an enemy of God. The truth of God's word will be standing tall after all the lies have been told. When light comes darkness has to flee.

The more comfortable you get in sin the harder it will be for you to get out of sin. All the nations are trying to agree with Satan and turn their backs on God. All the nations of the earth together weigh less than air against Jehovah. The Holy Scriptures say to the nations in Isaiah 40:17, "All nations before him are as nothing; and they are counted to him less than nothing, and vanity." Ask God to help you to hate sin. You want to agree with God and if God hate sin then you need to hate it too. Those who hate wisdom love death.

The Word of God has created me and the spirit or the breath of the Almighty has given me life. I agree with the word of God our creator who formed us out of clay and I speak against all those who are living contrary to him. Satan is speaking loud through media and all his agents are mentally kidnapping creation through lies and deception. The spirit of the devil use women as tools against men as distractions of intimidation, domination. God already set the standard for man and woman so everything else is just a distraction. God is greater than man. God is speaking to you and you don't understand him. He speaks to you in Job 33:15-17, "In a dream, in a vision of night, when deep sleep falleth upon men, in slumbering upon the bed; (Vs.16), Then he openeth the ears of man, and sealeth their instruction, (Vs.17), That he may withdraw man from his purpose, and hide pride from man."

Satan gives humankind a selfish plan and purpose to keep you from hearing God's plan and purpose for your life. Our government is selling fear in every form and sin in every fashion. Television is selling sin and fear. Covid fear, fear of war, drug fear, news fear, and crime fear is putting the full court press on the mind of God's creation. They even sell the fear of death and Jesus Christ has already defeated death and the grave. Choose this day whom you will serve. People choose to go to hell. When the only thing we should fear is God and the loss of our souls burning in hell.

There are men having the zeal of God but not according to righteousness. Mathew 15:8KJV speaks loud for God saying, "This people draweth nigh unto me with their mouth, and honoureth me with {their} lips; but their heart is far from me." God speaks again in Isaiah 29:13KJV saying "Wherefore the Lord said, For as much as this people draw near me with their mouth, and with their lips do honour me, but have removed their heart far from me, and their fear toward me is taught by the precepts of men."

Isaiah 9:16, "For the leaders of this people cause them to err; and they that are led of them are destroyed." We must understand that, "Great men are not always wise: neither do the aged understand judgement." Their Watchman are blind. People are going to church and dying slow spiritual deaths. Members are not being told how to stay out of hell. Jesus Christ said go, not sit. All people are doing is sitting down and getting obese in the word of God with no corresponding action.

Isaiah 56:10-11 Paraphase talks about leaders who are greedy dogs who never have enough. All the priest should be thinking of is the saving of the souls. They can't preach what is not in them. They are not convincing the people about the dangers of hell. Eternity is longer than this brief moment that we struggle to live in this life. Who wants to burn in eternity always and never ending for money that you can't take with you when you die. Funeral homes are prepared but the people that will be placed in the casket or cremated are not ready for eternal life. We put our trust in money, leaders and friends instead of trusting in God who created all things. Sin is a moment of pleasure and what's so bad about it is you don't even get the whole moment. There are too many perils pursuing pleasure.

God wants his servants to "Cry loud and spare not." There will come a time in all of our lives when there will be a fight for your life. It reminds me of the men that said "why should we sit here and die." People are afraid and famines are in the land because of the curse but who cares? You may think that thou doest well in that it was in thine heart. Most folks say God knows my heart. I don't sin that much. God don't bless sin. In the book of Job 32:8 that says, "But there is a spirit in man: and the inspiration of the Almighty giveth them understanding." Sin is a cause for repentance. Adam sinned and he was the Son of God and so was Jesus Christ who also was the Son of God came later to deliver us from our sins and he never sinned found in, Genesis 5:1-2, Luke 1:35, 4:38.

God blesses obedience. Black Women's communication says, in the women archives of 1832 Maria W Stewart one of her four public lectures in Franklin Hall in Boston that says "Why should we sit here and die? There are women and men in America who are against God and God will let you defeat yourselves. He will let men and women defeat themselves by their own craftiness. They are the ones who say they trust in the Lord but they are still leaning to their own understanding.

In the book of 2 Kings 7:3-4, says, "Now there were four men who were lepers at the entrance to the gate. This happened after the two women who were boiling each other sons to eat and then they had an argument. They fell out because one of the women reneged on the deal and did not do what she had promised or agreed to do and that was to eat her son next. If you want to know and see excitement you need to read your Holy Bible.

There is not one person on earth that I would like to go to hell with. I have not found one person that I would go to hell with or for; not even mother, father, sister, brother, daughter or son. Every person is responsible for his or her own soul. No one in their right mind should want to qualify to go to hell fire burning continually. There are people that are sitting around as though they are not going to die. They go to funerals and have heard of heaven and hell but they are not preparing themselves for where they are headed. They may have earthly insurance but not heavenly assurance.

Back to the four lepers who said in 2 Kings chapter 7:3-4, "And there were four leprous men at the entering in of the gate: and they said to one another, "Why sit we here until we die? In chapter 7 (Vs.4) of 2 Kings, "If we say, We will enter into the city, then the famine is in the city, and we shall die there: and if we sit still here, we die also. Now therefore come, and let us fall unto the host of the Syrians; if they save us alive; we shall live; and if they kill us, we shall but die." When you are in the valley of decision and your backs are against the wall keep moving forward. The only thing that can beat a failure is to try. They said we did not come this far to sit down but get down and so they did not run but went and faced life head on.

This is the attitude of people who have faith in God. Since Coronavirus and even before Omicron some have faired-well without work but a lot of businesses went under. Women have a new man in town and his name is Uncle Sam. In Vs.5 in Chapter 7 the last four words read "Behold, there was no man there." Since the Left have taken control of the White House people have stopped working and in many homes "Behold, there was no man there." There is no man there but babies are still being born in fornication and adulterous relationships.

In the 1st ten days of 2021 over a million abortions were performed. Some men and women have received a murderous spirit because our government has chosen and released Barabbas the murderer. He was charged with treason against Rome and released instead of Jesus Christ the Savior of the whole world. Barabbas was arrested and he was freed by Pontius Pilate and sent to the Salt Mines. Wherein he is then sold as a slave and eventually becomes a gladiator. He is finally converted to a Christian" (New World Encyclopedia).

Now back to 11Kings 7:3-20 before I go too far and stay too long. The four lepers decided to go into the enemy camp. Follow me in Vs. 6, 'For the Lord had made the host of the Syrians to hear a noise of chariots, and a noise of horses, even the noise of a great host: and they said to one another, Lo, the king of Israel has hired against us the kings of the Hittites, and the kings of the Egyptians, to come upon us. Sin and the curse will make you run in fear if a leaf shakes.

What are the voices that women and black men are hearing to make them panic? Some women are leaving their post as mothers as the nurturer of babies and men that would rather go to hell or jail throwing their whole life away in hopeless crime rather than to go and work on a job. They end up working anyway for free in the prison system. They were a slave to sin and now a slave in the prison system. Fear of death made them run from the frying pan into the fire and get delivered from the trap and fall into a snare. Satan keeps them in bondage. Their only hope is Jesus Christ who is the only one who can save them whether bond or free.

The country is divided and all nationalities believe that coronavirus is a trap against them. Our country is holding on unto the last few threads of morality and other countries are waiting like vultures circling America waiting for it to self-destruct. You can keep acting as though you don't see thousands of black men are daily and annually dying until you become that casualty.

This leads us to think the unthinkable about our leaders of America when trouble comes their way in 2 Kings chapter 7 Vs. 17, "And the king appointed the lord on whose hand he leaned to have charge of the gate (in this case the nation), and the people trode upon him in the gate, and he died." Leaders don't want to recognize the problem until it comes home to roost or to their front door then they want to do something about it. Who would have thought that the citizens of America would be the one who storms and try to destroy leaders in the White House. This happened to show lawmakers that their decisions of death like human trafficking, abortions are boomeranging right back to them. If you live in a glass house don't throw no stones. Especially those working in the White house who have the same faults.

God forbid, Repent! Could it be the spirit of greed from money earned from Opioids, abortions, fake marriages contrary to the Word of God and other tailor made drugs for dishonest gain? Opioids are substances that act on opioid receptors to produce morphine-like effects used for pain. The world is in pain. Designer drugs are on the rise in America. China and Russia or any other Country don't have to worry about America because our country is on the route that will surely self-destruct. It is sad but it is true. All these countries have to do is wait on America to kill itself in a civil rights power struggle.

Women are aborting babies and killing the future by the millions and young black men are killing by the thousands. Then we have those dying of natural death and now coronavirus has stepped up its game to Omicron to get the rest. It seems as though all America can think of is sin, sin, sin that only pay the wages of death. Satan and those denying God's laws is saying death by the pleasure from drugs, perverted homosexuality and sports and gambling that produce some form of death.

Smart intelligent men and women in America are destroying the family because of selfishness. Then coronavirus variants and other designer made diseases will get the rest. Pulpits are less than business as usual. They are the ones that have moral standards that men should live by but they are stuck on worldly things and not the soul business. Human rights have taken over the stage and no one is putting emphasis on being right with Jesus Christ when he returns.

TV is preparing us for the worst showing us how to run to the hills featuring the show Survivor. TV has trained the public to hear gunfire making it part of the New Normal. This is a form of "Mental Kidnapping" as they program and reprogram our society with crime shows. They are forms of programming and reprogramming the minds of the public. There are shooting galleries where all Americans can buy and learn how to shoot automatic weapons. As soon as you turn on your TV you hear rapid fire from automatic weapons from crime shows aired on TV. They show the movie series Survivor on a regular basis getting you ready for the worst. Hearing automatic weapons is going to be a normal sound. What is really going on? Satan is trying to slick take us out with his number one attribute fear.

My new book "The Battle for Souls is a trumpet warning America to Repent and be baptized in the name of Jesus Christ and receive the gift of the Holy Spirit. There is definitely a "Battle for Souls" in the spirit realm. Souls are being snatched off the planet at a fast rate with rapid fire of disobedience towards Jehovah. To get into God's kingdom you must have God's spirit. All other rebellious and wicked spirits that have the merchandise of Lucifer was kicked out of heaven and should be cast down and avoided. These other spirits that are not of God wants to exalt itself against the true knowledge of God.

There is only one way to the Father. Thomas was trying to find that way from Jesus. John 14:6 "Jesus told Thomas I am the way, the truth and the life; no one can come to the Father except through me." Communion with your creator is what this war for souls is all about. Satan is an imposter who hates Jehovah your creator and hates you too because you were born in his image. Soul snatching is where wrong information is used by the enemy and he makes many other ways to get to the Father other than Jesus Christ to throw you off course. He throws you off course to make you think you are serving God but you are serving Satan thru man made religion.

Your soul is your mind, will and emotions. The Bible says in Romans 10:13, "For whosoever calls on the name of the Lord shall be saved." These are the last days and this could be your last chance to come to Jesus Christ who is the God of heaven and earth. There is a race for souls and one soul is worth all the silver and gold on the earth. This war for men and women's inner man is their spirit that lives in their body. They have a soul. That mind, will, and emotion was meant only for God's purpose who gave it for his glory, honor and praise.

When you die your body called dust, "Then shall the dust return to the earth as it was: and the spirit shall return unto God who gave it" Ecclesiastes 12:7. How was man created? Genesis 2:7, "And the Lord God formed man from the dust of the ground, and breathed into his nostrils the breath of life; and man became a living soul." Your soul is a living, breathing consciousness in your body.

When God first formed man he was a shell dead just a form made of clay or dust. God is an eternal spirit and he breathed his eternal life into man and he became animated. He formed man from the dust and made him in his image. Dust thou art and to dust thou shall return.

When God breathed the breath of life into that dust he made man part heaven by the spirit of God that he breathed into man and part earth from the dust of the ground. Man was meant to live eternally with God his creator until he disobeyed and transgressed the command of God.

Those who truly trust God believe that the soul continues after the body is dead because the spirit is from Jehovah and it is eternal and will return to him that gave it. Ecclesiastes 12:7 says, "Then shall the dust return to the earth as it was: and the spirit shall return unto God who gave it." This is what believers seek for and that is a promise of eternal life with God our creator. The body without the spirit is dead. When you die your body goes back to where it came from (Dust) and the spirit returns to Jehovah who created you. Ecclesiastes12:7 says, "Then shall the dust return to the earth as it was: and the spirit shall return unto God who gave it."

We refer to someone as a particular kind of soul by describing their character or condition by the way they live. Your soul is the part of you that consist of your mind, character, thoughts, and feelings. In Mathew 22:37, "Jesus said unto him, Thou shalt love the Lord thy God with all thy heart, and with all thy soul, and with all thy mind." When you finish reading this book you will be able to see why the road to heaven is narrow and there will be few that get in.

The road to heaven and hell starts in your mind by the choices you make and this is the first place the enemy who is Satan attacks. He wants to keep you distracted. We need God in our life because he restoreth our soul. Since the fall in the Garden of Eden man has been on recall like car manufacturers that call back cars that have defects. Psalms 23:3 says "He restoreth my soul." God gave us the church or the spiritual hospital to help repair defects in his creation starting with "Repentance."

Everything we do begins with a thought. For some reason humankind has been sold on thinking they have more time to live. Your soul is your mind, will and your emotions. God gave humankind the will to choose right and wrong. Transgression started in heaven with Lucifer who committed the first sin. Lucifer full of pride, selfishness became "Mentally Kidnapped, Brainwashed, and had Group Therapy with the angels in heaven by Reeducating them bringing on a division and convinced a 3rd part of the angels in heaven to rebel against Jehovah. This is when war broke out in heaven. There was a separation. Sin is separation from God similar to darkness Vs or is opposite to light. Church since we represent Jehovah here on earth "War," need to break out down here.

Your home was nice and peaceful until bad John came in and planted evil seeds in your kids mind to turn them against you. You had to kick bad John out and a couple of your kids who cause havoc in your home. They thought acting like John was alright and did not know that John was sent from Satan on a mission to get their soul. Association brings about assimilation. Your kids became guilty by association. Sin is contagious and if you are not rooted and grounded in Jehovah and his word sin will uproot you from your position in life and your home with God and it will lead you straight to hell. You become guilty by association.

Mathew 10:28 reminds us, "And fear not them which kill the body, but are not able to kill the soul: but rather fear him which is able to destroy both soul and body." Those who sin don't understand that their soul is at state. This is another one of Satan's tricks. He dangles bait that looks good to us all because he knows what sin we like. It looks good to us in the beginning but he never shows us the end that leads to spiritual death and sometimes physical death. There is a battle for souls and souls are the least talked about thing in Religion today. In Ezekiel 18:4 God says, "Behold, all souls are mine; as the soul of the father, so also the soul of the son is mine: the soul that sinneth, it shall die." Sin is separation from God.

Your mind is a terrible thing waste and you will be surprised at who is playing with it in every area of your life. God gives us grace to come to him but if we continue to duck and hide from him he will give you up to what you believe. We must stand strong in the Lord and in the power of his might, not yours. Revelation 6:9 says, "And when he had opened the fifth seal, I saw under the altar the souls of them that were slain for the word of God, and for the testimony which they held." Satan is snatching all minds, wills and emotions who do not know why they were born. Those who are openly rebelling against God is fighting for a lost cause.

2 Thessalonians 2:11-12, "And for this cause God shall send them strong delusion, that they should believe a lie: (Vs.12), "That they all might be damned who believed not the truth, but had pleasure in unrighteousness." There are some that say there is no help for them from God for their soul, but God said in 3rd John 2, "Beloved, I wish above all things that thou mayest prosper and be in health, even as thy soul prospereth." God wants you to dwell in safety and cover you all the day long. God wants to dwell between your shoulders. Between your shoulders is where your mind and head is. This is where you put on the mind of Christ and hold the thoughts, feelings and purposes of his heart. Your mind and heart is where you abide in him and he in you.

God is going to render to every man and woman according to their deeds. In 1 Corinthians 15:51, "Behold, I shew you a mystery; "We shall not all sleep, but we shall be changed. Read Luke 16:19-31, "There was a certain rich man, which was clothed in purple and fine linen, and fared sumptuously every day. Read and see how he was changed after death and still had a mind, and he still had an emotion but no more will. He could still feel. He had a will to choose God or life while he was living but his soul ended up in hell where he could still speak, hear and feel. God gives every human the right to choose life or death or a blessing or the curse for our free will. People are still choosing death and the curse rather than life and the blessing found in Deuteronomy 30:19. We must choose now while we live. Now is the time for salvation.

Mathew16:26 "For what is a man profited, if he gain the whole world, and lose his own soul? or what shall a man give in exchange for his soul?" We must become aware of everlasting life and eternal life. Right now some only have tunnel vision where they only see what is in front of them and that could be eternal damnation. If you are still breathing God's fresh air you still have another opportunity to make the right choice today.

Just confess your sins and be baptized in the name of Jesus Christ and receive the gift of the Holy Spirit with evidence of speaking in tongues. You need God's Holy Spirit to belong to him. Without holiness no man shall see the Lord. Everlasting is always and never ending. Naked we came in this world and naked you are going to leave. You did not bring anything into this world and you are taking nothing out, only your soul.

Satan has shown humankind all the kingdoms of the world and has promised it to them if they would only bow down and worship him. He cannot offer what is not his because the earth is the Lord's and the fullness thereof and all that dwell therein." Although he is the prince of this world but King Jesus still rule. A prince is not above a king. Remember Lucifer lied and mentally kidnapped the minds of a 3rd part of the angels from heaven by reeducating them. God made all things even evil for the day of judgement.

So we must take heed and don't get caught up in his lies unless we fall. He is a fallen angel and wants us to fall because misery loves company. Our world has fallen men and fallen women that fell from their natural state. The devil hates God and he hates you because you are his creation, created in his image. He wants to get back at God by destroying his children. He lied to Eve the mother of all creation in the Garden of Eden and is still lying to us today. Look out men who think they are a woman and women who think they are a man. Satan lied to you and you believed the lie. He don't care about your position in life but he will tell you anything to gain your soul that is always and never ending.

The American Heritage College Dictionary defines a lie as to remain in a specified condition, and sin being that condition where motives lie hidden; A lie is the way things are situated or arranged to give a false impression, strictly to evade the truth of a point by resorting to trivial fault finding, to confuse the issue or evade the truth, to equivocate to use two or more meanings, not clear or uncertain, to fabricate, an invention of a false story. A lie has its own uniform. Living a lie can place an image in your mind that you cannot get out. Only God has the power to deliver you from that bondage. The world has more hope in a lie than they do God their creator.

Don't feel like the lone ranger because you have a lot of company when it comes to sin and here will be your company. Here are some others without Christ in Revelation 22:16, "For without are dogs and sorcerers, and whoremongers and murderers, and idolaters, and whosoever loveth and maketh a lie." This will be your guest of honor in hell Revelation 20:10, "And the devil that deceived them was cast into the lake of fire and brimstone, where the beast and the false prophet are, and shall be tormented day and night forever and ever. It will be always, never ending, in darkness, falling, never coming out and always cursing God because of your own disobedience. You denied Jesus Christ the one who came to deliver you from the lie that you were living.

Proverb 12:22 KJV), "Lying lips are abomination to the Lord, but they that deal truly are his delight." Jonah 2:8 says "They that observe lying vanities forsake their own mercy." God gives us new mercies every morning and his grace is giving us what we don't deserve another opportunity to get it right, but people go right ahead living a lie. God throws a rope to rescue us from our sinking quick sands and to keep us from drowning in our sins daily. He wants us to repent and turn to him but some lie and say, tomorrow! Tomorrow never comes because it is always a day ahead. Even God's children lie when selfishness and greed that is two of Satan's merchandise or attributes that enters into them.

As Ananias and Sapphira his wife sold a possession when she knew privy to it and Satan filled their heart to lie to the Holy Ghost. Satan is filling the hearts of humankind with the multitude of his merchandise. These are the people who put things before God who made all things. Anything contrary to the word of God is a lie from Satan's merchandise and should be repented of and turned away from.

They are not lying to men but unto God. The Old Testament gives us examples of different types of sin. When you read the Old Testament you should have seen all those who went under before you for disobeying God. Thank God for Jesus Christ who brought us repentance and dying on the cross for our sins covering us with his blood giving us his grace, another opportunity to get it right. Thank You Lord!

When you attend the funeral of a friend in crime you wander what are people and the preacher going to say about him or her. They knew at the funeral the preacher tried his best to lie for the family trying to preach your friend into heaven and you know that the person was living a lie in sin. Pastors have to repent of that sin for lying. There was a sinner in that casket at this funeral and the preacher was preaching them into heaven for much money. In reality he or she was a liar, thief, robber, prostitute or an undercover faggot.

We all need to repent, because you could be next. Our government needs to call for a "Special News Report" for everyone in America to put on sackcloth or pray and turn from their evil ways. Pray because God see the works from the violence of their hands and they need to turn from their evil ways. Disobedience to God only brings his wrath.

Our nation needs to go on a fast from sin for the fear of Devine Wrath of God to establish the pulpits in our nation for correction. Our government and even ministers of God are walking boldly in a prideful state refusing to be corrected. Our government should be leading us by example into righteousness instead they have gone to the Left.

"Therefore the law is slacked, and judgement doth never go forth: for the wicked doth compass the righteous, therefore wrong judgment proceedeth" HABAKKUK 1:4. God said in Malachi 3:7, "Even from the days of your fathers ye are gone away from mine ordinances, and have not kept them. "Return unto me, and I will return unto you, saith the Lord of host. "But ye said, Where shall we return?" Satan, the Lord rebuke you." It will not be by our own strength that we defeat the enemy. "This was the word of the Lord unto Zerubbabel, saying, "Not by might, nor by power, but by my spirit, saith the Lord of host."

Prayer: Heavenly Father I pray that whatsoever plague or sin sickness that be in the hearts of humankind, I pray that you reveal to every man that plague of sin and wickedness in his heart that he may "Repent" and be baptized in the name of Jesus Christ and receive your Holy Spirit Father God, because "thou only knowest the hearts of all the children of men." Heavenly Father if they sin against you for we know that there is no man that sinneth not, but if they bethink themselves and repent and return to you Father God with all their heart, and with all their soul I ask you to forgive them and I pray that You never leave us or forsake us as our hearts be perfected toward You Lord God in the mighty name of Jesus Christ I pray. Amen

The Truth is, 'The Supreme reality, the ultimate meaning and value of existence." Eternal truths being true and valid unchanged by time without beginning or end lasting forever, always, and never ending. There are essential truths where we see made by laws of this nation that are not insights about something but the apprehending of the immediate reality of the moment, for instance same-sex marriage. The Holy Scriptures is a means to an end and that end is the Truth about God to bring his creation back to him. Some people cannot handle the truth and have become enemies of God because of their fear of change.

Fear in unbelievers has become Forced-Energy-Against-Righteousness. Fear can also spell out False-Evidence-Appearing-Real. There is a strong force coming against believers and we must stand firm in the word of God. The thought of the heart of humankind is not right in the sight of God and repentance is needed for the forgiveness of their sin. Acts 28:27 states that, "For the heart of this people is wax gross, and their ears are dull of hearing, and their eyes have they closed; lest they should see with their eyes, and hear with their ears, and understand with their heart, and should be converted, and I should heal them."

God is no respecter of persons but he except all who works righteousness. Acts 11:26, "And when he had found him, he brought him unto Antioch. "And it came to pass, that a whole year they assembled themselves with the church, and taught much people. And the disciples were called Christians first in Antioch." A Christian is a person. Jesus never started a religion called Christianity. Satan is picking ministers to control and educate them in schools teaching them what the government wants by compromising the Word of God to bring them under his control. Believers are like the palm trees in the midst of the storms of life. We will bend but we will not break in the face of God's lawbreakers.

God's word is his will for our life. So stand firm in his Spirit centering in on the Gospel's work. Wait on God and stand still let God have his way in your life. The battle is not yours but it is the Lord's, but the victory is yours. We should be witnessing both to small and great saying none other things than those which the prophets and Moses did say should come. This is the truth about Jesus Christ and the resurrection. Jesus said in John 17:17 "Sanctify them through thy truth: thy word is truth." We need to share the Gospel of Christ. This is where the power lay in Jesus Christ.

People come to church as a formality. Ezekiel 33:31 says, "And they come unto thee as the people cometh, and they sit before thee as my people, and they hear thy words, but they will not do them: for with their mouth they shew much love, but their heart goeth after their covetousness." (Vs.32, "And, lo, thou art unto them as a very lovely song of one that hath a pleasant voice, and can play well on an instrument: for they hear thy words, but they do them not." To them God's word is like a pretty lovely song with a melody with a pleasant voice that sounds good. It serenades them and sooths them but they do them not.

Peter and the other Apostles said in the book of Acts, "We ought to obey God rather than men." God said, "Everything under heaven is mine." Palms 2:1-3 L B says, "What fools the nations are to rage against the Lord!" How strange that men should try to outwit God! (Vs.2), "For a summit conference of the nations has been called to plot against the Lord and his Messiah, Christ the king. (Vs.3), "Come let us break his chains, they say, and free ourselves from all this slavery to God." This is the fate of the Nations forgetting the Lord. They will fall in pitfalls they have dug for others and the trap they set for others will snap on them. Jehovah is angry because his people are being scattered and have become meat for the beast of field.

People are wandering trying to find the truth from man and not their creator. Men and women are only here for a moment and then they disappear. Jehovah has all knowledge and wisdom who made the heavens and the earth. People who don't know why they were born are like sheep without a shepherd. The truth is right there where you left it in your Bibles. In these cloudy and dark days Ezekiel 34:8 is coming to pass. God said, "As I live, saith the Lord God, surely because my flock became a prey, and my flock became meat to every beast of the field, because there was no shepherd, neither did my shepherds search for my flock, but the shepherds fed themselves, and fed not my flock." God wants us to seek those that are lost and those driven away who are broken and to strengthen the sick.

God will feed the greedy Pastors with judgement. Ezekiel 34:18-19 reveals to us, "Seemeth it a small thing unto you to have eaten up the good pasture, but ye must tread down with your feet the residue of your pastures? And have drunk of deep waters, but ye must foul up the residue with your feet? (Vs.19), "And as for my flock, they eat that which ye have trodden with your feet; and they drink that which ye have fouled with your feet." God will judge those who push their flocks until they were scattered. Shepherds drunk of the deep waters and fouled the residue with their feet leaving the flock to eat what they have trodden under their feet. The sheep ate that which is fouled up by the shepherd's feet." Now that is a dirty shepherd there.

PRAYER

Heavenly Father I pray that you arise and judge and punish the Nations and don't let them conquer your people. Make them tremble in fear; put the Nations in their place until at last they know they are puny men. They want us to flee to the mountains in back packs, but we are trusting in you Lord Jesus. They have set an ambush for your people. Law and order have collapsed we are told. But the righteous should stand firm in your spirit centering in on the Gospels work. Lord is still in his holy temple and he still rule from heaven. Father God we know that you watch everything that happens here on earth. God you put the righteous and the wicked to the test. Father God we are dealing with proud liars that lie to their hearts content. They say our lips are our own and who can stop us? Those who are yours know that your promises in your word are pure and you do not speak careless words because they are the purest of Truth. Heavenly Father, we thank you for preserving us from the enemy in Jesus mighty name we pray Amen.

CHAPTER 2

FELLOWSHIPPING WITH DARKNESS

How can two walk together unless they agree and what does light and darkness have in common? Church started out a battle against Satan but now it has become a playground. Playing with Satan is like taking fire in your bosom knowing you will get burned. If you let him ride he is going to want to drive you to hell. He likes to intervene into our lives to cause us to do his will other than God's will. He steals your time and keeps you out of God's presence where your safety lay. We are safe in God when we are cleanse, covered and protected by the blood of the Lamb and the words of our testimony. We are safe when we are somewhere bragging on God staying in his presence. The safest place to be is in the presence of God.

Sin only comes to steal, kill, and to cause to perish. Fellowshipping with darkness causes to perish young, old and little children. Saints this is not the time or the place to fellowship with darkness and sin. Hell is enlarging itself and the grave yard is not full. There is no certain age that people must be to die. The funeral homes have all size caskets. No man or woman knows the day or hour when Jesus Christ will return as a thief in the night.

James 4:4 say "Ye adulterers and adulteresses, know ye not that the friendship with the world is enmity with God? Whosoever therefore will be a friend of the world is the enemy of God." God said, to Moses in Exodus 6:2-3, "And God spake unto Moses, and said unto him, I am the Lord". (Vs.3) "And I appeared unto Abraham, unto Isaac, and unto Jacob, by the name of God Almighty, but by my name Jehovah was I not known to them." Our government is causing its citizens to be in open rebellion against Jehovah by passing laws contrary to his commands.

Like Moses and Aaron in Exodus 8;26 Paraphrase, America's children of God need to sacrifice the abominations of Egyptians or (America) to the Lord our God: lo, shall we sacrifice the abomination of Egyptians (America) before their eyes, and will they not stone us?" Our sacrifice to God is against their abominations. "Moses said It is not meet so to do" Like the native Shepherds in Egypt did not eat with the Hebrew. Shepherds raised large number of cattle for meat.

When Joseph's brother came to Egypt during the famine Joseph did not eat at the table with his brethren. Joseph ate by himself at another table because there was the assumed distaste between vegetarians and carnivores. Our government leaders have an evil eye and the book of Proverbs 23:6-7, tells us to, "Eat thou not the bread of him that hath an evil eye, neither desire thou his dainty meats" (Vs.7),"For as he thinketh in his heart, so is he: Eat and drink, saith he to thee; but his heart is not with thee."

Our world has seen very grievous murrain from cattle as the Egyptians. Murrain is a plague, epidemic, or crop blight. It is an infectious disease especially Babesiosis affecting cattle or other animals. "Babesiosis or Babesia is a rare and life threatening infection of the red blood cells that's usually spread by ticks to humans. They enter your blood stream similar to the Lyme disease when bitten by an infected deer tick. This disease has an circular rash that expands at the site of bite around 3to 30 days and have a bulls-eye or target appearance, that is, it may have a red, brown, or purple center with a ring around it." America has its own pestilence called lust from bedbugs and ticks.

God send plagues and there is a plague of the heart in Vs. 14 of Exodus 9. Like Pharaoh our leaders need to repent for our nation. Repent! Pharaoh said in chapter 9:27, "And Pharaoh sent, and called for Moses and Aaron, and said unto them, I have sinned this time: the Lord is righteous, and I and my people are wicked." Pharaoh begs Moses to "Entreat the Lord for me, that this plague be removed." He begs for the prayers of Moses like those who will not pray for themselves do. There is a lack of fear and understanding in our leadership that the earth is the Lord's. As soon as the vaccine that cured Covid came out America's heart hardened and they could not wait to sin yet more and more. It was sin business as usual.

America has on its money "In God we trust" and in their court houses. How can you trust God when you have God on one side and the rainbow flag on the other side? Will America continue like Pharaoh until it is destroyed? Covid 19 was covering the whole earth. Now there is a new virus called The Delta Virus and the world should be asking the Lord to forgive them of their sins to take away this death only. There is another virus that has a name that sounds like it is from the movie Transformer called Omicron. Now here comes the "Trans" representing Satan and his agenda. It came to steal your health, to kill and to destroy. It is called Omicron Coronavirus Variant and it is the newest in 2021 & 2022 first identified in South Africa and Botswana. Now Monkey-pox has entered the arena.

The government can give you what you want but God gives you what you need. We need God's word for instruction. We must thank God for the blood of Jesus Christ to protect us from all hurt, harm and danger. "The bloodthirsty hate the upright: but the just seek his soul." We have rulers that hearken unto lies and all their servants are wicked. The servants of Satan are lying to us because of our lack of knowledge. His agents are in many different uniforms from the top to the bottom.

Americans have to listen to investigative reporters to get the right news. Everything that our leaders tell us has to be investigated. They will lie to us just because their mouth is moving. They will lie in a minute. Even some of our priest will hide and hold the truth from us.

The Holy Bible tells us "like people like priest." "Hosea 4:9 says, "And there shall be, like people, like priest: and I will punish them for their ways, and reward them their doings." False prophets are holding the truth for money sake. All children of God are looking for that blessed hope, and the glorious appearing of the great God and Saviour Jesus Christ; Jesus Christ has the government that has peace with no end.

Isaiah 9:6, "For unto us a child is born. (God is not a child and He has no beginning and no end, "unto us a son is given: and the government shall be on his shoulder: and his name shall be called, Wonderful, Counselor, The mighty God, The everlasting Father, The Prince of Peace." Jesus Christ is our Mighty God, our everlasting Father. "For unto us a child is born" by God. Jesus was also born again being baptized and after he received the Holy Spirit giving us an example about what it will take for us to get back in good standing with our creator. He did not have to repent of his sins. He was born in sinless flesh because of Adam all mankind is born in sin. God needed and made a sacrifice without spot or wrinkle.

This was prophesied before Mary was born. Christ the anointing on Jesus was in the prophets of the Old Testament. He was in Moses. Acts 3:20-21"And he shall send Jesus Christ, which before was preached unto you; (Vs.21), "Whom the heaven must receive until the times of restitution of all things, which God hath spoken by the mouth of all his holy prophets since the world began." The same spirit that descended like a dove on Jesus after he was baptized and the same Holy Ghost was for those in God's church. That spirit makes us his and this is where the power is.

God is Spirit and his name is Jesus Christ who sent us a piece of himself as a helper called the Holy Spirit to dwell in us. Jesus Christ is not only a mighty God in Isaiah 9:6 but he is also a great God in Titus 2:13-14. Isaiah 9:6 "For unto us a child is born, unto us a son is given: and the government shall be upon his shoulder: and his name shall be called Wonderful, Counsellor, The Mighty God, The Everlasting Father, The Prince of Peace." Jesus has been here before the world began. Even more Mary was not even born yet when Isaiah 9:6 was prophesied. God's spirit got in Mary and she birth a Holy Thing then God's spirit got in Jesus after his baptism that fell upon him like a dove. God hid himself in Mary because he is a God that hides himself.

Jesus is a Just God. Psalm 89:14, "Justice and judgment are the habitation of thy throne: mercy and truth shall go before thy face." God is just. It is part of his character, which means He is always just. It is because of Jesus and his work on the Cross that we can be justified and made right with God. He is also that Great God. Titus 2:13-14"Looking for that blessed hope, and glorious appearing of our great God and our Saviour Jesus Christ; (Vs.14), "Who gave himself for us, that he might redeem us from all iniquity, and purify unto himself a peculiar people zealous of good works." John 8:58 says, "Jesus said unto them, Verily, verily, I say unto you, Before Abraham was, I am." Jesus is the One Lord the only Lord. I am lord over my house. I am the lord that said to the Lord. I pray to the Lord who made the heavens and the earth. Mathew 15:14 says, "Let them alone: they be blind leaders of the blind. And if the blind lead the blind, both shall fall into the ditch." The truth about God is not hidden.

Jesus is also a True God in 1 John 5:20-21 says, "And we know that the Son of God is come, and hath given us an understanding, that we may know him that is true, and we are in him that is true, even in his Son Jesus Christ. This is the true God, and eternal life." (Vs.21), "Little children, keep yourselves from idols." 1Timothy 3:16, "And without controversy great is the mystery of godliness: God was manifested in the flesh, justified in the Spirit, seen of angels, preached unto Gentiles, believed on in the world, received up in glory."

1 Timothy 4:1, "Now the Spirit speaketh expressly, that in the latter times some shall depart from the faith, giving heed to seducing spirits, and doctrines of devils; (Vs.2), Speaking lies in hypocrisy; having their conscience seared with a hot iron; (Vs.3), "Forbidding to marry, and commanding to abstain from meats, which God hath created to be received with thanksgiving of them which believe and know the truth." (Vs.4), "For every creature of God is good, and nothing to be refused, if it be received with thanksgiving."

2 Timothy 4:1, "I Charge thee therefore before God, and the Lord Jesus Christ, who shall judge the quick and the dead at his appearing and his kingdom; (Vs.2), "Preach the word; be instant in season, out of season; reprove, rebuke, exhort with all longsuffering and doctrine. (Vs.3), "For the time will come when they will not endure sound doctrine; but after their own lusts shall they heap to themselves teachers, having itching ears; (Vs.4),"And they shall turn away their ears from the truth, and shall be turned unto fables."

The devil is mocking the Gospel of Christ by making cartoons. The church mocks with Christian comedians. Instead of the world desiring God the Church miss the world and they are reaching back for everything they love so much like Lots wife looking back. The church is jealous of the money that the world entertainers make. So they charge like the world when God says, "Come without money." Isaiah 55:1 tells us, "Ho, every one that thirsteth, come ye to the waters, and he that hath no money; come ye, buy, and eat; come, buy wine and milk without money and without price."

2 Peter 2:17-18 tells us that, "These are wells without water, clouds that are carried with a tempest; to whom the mist of darkness is reserved for ever." Their music is noise to God in their song in Amos 5:23. God wants his children to put a difference between the Holy and profane or holy and the unholy. Take God to the world, not to take the church

back into your old stomping ground the club that shows you are not all clean like Jesus told his disciples. What has light to do with darkness unless it is bringing it into the light. People in darkness are trying to escape darkness not walk into a church full of darkness.

God said be ye Holy for I am Holy. Churches don't have to be that desperate for a member or the lost that you have to look like the world to get one. What will they be transforming into? Where is the difference between Holy and unholy? "The Lord is not slack concerning his promises, as some men count slackness; but is long suffering to us-ward, not willing that any should perish, but that all should come to repentance" 11 Peter3:9. Some churches loosen their Halo and neglect Holiness to draw members. They use rap songs as long as they stick Jesus in your song every now and then. If they can do the same as the world where is the transforming taking place? Where is the difference between the Holy and the profane?

The Church of Jesus Christ is to change the lost, not the lost change the church. Jesus said, "If I be lifted up I will draw all men unto me." Rappers started war in the streets and Satan has slick made it into the church. The church is giving new converts time to receive God's Spirit. Let the Holy Ghost make women pull your bra up and men pull your pants up. How can the love of money make leaders of the church forget that? 2 Peter 2:18 says, "For when they speak great swelling words of vanity, they allure through the lust of the flesh, through much wantonness, those that were clean escaped from them who live in error." They lure back into sin those who have barely escaped from a life style of deception. We know we have victory in the end but those who are babes in Christ are being led astray. When new believers come to Christ they must repent to God and do works meet for repentance.

The Holy Bible says to those on the Lord's side in Daniel 12:1-2, "And at that time shall Michael stand up, the great prince which standeth for the children of the people: and there shall be a time of trouble, such as never was since there was a nation even to that same time: and at that time thy people shall be delivered, every one that shall be found written in the book." (Vs.2), "And many of them that sleep in the dust of the earth shall awake, some to everlasting life, and some to shame and everlasting contempt." This is when we will find out who was wise. Was it the rich or those who delivered souls? (Vs.3), says "And they that be wise shall shine as the brightness of the firmament; and they that turn many to righteousness as the stars for ever and ever."

Those who are rich should not be high-minded trusting in uncertain riches. Trust in God who gives us all things to enjoy. We brought nothing into this world and we will take nothing out. Avoid vain babbling and opposition of science falsely so called that some professing has erred from the faith. Speak out against sin and the lie. Stand for Truth. God wants to cause you to come up out of your graves and prisons of your mind and put his spirit in you so that you can live in Him.

Isaiah 50:4-5, "The Lord hath given me the tongue of the learned, that I should know how to speak a word in season to him that is weary: he wakeneth morning by morning, he waketh mine ear to hear as the learned. (Vs.5), "The Lord God hath opened mine ear, and I was not rebellious, neither turned away back." (Vs.7), "For the Lord God will help me; therefore shall I not be confounded: therefore have I set my face like a flint, and I know that I shall not be ashamed."

Sinners must be warned not to trust in themselves because in Isaiah 50:11 says, "Behold all ye that kindle a fire that compass yourselves about with sparks: walk in the light of your fire, and in the sparks that ye have kindled, This shall ye have of mine hand, ye shall lie down in sorrow." Those who trust in themselves, kindles a fire, and walk in the light of their own fire. They walk in their own righteousness and burn their incense with the fire as Nadab and Abihu and not with the fire from heaven.

They compass themselves about with sparks of their own kindling. As they trust in their own righteousness, and not in the righteousness of Christ, so they place their happiness in their worldly possessions and enjoyments and not in the favour of God. Creature comforts that contribute to physical ease and well-being, such as good food and accommodations are sparks short lived and soon gone. They walk in the light of their own fire. Those that make the world their comfort, and their own righteousness their confidence, will meet with bitterness in the end. A godly man's way may be melancholy expressing sadness or depression of mind or spirit, but his end shall be peace and everlasting light. A wicked man's way may be pleasant, but his end will be darkness.

CHAPTER 3

COME

I saiah 55:1-3LB says, "Say there! Is anyone thirsty? Come and drink even if you have no money! Come, take your choice of wine and milk it's all free! (Vs.2), Why spend your money on foodstuffs that don't give strength? Why pay for groceries that don't do you any good? Listen and I will tell you where to get good food that fattens up the Soul!

Continue: (Vs.3), "Come to me with your ears wide open. Listen, for the life of your soul is at state. I am ready to make an everlasting covenant with you, to give you all the unfailing mercies and love that I had for King David." Our laws in America and the courts are telling us by the outcome of injustice; Are you going to believe me or are you going to believe your lying eyes?

A man is blessed who checks himself from doing wrong. We should serve the Lord and declare ourselves Sons of God in Romans 8:14, "For as many as are led by the Spirit of God, they are the sons of God." We do this so that we may have power according to the spirit of holiness by the resurrection from the dead being raised from the dead through water baptism in the name of Jesus Christ.

God is talking in Isaiah 57:7-8 LB, "Behind closed doors you set your idols up and worship someone other than me. This is adultery, for you are giving these idols your love, instead of loving me." God destroys in his anger but he will have mercy on you through grace. God wants the walls of our nation to be made of salvation. Brokenness?

We have leaders that rule over us that have no self-control. Proverbs 25:28 says, "He that hath no rule over his own spirit is like a city that is broken down, and without walls." They have no defense. God works for those who wait for him. God know that our world is infected and impure. We must stick with God's ordinances and stay away from abominable customs defiling ourselves.

Repent! "If we confess our sin he is faithful and just to forgive us of our sin and to cleanse us from all unrighteousness." Owning your sin is the first step to deliverance and recovery. God wants us to be holy because he is holy.

Lord God we pray that you don't turn your head away from us and leave us in our sin. Some still go out in the night and worship idols at grave sites and caves worshipping evil spirits. Some of these sins have been passed down through posterity. God sets his face against the soul of those who go after familiar spirits and wizards. Generational curses were passed down to us all the way back to the Garden of Eden but now every man dies for his own sins. There are still generational curses that can be broken when you repent and walk in Gods ways and purpose for your life.

Prayer: Father God we thank you for not destroying the whole cluster of grapes because there are some good grapes in a bad bunch. Heavenly father we pray for women who are discovering and uncovering each other's fountain. The good are standing tall and strong in your word in obedience as we continue to be a product of your holy eternity. There is a separation of the clean and unclean because we are Jehovah's children.

Continue: Your word says in Isaiah 57:15, "For thus saith the high and lofty One that inhabited eternity, whose name is Holy; I dwell in the high and holy place, with him also that is of a contrite and humble spirit, to revive the spirit of the humble, and to revive the heart of the contrite ones." God says there is no peace to the wicked in the name of Jesus Christ. Amen.

We need to learn the Lord's thoughts. You must have the understanding of God right in your mind and heart to truly serve him. How can you praise God not knowing who he is? His thoughts are higher than our thoughts. We are able to have God's ability within us a portion of the very thoughts and the mind of Christ by doing his word. This is how we put on the mind of Christ and hold the thoughts, feelings and purposes of his heart and God said, "Let there be light.

It is written is how we daily overcome the devil. It is important to understand that our time left here on earth is very short. We don't have a lot of opportunities left to do God's work as we think. It might not be the end of the world but it could be the end of your world. It is possible that a person could lose his or her life around the next corner. No man knows the day or the hour.

I don't have time for worry and I have to make good use of my opportunities. I can't let distractions such as emotions and getting money block me. Our world as we know it could soon be gone. This is not the time or the place to let your interest get divided. Keep a single eye on your God ordained destiny.

There is only one God and Father of all spirits who created all things. We have one Lord Jesus Christ who made all things 1Corithians 8:6 L B Paraphrase). Stay encouraged and don't desire evil things nor worship Idols as the children of Israel did by making the golden calf. The world has the interest of sin and wickedness and this is the devils interest. All wicked people side with that interest.

The interest of truth and holiness is God's interest, with which all Godly people side. There is no gray or neutral ground. It is right or wrong or heaven or hell. God not only see what we do, but what we are. God see who we do it with. God is not mocked; meaning he is not a stupid god. Some people treat God like they treat their mate like he is a fool, but God is not your mate. He is an all seeing, all knowing Father God. He is a faithful God. Are you a faithful child?

Isaiah 58:14 says, "Then shalt thou delight thyself in the Lord; and I will cause thee to ride upon the high places of the earth, and feed thee with the heritage of Jacob thy father: for the mouth of the Lord hath spoken it." Psalms 37:4 tells us to, "Delight thyself also in the Lord; and he shall give thee the desires of thine heart."

Trying the Lord's patience can be similar to when snake bites came on Israel. Covid 19 is our example today for disobedience. The scripture tells us in different ways how God's people corrupted themselves. The people sat down to eat and drink and then got up to dance in worship of the golden calf. They had corrupted themselves. There were also those who slept with other men wives and 23000 fell dead in one day (1Corinthians 10:8-9).

Continue; 1 Corinthians 10:11-12 LB explains, (Vs.11) tells us that, "All these things happened to them as examples—as object lessons to us—to warn us against doing the same things; they were written down so that we could read about them and learn in these last days as the world nears its end." (Vs. 12), "So be careful, If you are thinking, Oh I would never behave like that—let this be a warning to you. "For you too may fall into sin." "A trap does'nt snapped shut unless it is first stepped on: your punishment is well deserved" (Amos 3:5 LB).

We must all take heed when we think we stand unless we fall. 1 Corinthians 10:12 LB says, "So the one who thinks he is standing firm should be careful not to fall. Therefore the one thinking they stand, let him take heed lest he fall." Everything God says he put a period behind it. The devil come and say what God says and put a question mark behind God's statement and let man or woman figure it out for themselves. Satan hung out with God and man is no match for him.

Amos pleaded with God to relent his judgement in their place, God places a plumb line. A plumb line is a weight suspended from a string used as a vertical reference line to ensure a structure is centered. We must be centering in on the Gospels work. This has a lot to do with having a right relationship with God and loving your neighbor.

In the book of Amos God was speaking to Israel telling them that after all his warnings they still would not return to him. Now they were ripe for punishment. God will allow sin until your cup of sin is full and he will bring judgement. Don't think you want get paid for your sins. "For the wages of sin is death." It could be first spiritual death and sometimes physical death. Sin came to slick take us out of here.

God is telling us no matter where you go and hide in space, ocean, or on top of the mountains he is there. In Amos 9:2, warns us, that we must stop taking his mercies for granted. "Though they dig into hell, thence shall mine hand take them; though they climb up to heaven, thence will I bring them down." We have to guard our passions. God's word is his will for our life. The word that is coming out your mouth now is reflecting your faith then. Either you are speaking life or death, a blessing or a curse. The words you speak will justify you or condemn you. Be a believer and not a doubter and hold fast to your confessions of faith in the word of God. Speak good things into your life and into the lives of others.

Jonah preached to Nineveh and they repented and they returned to God from their evil ways. In our society today certain groups would rather try to outwit God and fight it out. They refuse to believe in God's word because they are possessed by demons. Stay close to God who is ready to save you. This could be your last warning. America can't heal its wound by saying it is not there.

It is time to ask God to help us understand what he want us to do. The wicked has set traps along sides of the roads of life. We must keep our focus and remain on God's Holy Highway and we must not pull over. There are people that want to live in their scum. Lord God, I don't want to be in that batch of scum that you throw away.

I can't look to men for help. I only have your word to lead me to the path of everlasting life. Our government can see the traps they have set and they act as though they want to fall in themselves. Technology is a booby trap that is taking us down the road of self -destruction. Our government is fighting the facts as they deny God's wisdom. Read Proverbs 1:24-33. This could be your last chance. God knows the secrets of every heart.

I will continue to go forth in truth, humility, and justice because this is God's royal scepter. We need not fear if the world blows up and the mountains crumble into the sea. The laws that are passed are thorns in America's side and they are only a constant temptation to its people to be evil continually. Common sense has turned into non-sense.

The laws that are passed opened the door for all kinds of sin and have given sin a wide open door to make wrong right and right wrong. God wants us to stand silent! He says, "Know that I am God! The battle is not yours it is the Lord's, but the victory is yours. Thank you for the victory in advance Lord God.

God wants us to know that, I (He) will be honored by every nation in the world. What is happening in America happened in the days of Joshua after Israel crossed over to the promise land and he died in Judges 2:7-10. The next generation had stopped being true to God. The old generation had died off that knew and saw the power of God.

After years have passed away with no posterity the younger generations ended up not knowing the God who made the heavens and the earth. This is not the first time young people are trying to throw God out of their lives. They wander why curses are upon them because, Isaiah 59:2 tells them, "But your iniquities have separated between you and your God, and your sins have hid his face from you, that he will not hear."

The next generation did not worship Jehovah as their God and did not acknowledge the God who brought them out of bondage into the land of milk and honey. Kids today only see milk and honey they don't know nothing about the struggle. They did not care about the mighty miracles that God had done for their ancestors.

Moses told Joshua that they would forget and start to disobey God and make him angry. This is when we must acknowledge 1 John 2:19 "They went out from us, but they were not of us; for if they had been of us, they would no doubt have continued with us: but they went out, that they might be made manifest that they were not all of us." Those who leave God is another battle and harvest for souls to save them from a multitude of sins.

The same is happening in America today as the world we live in changes little by little. Our government officials have a long foresight when making changes. They look down the road to the next 20 years and all of a sudden we wonder, how did we get here? Where did our worship to God go to?

America or the world and Satan's agenda is to get God off the set. Covid 19 is a training ground to get us prepared for the Socialist or One World Government set for the year of 2030. This is the year where every person will be in the new world system. They will use the media and pass laws to make sure everyone is reprogramed. The new norm is elevating Satan's agenda.

The type of government that we are being led into will be doing everything the Lord has forbidden including worshipping heathen gods from other nations. As you have noticed in 2020 Covid 19 was a plan to de-populate the earth. It was designed to kill off the elderly to prevent posterity. In 2021-22 kids are dying in a fast rate. The rush to open schools and businesses increase the death rate by school shootings. It seems as though they are keeping count. Parents are now marching their 5 to 11 year old children and holding their hand to get shots like the Holocaust.

There are also food shortages that is about to bring world-wide mass de-population. With God taken off the set the new generation 20 years from now will not know anything about Jehovah God. They will be untaught, and unlearned. By killing off the elderly the new generation will not know who they are or whose they are. They will be led by Tech giants like Nano Tech that will lead them into the world of Robotics. Thank God there will always be those who honor and worship God.

After this when the elderly dies off the children are being taught they can be anything they want other than who God created them to be. They can be anything other than what God created them to be. It is sad but it is true. How can you be confused about what's between your legs? We need to thank God for a sound mind because we are living in times when some of our leader's minds are twisted. For the love of money song by the O Jays is why our world is so twisted. The love of money is the root to all evil.

If the God who made the heavens and the earth is taken off the set then the next generation will be lost. If they don't know who God is they will be open to and grabbing for every wind of doctrine that looks like Jehovah. They are open for suggestions. When the New world government arrives in full force then you will really have a new normal. It is changing right before our eyes in all this confusion. In a couple of decades we will be saying how did we get here?

God always spanks his children for disobedience. America has already been intermarried to every wind of doctrine that comes from other nations. If you are not rooted and grounded in the Holy Bible you will surely be a target for Satan's agenda. People who teach these false doctrines are looking for everyone who is not tied down or rooted and grounded in God's word.

We have men and women in authority and bums and loafers saying how can Jesus Christ save us? God told Samuel the prophet to tell King David not to build him a temple because he will let his son build him a temple. God explained in 2 Samuel 7:14 LB that, "If he sins, I will use other nations to punish him." You have to watch out when your sins are piled higher than your head; meaning that your sins are full and over flowing ready for judgement. Those who don't believe is damned already.

It is a strange thing how a person can be a slave to his sin and not know it because of God's love, grace and mercy. He or she thinks because God has not punished them yet that they have gotten away. So they continue in their sin slavery. They think since nothing has happened yet God is not going to judge their sin.

(Ezra 9:9), "For we were slaves, but in your love and mercy you did not abandon us to slavery; instead you caused the kings of Persia to be favorable to us." We leave God but God will not forsake us when we cry out to him. In the use of Technology and research humankind finds new wickedness thru experimentation. Wickedness jumps out at you through the dark web of computers.

I want you to be encouraged because it is God who made the heavens and the earth and all that dwell in it. There is nothing new to God under the sun. We are Jehovah's guest here on earth and God knows where all the traps and snares are. This is why he gives us his word to warn us ahead of time so that we don't fall into them. Reading and obeying God's word keeps us in safety wherever we go when we obey them.

There are those who try to get rich and make money their God, but all the money on earth can't compare to the value of one soul. If you get all the money on earth you will not be able to buy your way out of death or hell. When a man dies the power of his money will die when he dies and he will not be able to take it with him. It will be left to others.

God wants to supply all of your needs so that he can receive thanksgiving from you. He wants to fulfill your needs. Jehovah wants you to trust him. When trouble comes your way he wants to be there for you to bring you out. He wants to be your super hero and rescue you so that he can receive your praise. Faithfulness is his character. In relationships you want someone faithful to you as you are to them. Delight yourself in the word of God giving him due respect. He is the one holding you up and catching you when you fall.

I want to remind you that we are the Lord's assistant down here on earth helping one another. Our theme should be God is so good and his loving kindness last forever. Those who bless God through their body or their temple receive God's blessing with his presence in them, on them, around them and for them. We are walking temples praying and praising and doing the will of God in love. Jesus died and rose again victoriously over the enemy so that we could stay in fellowship with him who is the Lord thy God.

This was God's perfect plan for imperfect people. Now all we have to do is admit it, quit it, and get back with it. Get back in line with the word of God. In other words "Repent." When we repent God will listen to every individual prayer concerning their private sorrow and your public prayers. When you find yourself in bondage tied up in your sin, repent, and cry out to the Lord with a sincere heart. God will hear your cry and forgive and forget your sin and help you.

God said in 2 Chronicles 7:14-15 L B, "Then if my people will humble themselves and pray, and search for me, and turn from their wicked ways. "I will hear from heaven and forgive their sins and heal their land." (Vs.15), "I will listen, wide awake, to every prayer made in this place."

Keep your communication lines open because God will stay with you as long as you stay with him. God will never leave you nor forsake you. If you walk out on God and serve other gods he will turn his head on you and eventually spank you back into repentance. 2 Chronicles 16;9 LB tells us, "For the eyes of the Lord search back and forth across the whole earth, looking for people whose heart is perfect towards him, so that he can show his great power in helping them."

We should have leaders who have a constant relationship with God to guide us. We don't need leaders who think they are better than the people they serve. As Covid 19 brings us closer to the use of robots men and women should reevaluate his or herself. Mad science is looking for a way for us to self-destruct by experimenting with the human body trying to improve and find eternal life with computers that break down.

Science is looking for control of your thoughts and looking for ways to stop criminal thoughts as they think them. We must watch as well as pray because someone close to you wants to try and control your life.

Have you noticed there is always someone fighting for control in your life? They are preying on the weak. They come in a help suit and some get mad when they can't get in where they fit in.

Drug dealers have many followers controlled by drugs. People deliver their strength over to them because drugs have broken them down to the last denominator. Remember that people are being trained by the government to follow instructions. The media is a strong teacher when we panic and know not what to do. We turn to the media for advice and they will lead you straight into the New World Order. Like children we could not even go outside or to work as we received the training from government control. We was even being trained how to get in line for handouts. The TV show Survivor is becoming very popular these days.

Let no man think that he will continue to prosper walking in stubbornness against God. Romans 1:18-19 warns us "For the wrath of God is revealed from heaven against all ungodliness and unrighteousness of men, who hold the truth in unrighteousness." (Vs.19),"Because that which may be known of God is manifest in them; for God hast shewed it unto them."

Whenever a people of a land walk contrary to God it will bring devastation and disease that the Lord allows to come upon it. When man keep breaking the contract God allow curses to come on this people because of their disobedience. Obedience is not beyond their reach because it is in their hearts and in their mouths is how you obey.

Disobedience is the reason for your woes today. Only the repentance of your sin can and will bring you out of curses, woes and sin. Jesus Christ came to bring the world peace. Whenever people want to live anyway they want to without law and order their own evil will crush them. Our new leaders detest God's word and his order especially the gays and women groups. God made our bodies and set the standards for our bodies. Modern churches preach everything but change. They don't tell you that you must change your wicked ways.

This imaginary government that they are dreaming about will explode in their faces. Did you see how many lives that was lost just in the first stage of their dream. What is a dream? "A dream is a succession of images, ideas, emotions, and sensations that occur involuntarily in the mind during certain stages of sleep. It can also mean a personal ambition or goal." They are making images in their mind that becomes our reality. America is a melting pot of different religions that do not have the contract with the God that made the heavens and the earth. These different religions bring their altars into America and become a thorn in our sides.

Satan has it's bondages that make sin their paradise. Satan's grip on those who serve him will become his merchandise. Everything that is contrary to the word of Jehovah is Satan's merchandise. Remember Lots wife loved sin so much that she did not want to leave sin and break sins heart. Not knowing that her soul was more precious to her than to put it on the line than all the lust from gay movements and women's movement money and sins for a moment.

Women, all the makeup in the world can't give you beauty forever. It is only a temporary fix. None of these things can give a woman eternal life and keep your soul from hell. If you are a rich man, proud man or wise man, all will die like the foolish man.

Death is the shepherd of all humankind. Those in charge of our government are turning away from Jehovah by passing laws and they will be responsible for destroying God's people and bringing disaster upon the whole nation. You can be sure that all the sins of the people will catch up with them by the contrary laws against God that they have passed.

Misery loves company. Our government is being led by pedophiles. When you look at milk cartons that say have you seen her or him and it makes me wonder, where are they? Children are missing in vast numbers used in research and never seen again.

Scientist wants to be like God and find a way to live forever. They will live forever when their body die and go back to the ground and their soul will either end up in heaven or hell. We are choosing right now for ourselves heaven or hell. They will still be quoting that these people had great wisdom.

So don't be dismayed when evil men grow rich and build their lovely homes for when they die they carry nothing with them. Money, houses and cars are things God let us use while we are here on earth. The poor you wil have always.. This could be the reason why some are trying to buy eternal life because through Jehovah our God standards they do not qualify. Their honors here on earth will not follow them but their sins will fly them straight to hell.

There is a group called the Left in our country that calls him or herself happy all through their life and part of the world applauds their success --- yet in the end he dies like everyone else, and enters into eternal darkness. For humankind with all its pomp must die like any animal but men and women have a soul. They have a mind, will and emotion and they are able to communicate directly to their creator.

Humankind is fast at work trying to use cybernetics to find out how to modify human genes functions. They want to use such things as Neuro dust implanted in the body to be implemented censors to your brain. They want to use a remote to control your mind and body to turn you off or on at their will. They want to capture your soul.

Our government is seeking your mind, will and emotions. They want to place your soul in a computer so you can live forever. They want to preserve your soul in a computer library. They want to save your individual thoughts for future reference. This is how scientist see us living forever.

The rich wants to live forever without the Holy Spirit so that they can keep their sins and take us all to hell with them. They want to download your brain into quest bionics body parts by 2050. By 2030 every individual should have received their Covid 19 shot to bring in the New World Order. The war with Russia and Ukraine is fighting to corner the market over Neon Gas. This gas helps provide a needed ingredient to make chips for computers, phones, credit cards, and T V's.

God's people should never forget what he has done for them. We have that blessed hope of eternal life. Some hope is better than no hope. We have hope and that is our earnest, intense, favorable, confident expectation of eternal life. The wicked know when he dies there will be know hope.

Over the portals of hell should be written; abandon all hope ye who enter here. God's miracles has had a strong effect on those lives who encountered them and those who seen them and his miracles leave a lasting impression. Jehovah's miracles have a deep and permanent effect upon our lives.

We have choices all day long. Good choice good consequence, bad choice, bad consequences. God moves gradually to help you. Like a father that pities his children so the Lord pities them that fear him. The atheist are running this country because they have no experience with God who made the heavens and the earth. They have tunnel vision. They still have time to experience Christ. The only reason the atheist don't know Christ is because they have never experienced Him.

Our government has another agenda other than what God said life should be like. We are headed into Marxism and that is the gateway to communism and there is a new slavery in town, not a new sheriff. In the book of Daniel we read how Daniel pray to his God 3 times a day. Shadrach, Meshach and Abednego did not bow down to government idols.

God sends his angels before those whom he loves who are careful to obey him. The angel will clear the way before them and defeat all who come against them. As we pray our prayer of protection and as we plead the blood and the oil of the anointing over our lives we sanctify ourselves unto the Lord. Plead the blood and the oil over all that belongs to you anointing all that you own with the oil of the anointing, Sanctify your tabernacle or your body, home, at work, your car and over all that belongs to you because you are children to the Lord.

Revelation 12:11 "And they overcame him (the devil) by the blood of the Lamb, (Jesus) and by the word of their testimony; and they loved not their lives unto the death."

Isaiah 10:27 "It shall come to pass in that day, that his (the devil's) burden shall be taken away from off thy shoulder, and his yoke from off thy neck, and the yoke shall be destroyed because of the anointing."

PLEAD THE BLOOD AND THE OIL

Father, I thank You for the blood and the oil of the anointing. I thank You for the scriptures teaching me about Your blood and the oil. I apply the blood of Jesus over me and my household today, and also over my physical body, mind, and soul. I also apply the oil of the anointing to my household, body, mind, soul, and spirit. I thank You that the blood of Jesus protects me from physical harm, destruction, inconvenience, physical disease and danger.

Thank You Father, that as I apply the blood to my body that I am empowered with strength and energy with the life of God. I thank You for the oil of anointing upon my life; I apply it to my soulish realm. I apply it to my soul that I might be protected from the lies, the influence, and the deception of the devil. I thank You that the blood protects my soulish realm and that I am cleansed from the things in my mind that are not of God.

I thank You Father, that as I apply the oil of the anointing to my soulish areas, that my mind, my will, and my emotions will change as the anointing protects me from the lies and intents of the devil and as it protects me from the world, the flesh, and the devil on a day to day basis. I thank You Father, that I am protected from what I hear or see. I thank You Father that I am a person that goes by what I know and not by what I see or hear. I thank You Father, that my household has the mind of Christ, the wisdom of God, and the personality and emotions of the Holy Spirit. I thank You Father, that the blood protects me from evil spirits that would try to attach themselves to me or my household.

Father, I invite You into my life as never before. I thank You Father, for the blood and the oil and the scriptures you gave us for teaching us to better understand how to apply each to our lives. In the Mighty Name of Jesus Christ we pray. Hallelujah! Thank You Lord God!

We also give offering to the Lord to make ransom for our soul. To atone is make amends to; to provide or serve as reparation or compensation for something bad or unwelcomed--- usually + for. To make reparation or supply satisfaction for expiate. Reparations should be taken to repair the wrongs that were done. Amends need to be made for the wrong one has done by paying money to or otherwise helping those who have been wronged. Our government would rather turn America into a welfare state than to give each person reparations.

There are a lot people who don't even know they already have a God who made the heavens and the earth. They walk around breathing his fresh air and don't even know that God breathe the breath of life into man and he became a living soul. Satan snatches the souls of those who are ignorant about God their creator. Ignorance about the word of God makes the war for souls a hard task.

God is inside those who are saved and when we walk away and serve other gods he is tempted to turn his head and allow sin without repentance to have its wages which is death. God's spirit inside believers makes them God's children and makes them qualify for the return of Jesus Christ. Those who don't have God's spirit is already damned but they have God's grace. They have another opportunity to get it right.

God said in Psalms 50:22 LB, "This is the last chance for all of you who have forgotten God, before I tear you apart--- and no one can help you then." There are fools who say to themselves, there is no God. They have a wicked heart and their life is corroded with sin. They have turned their backs on him. They are corrupt and rotten and their lives are filthy with sin. Our government is seeking the lives of your people Lord God. Let their evil deeds boomerang upon them.

Their real problem is inner debate, inner conflict and inner disharmony making their real problem internal. Wickedness and dishonesty are entrenched in their hearts. They pervert the children. They rob and murder and refuse to fear you Lord. Their words are oily smooth, but in their heart is war against you Lord God.

They made sweet promises to our nation but underneath there were daggers. I am casting all my cares on you for you care for me. I thank you in advance for not letting me slip and fall to murders and robbers because I am trusting in you to save me. What can man do to me?

Lord God all I am looking for is justice. Psalms 58:1-2 LB, "You High and mighty politicians don't even know the meaning of the word! Fairness? Which of you has any left? Not one! All your dealings are crooked: you give justice in exchange for bribes. (Vs.8),"Let them be as snails that dissolve into slime, and as those who die at birth, who never see the sun." Put the turn around on them Lord God aborting over 1 million babies in the first ten days of 2021. Over 100 thousand a day all over the world denying you the fruitfulness you commanded. They are proud and need to know that God rule and reign throughout the world.

God likes absolute loyalty and exclusive devotion. As you read the Old Testament the death of an animal was excepted by God instead of Jesus Christ the spotless Lamb of God. Jesus Christ the spotless sacrifice came to deliver humankind from sin once and for all. They had to have an inspection of every animal to make sure it was spotless.

There are too many spots and wrinkles in the church Lord God and we still need some more of your grace to give us time to get it right. In those days the offering was seasoned with salt as a reminder of God's covenant. Today we are the salt of the world. When we get saved we have the rainbow in the sky as a reminder of the covenant not to destroy humankind by flood again. Satan through homosexuality has "Mentally Kidnapped" the rainbow as a sign of rebellion against God.

The enemy is waving its flag of disobedience. Deuteronomy 32:31-33 "For their rock is not as our Rock, even our enemies themselves being judges, (Vs.32), "For their vine is of the vine of Sodom, and of the fields of Gomorrah: their grapes are grapes of gall, their clusters are bitter: (Vs.33), "Their wine is the poison of dragons, and the cruel venom of asps." Mathew 16:18 L B says, "Now I say to you are Peter (which means rock), and upon this rock I will build my church, and all the powers of hell will not conquer it."

Jesus Christ sealed the New Covenant with his blood that we now partake of. He also gave us the covenant of Peace. There are people today that feel like Dathan and Abiram who protest against authority in and outside the Church. They would love to do the priest job but they have not been appointed. God said in Deuteronomy 32:39-40, "See now that I, even I, am he, and there is no god with me: I kill, and I make alive; I wound, and I heal: neither is there any that can deliver out of my hand. (Vs.40), "For I lift up my hand to heaven, and say I live forever."

Isaac carried the wood to Moriah to be a sacrifice and so did Jesus carry his cross as a sacrifice for us. We must carry our own cross to be a living sacrifice. Isaac had a ram in the bush and he was delivered from death. Jesus defeated death when he died was buried and rose from the grave to defeat death for all humankind.

We are living sacrifices but some of us keep crawling off the altar. Keep God first place in your life so that you can be successful in every area of your life. He is a first God. Why do you think you are still breathing? He is demonstrating his love for you by giving you another opportunity to get it right. He is giving you what is called grace. He is giving you what you don't deserve. Why are we still here? It is not because you are so good. God wish that all be saved and come to repentance.

Covid 19 reminds me of Exodus 9:18-21, when God sent a hail storm on Egypt. People that have no regard for the word of God's warnings suffer the consequences of disobedience. During this epidemic people are just like Pharaoh who heart hardened again and again until death hit their door steps. Our officials talk about everything but God during these times. They have no regard for his word or power. During the epidemic people sinned yet more and more because of their stubbornness and refusal to follow and obey Jehovah.

God threw down on the priest in Malachi 2:1-2-3 saying, (1), "And now, O ye priest, this commandment is for you. (2), "If ye will not hear, and if ye will not lay it to heart, to give glory unto my name, saith the Lord of host, I will even send a curse upon you, and I will curse your blessings: yea, I have cursed them already, because ye do not lay it to heart. (3), "Behold, I will corrupt your seed, and spread dung upon your faces, even the dung of your solemn feast; and one shall take you away with it."

Jehovah is still making a distinction between those who worship and honor him and those who don't. Posterity comes from the parent to the children not the children to the parent. Moses had a son named Eliezer that means "God is my help." Even in the epidemic people are still trying to keep up with the Joneses without faith in God. People are coveting that of another so they can live a good life without God.

They lose sight of what is right and what is wrong. Tech Giants are using aborted baby parts to make cosmetics for women and men to look younger. Using these parts now they can spray a younger look on their face from the tenderness of an aborted child. You can see on T V commercial when they do this by spraying on make-up to make their face as smooth as a baby behind. When they finish spraying on the make-up their face resemble that of a mannequin that businesses dress their windows with to display clothing.

This is the Mystery of Aborted Baby Parts. At all abortion clinics there are trucks that come and pick up aborted babies taking them to unknown destinations. The more babies are aborted brings an increase of breast cancer because the milk meant for babies has no-where to go and becomes hard in the breast of the mother like spoiled milk lumps up and hardens in a milk carton. This is part of the women and the alphabet group called the Lefts reward for their agenda. This Jezebel group can't wait to spray on rebellion. Jezebel painted her face and tied her head as a form of rebellion in 2 Kings 9:30-37.

Those who hate and resist God bring punishment on their family for generations. Jezebel and her whole family died because of her rebellion. You must honor your mother and father is one way to have a good long life. Knowing God is something each person must experience for himself. Our world is still wandering who is behind the curtain on the Wizard of Oz. If you have wandered away from God in your mind return to him so he can guard your soul and keep you safe from all the attacks of the enemy.

Jehovah will keep you under his wings and in the palm of his hand. He will set you high on a cleft where the enemy can't reach you. Resist temptation and stay plugged in to God and his word who gives you strength and power to overcome evil. Stay plugged into God's word until the flesh loose its desire to rule you and sin lose its power. God always make a way of escape. People who die in their sins are punished by the way they lived. They go to hell because they choose to go to hell. Our spirits live on because they were here before the earth was formed with Jehovah who is the God or Father of Spirits.

Our spirits are from God and will return to God when the body goes back to dust. Jesus Christ brings us back into fellowship with God after the fall of Adam and Eve in the Garden of Eden. There are those who keep on sinning against Jehovah. Satanic worship is out in full force and I want to remind you that there is a hell where Satan and all who reject Jehovah will be punished.

Isaiah 29:15 warns us, "Woe unto them that seek deep to hide their counsel from the Lord, and their works are in the dark, and they say, Who seeth us? And who knoweth us?" They just add sin on top of sin until their cup of sin is full and that will bring God's judgement. This is when they get paid their wages for sinning and that is death.

God is a forgiving God. People who sin are much like Adam when he told God I heard your voice, but I was naked and afraid. When you are in sin you run, duck and hide from the presence of God. You do it because you have guilt, shame and condemnation that come from your father the devil. Repent of your sins and ask God to restore you again to his favor.

Your strength will be to sit still and let God fight your battles casting all your cares on him by trusting in him with all your heart leaning not to your own understanding. God tells us in Isaiah 30:15, "For thus saith the Lord God, the Holy One of Israel; In returning and rest shall ye be saved; in quietness and in confidence shall be your strength: and ye would not." You were not willing to act right, but God has the power to cause you to come to him because God draws men and women to himself. John12:32, "And I, if I be lifted up from the earth, will draw all men unto me."

CHAPTER 4

GOD WILL CAUSE

God know how to bring the world to its knees. God has a way of getting your lying, hardheaded, rebellious, and disobedient-selves attention. God caused water to flow out of the rock for Israel. He does not try to get your attention but God know how to get your attention. Psalms143:8 David ask God to, "Cause me to hear thy loving kindness in the morning; for in thee do I trust; cause me to know the way wherein I should walk; for I lift up my soul to thee." Think about Moses and the burning bush. What about Paul's Damascus Road experience. God knows how to get your attention.

How do we avoid mistakes? If we do not hear or ignore God's instructions by not doing what God tells you to do, instead you blame others for your own shortcomings. Examine yourself and deal with any open doors to the enemy in your life. This is how you honor God and cause His plan for your life to succeed!

Don't blame God or other people for your troubles. Be honest before God and examine yourself. Teach your children fairly and justly in love while there is still hope. Live a Godly and righteous life before them in God's way of doing and being right at an early age. Keep them away from the school of hard knocks to learn life's lessons. Let God's word make them wise.

We all have an appointed time when we will cry out for God's help. Isaiah 30:21says, "And thine ears shall hear a word behind thee, saying, This is the way, walk ye in it, when ye turn to the right hand, and when ye turn to the left." This is when you will resist the devil and he will flee.

You hear the voice of the Good Shepherd and you will be hearing your Father God voice and the voice of a stranger you will not follow. You will roll your works upon the Lord. You will commit and trust them wholly to him, and he will cause your thoughts to become agreeable to His will, then so shall your plans be established and succeed.

God got my attention when I got hit by a car knocked up eight feet in the air landed on a windshield. I died twice on the way to the hospital. The emergency fire department said that they lost my pulse twice on the way to the emergency room. I was in a coma for fifteen days. I came out the coma and found out that I was paralyzed. I stayed in a nursing home ten months and God blessed me to walk out the nursing home. My previous job was that of a lying used car dealer but I learned to love the truth. So while I live I will praise the Lord.

God did not cause or let me stop breathing and let my body return to the earth and all my thoughts perish at death. Instead, I shall live and not die and declare the works of the Lord. In Isaiah 30:30 Abbreviated version, "And the Lord shall cause his glorious voice to be heard, and shall shew the lightning down of his arm, with the indignation of his anger, and with the flame of a devouring fire, with scattering, and tempest, and hailstones." (Vs.33) speaks a warning, "The breath of the Lord is like a stream of brimstone, so don't kindle it."

My son, despise not the chastening of the Lord. Either you are going to do what God wants or go to hell. God spanks his children. Don't get mad when God say "Thou shall not." It don't matter who you are you must prepare for a beaten when you disobey. Men and women walk around with their skirts up and pants hanging down because they are prepared for their beaten.

God deals with the heart. God also draw souls to him. Let God change those around you as you humble yourself and pray. If my people, which are called by my name, shall humble themselves, and pray, and seek my face, and turn from their wicked ways; then will I hear from heaven, and will forgive their sin, and will heal their land. "If my people who are called by my name will humble themselves and pray. We must first,

(1). Humble yourself.

(2). and pray, Pray in humility.

(3). Seek his face.

(4). Turn from wickedness. This is what you got to do. That's right you got work to do. God wants a broken and contrite spirit.

(5). Then will I hear from heaven. Then you will get through to me.

(6). And God will forgive your sin.

(7). Then I will heal their land.

There is no repentance without remorse. God is calling for humility. God don't just want you to swallow your pride but he wants you to get rid of it. Submit to God and stop asking God why has God made me such? Who are you to inquire against God? We are only clay on the wheel of God and have a need to shut up and let God finish forming us. Who are thou that repliest against God? You are an arrogant, self-willed heathen when you inquire against God. Has not the potter have power over the clay? God said shut your mouth and do what I tell you to do. Jonah replied against God and went the other way but ended up going to Nineveh any way.

We are the same today and we need to examine ourselves and see if Christ is in you. Humankind is still hitch hiking on every boxcar or wind or doctrine that comes along. Where did all these different religions come from that man has created. Who told them to be these different religions that they can't find in the Holy Scriptures they preach and study from. My people are destroyed for lack of knowledge.

They start out Baptist, Methodist, Catholic, Islamic, Mormon and every other religion that comes along. Hebrew Israelites believe that God is all black because the Garden of Eden was near Ethiopia. Roman 2:20 says, "An instructor of the foolish, a teacher of babes, which hast the form of knowledge and of the truth of the law." Romans2:28 reveals, "For he is not a Jew which is one outwardly; neither is that circumcision, which is outward in the flesh: (Vs.29), "But he is a Jew, which is one inwardly; and circumcision is that of the heart, in the spirit, and not in letter; whose praise is not of man, but of God."

Ephesians 4:3 says,"Endeavouring to keep the unity of the spirit in the bond of peace." (Ephesians 4:4 "There is one body, and one Spirit, even as ye are called in one hope of your calling." There is one God and he is spirit in John 4:24, "God is a Spirit: and they that worship him must worship him in spirit and in truth. There is one faith and one baptism in Ephesians 4:5.

Every group have a different song but all reading the same Holy Scriptures. Groups like these are nothing but confusion from the synagogue of Satan. God is not the author of confusion. The KKK believes that God is white. God is not a man. God is Spirit and spirit don't have color but a spirit will get into men and women of different races. God gave to all nations one blood. Obedience is better than sacrifice. "For all have sinned, and come short of the glory of God."

Therefore let all the house of Israel (in America and the world hear) that God has made all men of one blood and all men must repent. Repent of their sins and go down in water and wait on the Holy Spirit when you ask God for his Spirit in you. Acts 2:38 says, "Then Peter said unto them, Repent, and be baptized every-one of you in the name of Jesus Christ for the remission of sins, and ye shall receive the gift of the Holy Ghost." Acts 17:26, "And hath made of one blood all nations of men for to dwell on the face of the earth, and hath determined the bounds of their habitation."

We all must stand before God to be judged for the things done in the body and black and white is not even on the test. Are you going to tell God that you were black or that you were white on Judgement Day? Followers of these hate groups have become the Black Klan in the name of Jesus Christ. In Colossians 3:17 tells us to, "And whatever ye do in word or deed, do all in the name of the Lord Jesus, giving thanks to God and the Father by him.

1Peter3:9 says do not repay evil for evil or insult with insult." Now blacks groups think that they are doing God's will by terrorizing whites using religion as a covering. This makes Hebrew Israelites no better than the KKK and the world know where they stand being soldiers who so called protect their race.

If there is any type of harm done to another using God's name reveals that they have not known God. Mental Kidnapping from Satan has people thinking that they do God a service. Satan has put on religion and made Jesus as their purpose, not their scape goat. God wants your obedience. God wish that all should be saved and come to repentance.

God is no respecter of persons. We worship one Lord and he is the only Lord and we should love the Lord thy God with all thy mind and heart and with thy entire being and with all our might. Whites try to make blacks think they are better than blacks and now blacks want to return the favor with black supremacy. We are mixed with each other. God said that we should be holy, not black. God said we should be holy for I am holy, not white. Satan will get in anyone who allows him and obey him.

Then Churches jumped on the Non-Denomination train and now they want to catch the Holy train because it is the only train that God want his people to ride on. God said at least 3 times in his word "Be ye holy, for I am holy." This is the blind leading the blind. They will follow whatever new style of religion that comes on TV like new styles of clothing. They honor God with their mouth but their hearts are far from Him.

Humankind is always changing to different styles of religion. Every time a new train of religion comes by our leaders who lead by example want to jump on it so they can stay in style with religion on television. God is the same yesterday, today and forever. His word is unchanging. Churches are reminding me of this popular song that said, "If it feels good do it, if doing it is what you feel." They are letting their emotions lead them.

Satan is the prince of the air. God's word is settled in heaven and his Word says "Be ye holy for I am holy." God causes day and night to come on their schedule every day and night. Jeremiah 33:20 says, "Thus saith the Lord; If ye can break my covenant of day and my covenant of the night, and that there should not be day and night in their season." Humankind cannot control the sun called the greater light and the moon called the lessor light.

Everything God has the devil has a counterfeit. Man made a light switch and there are those who love darkness more than light because their deeds are evil. Darkness in churches now looks like you are in a movie theater, music concert or night club. This is what most churches replaced the pictures of the so called Jesus Christ with. They went from bad to worse.

The Holy Scriptures says that every knee shall bow and every tongue will confess that Jesus Christ is Lord. So we should not worry, fret, or have anxiety about anything we should not have a care. As God worked through Moses God can always causes me to triumph through Christ Jesus. 2 Corinthians2:14, "Now thanks be unto God, which always causeth us to triumph in Christ, and maketh manifest the savour of his knowledge by us in every place." God caused the sea to go back by a strong east wind and made the sea dry land and divided the waters when Moses stretched out his hand over the sea in Exodus 14:21.

God displayed his power over Egypt and caused Pharaoh to let his people go. Even though God cause good things to happen for those that are his after time they forget. When Covid the virus that had the world in fear the people mourned for Jehovah. When the cure was found humankind went right back into sin just like Pharaoh like nothing ever happened.

After every plague Pharaoh trembled with fear and lied to Moses and Aaron as though nothing had happened. The Lord showed Israel that he is a man of war if they only let him fight their battles. He is glorious in holiness, fearful in praises, doing wonders. Jesus Christ is still on the throne and no man knows the day or hour of his return. Jesus Christ died to atone for our sins. We must trust in God to fight our battles.

I was reading the book of Psalms 60:2 LB where it tells us in another way how God cause things to happen. It says, "You have caused this nation to tremble in fear; you have torn it apart. Lord, heal it now, for it is shaken to its depths." (Vs.3), "You have been very hard on us and made us reel beneath your blows." God's displeasure causes hardships. Our whole nation has convulsions by drugs with consternation with feelings of anxiety or dismay from things unexpected.

Men are running around killing like they are drunk out of their minds and things have been long bad but it is now time for them to start to mend. (Vs.4-5) of Psalms 60 LB tells us, "But you have given us a banner to rally to; all who love truth will rally to it; then you can deliver your beloved people. Use your strong right arm to rescue us." Heavenly Father our enemies weigh less than air on scales that is trying to destroy our peace in this nation. Oh Lord publicly avenge the slaughter of your people.

God's praying people remember your promises in the Word of God in hard times. Thank God for giving us your promises a flag of defiance against the enemy to resist the devil. It is for those that fear God that glory and take courage in him through Jesus Christ. We thank God for his spirit being in us, on us, around us, and for us. In the name of Jesus Christ gives us power to wage war against the powers of darkness.

Psalms 78:28, "He caused the birds to fall to the ground among the tents." God cause us to become righteous because God draws and Jesus is the Lord Our Righteousness. God told the people how Edom shall be a desolation and that he will cause her enemies to wipe her out in the book of Jeremiah 49:17. God will cause people to lack both bread and water in the book of Ezekiel 4:17). "That they may want bread and water, and be astonied one with another, and consume away for their Iniquity." God is due all praise and honor. He is the God that breathed breath into man and he became a living soul. Jehovah is above any god or idol and it is he that controls your destiny.

America, Jehovah desires your love and obedience. Self-preservation and pursuing a career is trumping out God's plan for women. Some women are telling God let the men have the babies they feel they can be more of a man than who they were born to be as a helper. The good merchandise that a virtuous woman brings to a Godly relationship is too hard for them. Confusion is from the merchandise of Satan and women group up and support the author of confusion (the Devil) supporting one another to give Satan power in their life choice.

Having abortions make women wombs become grave yards for unborn children. Disobedience like abortion brings more wombs that don't give birth and breast that cannot nourish. Example; Abortion=breast cancer and homosexuality=Aids. This is the reward of rebels that have a false heart towards God. God says, "All souls are mine." All people are mine. No matter what your nationality your soul belongs to God and he demands obedience. God made male and female. Anything called other is from their imaginations that have a rebellious heart toward God that is on its way to the pit of hell if not repented of.

The Left wants to sin, sin, sin like the men of Gibeah before they were wiped out. When they committed a horrible crime in the book of Judges 19:22 when the sex perverts gathered together. There are too many shrines on Capital Hill and the worship of idols on the high hills and under every green tree. Satan is setting up temples all over America duplicating churches on every other corner in America. This is open rebellion against the God who made the heavens and the earth.

It reminds me when Jeroboam reigned in 1ˢᵗ Kings 14:21-24 when there was homosexuality throughout the land. Women are deleting babies out of their stomach. In order to delete something it first had to be there. Satan has taken their heart and they love their bodies more than God making it equal to the love of money is the root of all evil. This land will reap the full reward of trusting in a lie as it cultivates wickedness that brings a crop of sin.

God is offering the world the seed of righteousness to reap a harvest of love. This is the time to plow the hard ground of your hard hearts by seeking the Lord. Their goal is money but riches can't make up for sin. (Hosea 14:9 LB), "Whoever is wise, let him understand these things. Whoever is intelligent, let him listen. For the paths of the Lord are true and right, and good men walk along them. But sinners trying it will fail."

Sin is separation from God. When light appear darkness has to flee. People refuse to see when they close their eyes and they have decided to choose evil and it becomes willful blindness. Romans 15:4 remind us, "For whatsoever things were written aforetime were written for our learning, that we through patience and comfort of the scriptures might have hope." "I hear the voice of the Good Shepherd. I hear my Father's voice, and the voice of a stranger I will not follow. I roll my works upon the Lord. I commit and trust them wholly to Him. He will cause my thoughts to become agreeable to His will, and so shall my plans be established and succeed." (John 10:27), (Proverbs 16:3)

CHAPTER 5

CHOOSE RIGHTEOUSNESS

We think 60 to 70,000 thoughts a day. Our brains are a record of the past. We all must do something different. Philippians 3:13-14 says, "Brethren, I count not myself to have apprehended: but this one thing I do, forgetting those things which are behind, and reaching forth unto those things which are before, (Vs.14), "I press toward the mark for the prize of the high calling of God in Christ Jesus.

Repetition behavior is subconscious behavior. When you learn righteousness you begin to make new connections. New choices and new thoughts begin to evolutionize your mind into a productive progressive development. Evolution is the change in the heritable characteristics of biological populations over successive generations. These characteristics are the expressions of genes which are passed on from parent to offspring during reproduction. The devil uses homosexuality and same-sex marriage or sexual selections trying to use evolutionary pressures on society to make their lie seem natural. Everything we do begins with a thought. When your mind begins to change to another or higher level of thinking it begins to reach toward godhood. You must choose the God (Jesus Christ) who made you or the god of this world (Satan) who wants to destroy you.

The Counselor Himself, the Holy Spirit, lives in your spirit to lead and guide you—but you have to take the time to draw out the deep waters of His counsel. Proverbs 20:5 says, "Counsel in the heart of man is like deep water; but a man of understanding will draw it out."

Isaiah 60:12 shows us that humankind know what they are doing is wrong in the sight of God. "For our transgressions are multiplied before thee, and our sins testify against us: for our transgressions are with us; and as for our iniquities, we know them; (Vs.13), "In transgressing and lying against the Lord, and departing away from our God, speaking oppression and revolt, conceiving and uttering from the heart words of falsehood." When you depart from evil it makes you a prey but your righteousness shall sustain you.

Our government wants to produce or change our minds by process of evolutions subject to a gradual progressive development. It wants to develop us into a process of continuous change from lower, simpler, or worse, to a higher more complex, or better state. They want to bring us into a peaceful social, political, and economic advancements. There will always be those who are poor.

Romans 12:1-2 tells us that, "I Beseech you therefore, brethren, by the mercies of God, that ye present your bodies a living sacrifice, holy, acceptable unto God, which is your reasonable service. (Vs.2), "And be not conformed to this world: but be ye transformed by the renewing of your mind, that ye may prove what is that good and acceptable, and perfect, will of God."

God want a messenger among you that can show a man or woman their uprightness and deliver them from going to hell. He wants us to walk in the path of wisdom on his Holy Highway that leads to abundant life. Show them how Jesus Christ paid the ransom. In order to do this we must be able to stand correction walking in the wisdom of God. We must be willing to be taught. However, you won't fulfill that call if you make the mistake of ignoring God's Word: Proverb 19:27 "Cease, my son to hear instructions only to ignore it and stray from the words of knowledge."

All those that despise correction hates himself. Help them pray to God so God will be favorable to them. Then God will see their face with joy and render unto them his righteousness. They need to repent of their sin for perverting that which was right. Isaiah 59:18 tells us that, "According to their deeds, accordingly he will repay, fury to his adversaries, recompense to his enemies; to the islands he will repay recompense." The spirit of the Lord shall lift up a standard against him." He will come up against those who walk in their own thoughts and wicked imaginations. He will come against those who action of forming new ideas or images and concepts of external objects not present to the senses against his kingdom.

Why are you lying against the right? Some people get offended when the Holy Spirit tries to correct them. As long as you transgress against God you will always have incurable wounds and pain. God can and will deliver their soul from hell and they shall see light. Stop running ducking and hiding from the answer and cure to your pain and sorrows. This is what God does all the time working in humankind to bring your soul from hell fire burning. He wants to justify you and sanctify you so you can just make the necessary adjustment.

God wants his creation to come to him and render their works unto his ways. Your sins don't hurt God only yourself. He wants to cause your thoughts to become agreeable to his will, so that your plans be established and you will succeed. There are those who will not confess Jesus Christ as Lord and Savior.

I am here to tell you that you are going to meet him. You are going to meet him (Jesus Christ) as Saviour or you are going to meet him (Jesus Christ) as Judge. When you obey and serve God you spend your days in prosperity and years of pleasure. You will have prosperity in his Word and in your relationships. God will supply your needs giving you all sufficiency in all things for every good work so you can abound in those good works. The joy of the Lord will be your strength. The wisdom of God will keep you away from the traps and snares of the devil and make those serving sin fall into them. They fall in their own traps.

You will gradually be transformed by the renewing of your mind. As you are being transformed you will have new experiences, feelings and emotions that will drive your thoughts away from your past thoughts of whatever lies that you were living. When you continue to talk about your past it will keep you in your past. Your past will become your testimony.

Our thoughts are the language of the brain. Our feelings are the language of the body. When you learn something different you begin to remove that record of the past. We can't let our emotions rule. Your external environment makes you put limits on your mind. Let God's Word open your understanding into the Truth about the real you as it leads and guides you into all truth and where your treasures are.

God calls us to Prophesy. To speak as a prophet and foretell your own future calling those things that be not as though they were. We must live in our future from the old man into the new. We must walk in our vision. We are destroyed for lack of knowledge. Our frontal lobe of the brain is the creative center. We have to write down what we want to achieve and speak it into existence.

We have to have a clear intent with an elevated emotion to move forward with our vision. Do not fear when you are moving from the known into the unknown. Use God's word or his wisdom to guide you. Let the wisdom from God's word transform you by the renewing of your mind. Romans 4:17 says, "(As it is written, I have made thee a father of many nations,) before him whom he believed, even God, who quickeneth the dead, and calleth those things which be not as though they were."

God's word is knowledge for the mind. Condition your mind and kill flesh thoughts and let the real you shine through. Share with others how you are being transformed from sin to righteousness. Be a witness and testify that you are cleansed, covered and protected by the blood of the Lamb and the words of your testimony. The way you think, act and feel is your personality and it will show that you have become someone else.

In the book of Habakkuk 2;2, "And the Lord answered me, and said, Write the vision, and make it plain upon tables, that he may run that readeth it. (3), "For the vision is yet for an appointed time, but at the end it shall speak, and not lie though it tarry, wait for it, for it will surely come, it will not tarry." Remember that your dream does not have an expiration date. aHabakH

Show them that you have become the woman or man who thinks he or she can be without abandoning who God made you. Don't hang out with doubt and unbelief and those who don't know who they are in Christ Jesus. There are people who have doubt and unbelief from Satan that twist their thoughts to confuse who they really are. The lie from Satan says, you are not a woman but a man. God made you a woman. The same goes for the man who listen to the lies of the devil. They call that coming out the closet. They are the ones who have just been convinced (completely) by Satan the father of lies.

Everything that you have learned in life from the Holy Scriptures, your culture and environment will help you bring your vision to past. You will have a before and after picture of how you see yourself. You will have to put some corresponding action and be empowered by the power of the Holy Spirit to get rid of past thoughts or (your old self) to create your success.

God wants you to have good success. Your future success will have you on a mission and you should be self- motivated and guided by the Holy Spirit. The spirit of God brings life and the blessing not death and the curse. God has a purpose for us all. Find your purpose and set your goals in line with your purpose.

Hint! "Seek ye first God's kingdom and righteousness and all these other things will be added unto you." Be on purpose minded. Be confident and hold yourself accountable by not playing the blame game as you trust in God. Stay away from stress, doubt and unbelief. Stress moves you out of balance and put your mind on trying to be your own god taking your mind away from God. Don't run but fight back because God has given you everything you need to win the battle when you got saved as you stay plugged in and feed and meditate on His word.

Watch your thoughts because wrong thoughts can turn on stress. You stop being creative when you are stressed out. Your thoughts and stress can make you sick and the doctor will have a hard time trying to figure out what is wrong with you. Stress will also bring selfishness and self-preservation which is the law of nature. Self-preservation will seem to be the right thing to do when you will be all wrong. Pride will set in and you will begin to have elevated emotions and think more highly of yourself than you ought to and forget about love toward others.

We all need to have knowledge about self and test our own actions so that we can have the appropriate self-esteem without comparing ourselves to anyone else. We need to know the truth about ourselves. Find out who you are in Christ Jesus your creator. We measure ourselves by being Christ like. Those who are unwise measure themselves by themselves.

The wisdom of God leads and guides us into all truths. We need to know the truth and that is the supreme reality and the ultimate meaning and value of our existence that comes from the Holy Scriptures. Each of us is an original and we should not lose our own originality.

Our government wants to take away your free will by programming our minds using computers doing the same thing daily. They want to use temperament which is the personality traits that determine how someone reacts to the world. The traits of temperament are mostly innate traits that we are born with although they can be influenced by an individual's family culture or their experiences.

They are catching our children at a critical period in life between age five and puberty. This is a sensitive period of time in development in which the effects of experience can influence a child's vulnerability to the adverse effects of life events. When a person is recalling an event for weeks and months and if this last for years it becomes personality. Your body and mind knows routine. They know things that must be done on a daily basis.

When the mind and body is not functioning together you could possibly have Parkinson or Alzheimer. They are progressive diseases that destroy memory and other important mental functions. The brain connections and the cells themselves degenerate and die, eventually destroying memory and other important mental functions. Elon Musk: Neuralink hopes to put brain chips in humans in 2022. Brain interface technology implants and help treat Parkinson and Alzheimer.

Brain implants connects the human brain with computers. Interface and robots are used to perform, record and stimulate brain activity. They are implanted by flush in surgery as it charges wirelessly. They also perform surgery for spinal cord injuries and neurological disorders. The war in Ukraine over where manufacturers are trying to corner the market over Neon gas used to make semi- conductor chips.

There is a lack of these chips. These chips are used in our TV, credit cards, cell phones and the war is causing a disruption in the chains in 70% of the world. China and Taiwan also have a strong desire for Neon gas that contributes to the manufacturing of these chips. These chips will be used to store and access information on a device such as cookies and to process personal data such as unique identifiers and standard information sent by a device for personalized ads and content ads and content measurement and audience insights as well as to develop and improve products.

They say with your permission they and their partners can use precise geolocations data and identification through device scanning. Like a Fitbit in your skull. Paralyzed patients could be able to operate smart phones and other technology like robot limbs with their thought. A Fitbit is placed in your skull about the size of a coin with tiny wires.

It is being tested on pigs and they somehow think that this study could enhance and optimize financial outcomes.

The flesh or the body is part of your unconscious mind because the body serves you and could become your master over time. The flesh and the spirit is constantly warring against each other. This is why we must prophesy into our life. We must speak good things into our lives and into the lives of others. We cannot let the flesh rule or we will feel like a victim other than a victor. We have to command our body to obey when it wants to do what it has been accustomed to doing. Meditate on God's word and use the word of God to get results for your future and control the flesh thoughts and the body. We must use one of the fruit of the spirit called self-control.

We have to practice doing right to become Christ like. Doctors ask each other all the time; how is your practice? We should ask fellow believers how is your practice being Christ like? There are some who are afraid to come back to Jehovah because of fear, guilt and shame. They feel condemned. They may have put the kingdom of God to shame having been mocked in public by others.

Thank God for Jesus Christ who said whosoever believes in him shall not be ashamed. We are delivered from guilt, shame and condemnation sent from Satan. Jesus died and rose victoriously for our sin nature and all we have to do is admit it, quit it, and get back with it. Repent with a sincere heart! Get back in line with the word of God. We get in line at the bank when we run out of money. When we need groceries we get in line. Why can't we repent and get back in line with God's word.

His word says in Romans 8:1 "There is therefore now no condemnation to them which are in Christ Jesus, who walk not after the flesh, but after the spirit." I'm in Christ therefore I am free from condemnation. Romans 10:11 says whosoever believeth in him shall not be ashamed." Don't be proud, stiff-necked and unteachable. Ask yourself is what is being said agree with the word of God? Stay teachable and change from sin into righteousness.

We don't have to worry about priest to go before God for us anymore. In Romans 9 tells us they are not all Israel which are of Israel and neither because they are the seed of Abraham are they all children. It is telling us that those of the flesh are not all the children of God but God shew us his mercy. Jesus was our sacrifice and our mediator and he will always be there before God as a reminder that he paid the price for our sin. Man could not stop doing wrong so this is when God's spirit got in that flesh (Jesus) to be a sacrifice for our sins.

God appointed by his oath his son who is perfect forever. We can now cast all our care on him for he cares for us. Romans 10:21says "But to Israel he saith, All day long I have stretched forth my hands unto a disobedient and gainsaying people." His mercy endureth forever and his love for us is everlasting. His ways are past finding out. No one knows the mind of the Lord and no one instructs him. Everything is, "For of him, and through him, and to him, are all things; to whom be glory forever." Amen. Romans 11:36

Romans 12:1-2 tells us, "I Beseech you therefore, brethren, by the mercies of God, that ye present your bodies a living sacrifice, holy, acceptable unto God, which is your reasonable service. (Vs.2), "And be not conformed to this world: but be ye transformed by the renewing of your mind, that ye may prove what is that good, and acceptable, and perfect, will of God." Romans 13:1-2 "Let every soul be subject unto the higher powers. For there is no power but of God: the powers that be are ordained of God. (Vs.2), "Whosoever therefore resisteth the power, resiseth the ordinance of God: and they that resist shall receive to themselves damnation."

When we sin or drop the ball repent immediately of that sin and move fast forward because God will forgive us. Then forgive yourself. We must live a repentant lifestyle because he is faithful and just to forgive us of our sins. When you repent remember your sins has been forever forgotten. Remember that our faith in God assures our soul salvation. Your fate is sealed to go to hell only if you reject Jesus Christ as Lord and Savior. "Repent" and receive forgiveness for your sins and then receive Jesus Christ as Lord and Savior and be baptized.in the name of Jesus Christ and receive his Holy Spirit.

We must remember God's warnings because God's word is our life. Hebrew 3:15LB, "But now is the time." Never forget the warning, "Today if you hear God's voice speaking to you, do not harden your hearts against him, as the people of Israel did when they rebelled against him in the desert." God was speaking to them in those days but did you notice he said, "Today! He is talking to you and me so that our days will be long on the earth.

Let the words of the Lord dwell between your shoulders, in your head, in your (mind). Let every man and woman be fully persuaded in his own mind. (Hebrews 4:12) reminds us, "For whatever God says to us is full of living power; it is sharper than the sharpest dagger cutting swift and deep into our innermost thoughts and desires with all their parts. Exposing us for what we really are."

Continue: (Vs13), "He knows about everyone, everywhere. Everything about us is bare and wide open to the all-seeing eyes of our living God; nothing can be hidden from him to whom we must explain all that we have done." We must put our faith and trust in the only true God who is the only one who can save us from premature death. Every one of us must give account of him or herself unto the Lord. Come to the Lord before your wound of sin becomes too deep to heal.

Micah 3:2 says, "I said, Listen, you leaders you are supposed to know right from wrong, yet you are the very ones who hate good and love evil. "You are the one who are to know judgement." "You give God's people useless medicine for their grevious wounds. "Are you true leaders? No misleaders! "You leaders who take bribes; you priest and prophets who won't preach and prophesy until you are paid."

You say all is well and the Lord is here among us until America becomes a heap of rubble. In Micah 3:11, reminds us about, "The heads therefore judge for reward, and the priest thereof teach for hire, and the prophets thereof divine for money: yet will they lean upon the Lord, and say, Is not the Lord among us? None evil can come upon us."

Our nation is so use to lying that it can't tell the truth from a lie. Justice is twisted and the straightest are more crooked as the rich pays them off and tell them who to take out. This is why we must all put our trust in God and not man. "Hast thou faith? Have it to thyself before God. "Happy is he who does not condemn himself in what he approves" Romans 14:22. Remember that whatever is not faith is sin.

Actions like these only bring confusion, destruction and terror. Yes a man's enemy can be found in his own home. Self can be your worst enemy. The only light that we receive will come from the Lord because sin is darkness. Satan tells you lies and becomes an angel of light. Man can imitate giving light with a light switch but he does not have a covenant with day and night. If God be for you, who can be against you? You are about to see the snakes and worms come out of their holes in our nation.

They will begin to destroy their idols and fear the Lord. We have a loving God who put our sins under our feet and remove them as far as the east is from the west. God's enemies are building an army millions strong but God declares they will all vanish. Have our government sold out to the enemies of God? Have we been sold out by our leaders?

We must understand that it is not easy to live a holy life. It is hard to be transformed by the renewing of your mind like the caterpillar. New converts must be patient while waiting on the change to come in their mind and heart. If not Satan is waiting on all backsliders.

CHAPTER 6

THE FAMILY STRUCTURE IS BROKEN

The church and the family both have become like a buffet dish. You can pick any church to suit your taste and any kind of mate even if there are abominations on the menu. True lies told by abominations are adopting young kids as they grow up with two mommies or two daddies being defiled by Satan's emissaries. A true lie is a lie that becomes true when announced. This formula is being used to confuse our society. Satan is the author of confusion. Kids should ask the two mommies which one is my father and ask the two daddies which one is my mommy. God wants his preachers to preach all the word. "Everything in the Scriptures is God's Word. All of it is useful for teaching and helping people and for correcting them and showing them how to live" 2 Timothy 3:16, CEV.

Some people think success is acquiring a big house or car. The greatest success in life is when you humble yourself and obey God. Seeking him first in Mathew 6:33 is our 1st priority, "But first and most importantly seek for, (aim at, strive after) first of all, His kingdom and His righteousness{His way of doing and being right- the attitude and character of God}. Then all these other things will be added unto you.

We can talk can't we? Let's make this conversation so plain that you can't get it wrong. 2 Corinthians 13:8 says, "For we can do nothing against the truth but for the truth." You must "Examine yourselves, whether ye be in the faith; prove your own selves, Know ye not your own selves, how that Jesus Christ is in you except ye be reprobates? Long life comes to those who honor and obey their mother and father. Children are born from a mother and father.

God is not a man that he should lie. God sent his Son so that man could come into the knowledge of himself. Jesus Christ was a reflection to humankind of how they should look while walking in the spirit of God inside them. Man was made to have the reflection of God but man cannot recreate heaven and earth.

Humankind wants to do what they want without God. Without God we can do no-thing. We must have the spirit of truth in us to reflect God. Family was God's idea. He told Adam and Eve to be fruitful and multiply and replenish the earth. God's creation chose evil continually and he destroyed all evil and then let Noah's family start again replenishing the earth.

God Jehovah gave us his word to live by since he manufactured us from the dust of the ground and breathed his life into man and he became a living soul. Our maker did not hide our instructions from us. He did not hide them in heaven where we had to go up to heaven and get them to hear and do them. He did not hide how to live from us across the sea for us to go and get it. But his instructions are very near in our mouth and the heart that we may do it. God set before us this day life and good and death and evil. It is a good thing to be adapted but not those who are confused about who they are when all they need to do is look down. They failed the aptitude test. They are confused because their relationships do not have the natural ability to be fruitful and multiply.

God Jehovah wants us to appreciate Him by walking in his ways and keeping his commandments so we can live and multiply. God wants us to multiply while Satan wants to steal, kill and to destroy everything that God stand for. God gave humankind a choice and men and women are choosing death and the curse. Deuteronomy 30:19 that says, "I call heaven and earth to record this day against you, that I have set before you, life and death, blessing and cursing: God even gave us the answer he said, "choose life, that both thou and thy seed may live."

Man was drawn away and man's heart turned away from God so that he could not hear but worshiped other gods that cannot hear, see, nor deliver. Sin comes in noise like lust, TV, radio and words of doubt. When you disconnect from God the source of all life you will perish and your days will be shortened. We were created by God to hear, love and obey him.

We should only fear, learn and hear the Lord your God and to observe to do all his words. Jehovah only wants us to be successful in life. God is our source and he fights all our battles as he goes before us to clear the way. All God tells us to do is hear and obey. He wants agreement. He wants us to be strong and courageous and fear not because he will not fail you nor forsake you.

God is not mocked when he says, "Ye shall not make any cutting in your flesh for the dead, nor print any marks upon you: I am the Lord." This is God talking in Leviticus 19:28, but our world says God is outdated and they can do whatever they want with their body. We see women in low riding jeans and put ink on their back parts where the jeans are low advertising their body as a billboard. This makes rape and prostitution human trafficking an open season.

Well some say, I got Jesus tattooed on me, but God wants his word written on the tables of your heart, not your body. There are some women so messed up that they got to put somebody else hair, nails, and silicone breast to get a man. Stop coveting what someone else has or what they look like and notice your own beauty. Satan is lying to you so strong you are dispensing Botox on your own selves. What happened that make you stop loving how God made you? Will the real you please stand up? What in hell is wrong with you? It don't take all that to get a man. What is wrong with the way God made you?

You let a fake woman that is in reality a man show you how to be a woman. Churches are full of women and they are even in the pulpit agreeing with abominations of the world. Don't get shy now! Have you taken an up close and personal look at yourself and the spiritual condition of yourself lately? There is not a man, woman or group that I want to go to hell with. God made us male and female and that is who Jesus Christ is coming back for. Every-(Thing) else is going to hell fire burning.

Your mothers should have taught you that. When you sit down you don't have one leg pointed east and the other west wide open. Then you want to hang out with friends and go partying half naked and someone spikes your drink and you end up with no control of mind or your body. You went out for a moment of pleasure and did not even get the whole moment and end up mentally and physically broken to pieces. This is when you run to God to help put the pieces back together. Thank God for repentance!

There is too much wickedness that we have to already go thru even in our own families. There are mothers and fathers sisters and brothers in incest and they call this, such fornication. 2 Corinthians5:1 talk about such fornication, "It is reported commonly that there is fornication among you, and such fornication as is not so much as named among Gentiles, that one should have his father's wife."

Children were having sex with fathers and mothers. They were having sex with step fathers and fathers and with step mothers and mothers. There are perverted parents that bath their kids at an early age and still bath them beyond child age. Mother's and father's still testing the water for their teenage kids. Perverted mothers running water for their sons and pervert father's still want to test the waters for teenage daughters.

It gets worse when families include their pets in their perverted life styles sleeping with their animals. Sleeping and eating with beast showing the beast their nakedness as the dog sniffs the woman to see if male or female. A dog knows the difference as he looks at her in confusion. The dog knows his kind but humans are the only species that don't know what they were made from, they was made for. They call it spite. The dog will put his sperm in that woman when she gets in that right position to hunch on her.

Scientist are being funded to experiment on women pregnancy with dogs. China is researching on how to get a man pregnant. It is said that dogs can get women pregnant shows how far mentally kidnapped and warped mad science has become. Our government passed laws for those who are sick like that. Two men and two women getting married are examples of that behavior. The Holy Scriptures say preach all the word that pertained to our life. Acts 5:20 states the angel of the Lord opened the prison door for the Apostles in verse 19 and told them, "Go, stand and speak in the temple to the people all the words of this life."

The book of Leviticus speaks about men and women having sex with animals. Deuteronomy 28:20 warns us that, "The Lord shall send upon thee cursing, vexation, and rebuke, in all that thou settest thine hand unto for to do, until thou be destroyed, and until thou perish quickly; because of the wickedness of thy doing, whereby thou hast forsaken me. (Vs.22) in chapter 28 thru vs.68 reveals all the curses that comes with disobedience.

People are choosing death and the curse rather than life and the blessing because of selfishness. Leviticus 27:21 says, "Cursed be he that lieth with any manner of beast. And all the people shall say, Amen." Men and women today are sleeping and kissing and performing sex act in cages with snakes. They don't want to be taught God's ways all they want to understand is that the Internet is their Intellect. They have a capacity for ill-rational intelligence and their thoughts are highly developed. They take it to the extreme. They seek money and internet fame.

If we stand firm in God's Spirit, "The Lord shall establish thee an holy people unto himself, as he hath sworn unto thee, if thou shalt keep the commandments of the Lord thy God, and walk in his ways" Deuteronomy 28:9. Despite God's warning as he get you prepared for temptations that will come your way your hearts harden as a drunkard. Idolatry is the ruin of a nation and it brings plagues upon the land that start at the root of bitterness. It is an infection that spreads across that nation.

Things revealed to us belong to us and our children, but secret things belong to the Lord. Parents are not preparing their kids for the dangers that they will meet in life by not acquainting them with the things of God. God's word warns the family ahead of time things to stay away from. Psalms 1:1-6 gives us fair warning. The whole book of Proverbs is meant to give us understanding for the simple, fool and those who are greedy of gain.

These are the things that we and ours are closely interest in. The Holy Scriptures are rules we live by. We should learn them diligently and teach them diligently. We should have our knowledge in order to practice it for this is the end of all divine revelation. This is not the time or the place for curious subjects of speculation and discourse, with which to entertain ourselves and our friends.

Money ventures are taking over and the church has become a night club with a cross on it. Education is good when used properly. Parents and government are helping kids to be lazy. Some parents have chosen to take their kids out of school. God wants men and women to be men and women in the world not of the world. Our children minds have not caught up with their bodies. They need a standard in their character. If the parents have a twisted version of life then we should pray that child break that generational curse in the mighty name of Jesus Christ.

For instance there are stages that a female go thru. You have a baby girl that must go thru stages of growth and development. She is a baby then she is a girl, a woman, and then she becomes a lady. A Baby needs training. A Girl needs more training. A Woman is development. In a Lady there is character. Women get the short end of the stick in life because they are most qualified for most jobs but get paid less. Young girls need to catch themselves before they end up giving what God gave them and the thing that is most precious to them away free. They become a bus stop to boys when one gets on right after one get off.

Satan makes the bait look good in the beginning to make you want to bite the hook. Women when you take the money you have bit the hook. Young men and young women need to stop playing. Young women breast all hanging out with the assistance of tattoos all over and young men trying to buy their way into that temptation that she is showing. I want to tell you both that the devil always shows you the beginning, but he never show you the end. If you knew what was at the end you would have never bit that hook. You only become a piece of meat to one another. Stick with God's wisdom because He knows the end from the beginning.

CHAPTER 7

VOMIT LOVERS

We are living with an untoward generation. This means that they are a generation hard to control. All the houses of God should be teaching God made Jesus Christ whom they crucified. True lies about our Lord and Christ are helping men and women souls go to hell. The church is to make known to us the ways of life. The church should be helping people recieve the spirit of wisdom and the revelation in the knowledge of Jesus Christ so the eyes of their understanding will be enlightened.

We are called and given authority over devils and to cure disease speaking about the resurrection of Christ. We do this so that we can know "what is the hope of his callings" and to know what is the exceeding greatness of his power to believers. Show believers how to use and work the power that we receive when we are born again. Being Christ like is imitating Jesus Christ by using the example that he left the Apostles when he walked this earth. We become his workmanship recreated in Christ Jesus.

We should be walking in his fullness by fellowshipping with him that filleth all in all. Jesus Christ our creator is all, in all, and God (Jesus Christ) is all in it. Jesus Christ who is the head of the church is being replaced by organized crime called church organizations by false prophets. Some of our government leaders are on the verge trying to kick the truth of God to the curve. They are determined to turn the Truth of God into a lie.

There are groups and churches that are on their way to hell because they are guilty of sins by association. There is not a man, woman or group that I want to go to hell with. No you are not that cool that I want to spend eternity in hell with you. They were supposed to preach the kingdom of God and to heal the sick.

Proverbs 26:11 says, "As when a dog goes to his own vomit, and becomes abominable, so is fool who returns in his wickedness to his own sin." As a dog returns to its vomit so a fool returns to its folly." I was just imagining one person but I can't imagine how a whole group of people being led by one could return to their vomit at the same time. Proverbs 14:12 reminds us, "There is a way which seemeth right unto a man. But the end is the way of death." There is a path before each person that seems right, but it ends in death."

There are some Church organizations that side track the Gospel of Christ by loving the ways of the world and can't wait to copy some of their ways. The reason why they look back is beyond my knowledge. Maybe they want to see how far God has brought them and there is nothing wrong with that. Staying in the past thought-wise will keep you in the past and that is dangerous after you have escaped from your past that was trying to take you out. America is defiled. Therefore God will show up and the land will vomit out her inhabitants for all the abominations that humankind have done by making the land defiled. Jesus Christ will do the separating the sheep from the goat and the wheat and the tares upon his return. Only if the whole world could hear the Gospel of Christ for this is the power of God to salvation.

A minister's charge is to preach the word. It is not their own notion, business or fancies that they are to preach, but the pure plain word of God. This must not be done with passion but with doctrine. The tongue of the false prophet is the tail of Satan also called that Great Dragon.

God gave ministers the Old Testament and the New Testament so they can break it down and make it plain mixing the Old and the New.

You must be direct in telling people their faults. Preach Jesus Christ to bring them from evil to good. 2 Timothy 4:2-3 KJV says, (Vs.2), "Preach the word; be instant in season, out of season; reprove, rebuke, exhort with long suffering and doctrine." Preach in season when some special opportunity offers itself. Preach out of season because thou may not know but the Holy Spirit knows exactly what he is doing and will fasten upon them. (Vs.3), "For the time will come when they will not endure sound doctrine; but after their own lust shall they heap to themselves teachers, having itching ears." Some of God's people think that it is hard to obey the word of God so they compromise and justify sin in their lives. Obeying is a job that we must keep your focus on.

Preaching has gone beyond the scope overlooking the Gospel of Christ that possesses the power of God to deliver. Joshua 22:5 warns us, "But take diligent heed to do the commandment and the law, which Moses the servant of the Lord your God charged you, to love the Lord your God, and to walk in all his ways, and to keep his commandments, and to cleave unto him, and to serve him with all your heart and with all your soul."

Abominations are being committed before you and I pray that you do not defile yourselves therein. Most people come to church to participate in church to help someone else get saved. How are the services getting off track when we have the teaching of Jesus Christ that gives us the power of God?

Vomit comes up from wrong past teaching and the body of Christ has a need to rid itself of it. This teaching did not go down right. In Mark 4 where the sower went forth to sow. Soon as the word went down from wrong teaching it came right back up. This is a spiritual illness that makes you throw up God's nutritious word.

We must watch what we put into our temple. We must lay aside every weight that so easily beset us. Vomit is flowing from the White

House to the pulpits of our country into the congregation into the streets. The laws being passed contradicts God's word supporting sin making hell numb to them. When no fear of God is preached it have no effect on those who disobey. Preaching no hell fire burning always and never ending seems to be an invitation to do evil other than preaching God's wrath to make them fear God to deter them from evil.

Throw-up or vomit in the church don't seem to bother leaders that are silent about abominations being passed by laws of men. Instead they change their diets from the truth of God's word and agree with the world. The sanctuary is being polluted. God's thoughts should run the church. We have to take God's word in the Holy Scriptures and eat it, All. God did not mean get a knife and fork and eat it. God wants us to feed on all his word and get it in the mind and heart.

Read it, meditate on it, and obey his word. He did not say that you have to like it. The truth is like a medicine that might not tastes good to you, but this good book is good for you. God said eat it All. Don't tear pages out or omit and avoid scripture that convicts your selfish purpose. We must have God's word and spirit in us or we are none of his.

Paul calls down a curse on bad preaching. Galatians 1:8 tells us, "But though we, or an angel from heaven, preach any other gospel unto you than that which we have preached unto you, let him be accursed." Paul wanted the Philippians 1:17 to be set for the defense of the gospel. In Vs.18 Paul says, "What then? not with standing, everyway, whether in pretense, or in truth, Christ is preached; and I do rejoice, yea, and will rejoice."

We need God's word to make us sick of lying, adultery, mammon, fornication, lust and all other teaching that is not on God's menu. What do you have in your spiritual daily diet? Jeremiah 15:16 says, "Thy words were found, and I did eat them; and thy word was unto me the joy and rejoicing of mine heart: for I am called by thy name, O Lord of host." Satan wants to push you out of your comfort zone. We must stay focused on God's word meditating at least 21 to 30 days before his word becomes habit.

Our world is fighting spirits that are from the use of video games, witchcraft, and sorcery. They meditate on these games to calm themselves from anxiety. The games they meditate on while playing is the cause of most murder and crime in our country. You read this as if you did not know this. This empowerment from these games became a mental illness to some and kidnaps the mind of the user of these games and this becomes their therapy for crime.

Leviticus 18:1-2 says, "The Lord speaks to Moses, saying, (Vs.2), "Speak unto all the congregation of the children of Israel, and say unto them, "Ye shall be holy: for I the Lord your God am holy." When sin revives itself and you begin to covet and lust that of another you must remember your covenant that you made with God. Obeying God will give houses you did not build and fields you did not plant.

You made a contract with God when you got saved. Isaiah 8:12-13, "Say not a confederacy, to all them to whom this people shall say, A confederacy; neither fear ye their fear, nor be afraid. (Vs.13), "Sanctify the Lord of host himself; and let him be your fear, and let him be your dread." Ezekiel 16:59 warns us, "This is what the Lord said: I will treat you like you treated me! You broke your marriage promise." God is asking his creation today where art thou, or in what place, or condition. Is this all you get for disobeying God. A moment of pleasure or 30years in prison, an incurable disease, and a few dollars to spend eternity in hell fire burning.

God see how you did not respect your agreement. Your reply is, Romans 7:15 says "For that which I do I allow not: for what I would, that do I not; but what I hate, that do I." There is a law in your members warring against the law of your mind. Men and women are still sewing fig leaves because of homosexuality to cover themselves as part of their shame from one another. God gave woman his grace after the sin in the Garden to be saved by child bearing so she could hold her head up after she was tricked by Satan in the Garden. Those who agree with Satan are Pro- Abortionist is declaring war with God is fighting a losing battle.

Isaiah 24:5 says, "They did what God said was wrong. They did not obey God's laws. They made an agreement with God a long time ago, but they broke their agreement with God." You have to understand that faith comes by hearing and hearing and hearing by the word of God. Becoming Christ like is a process that we all go through. We die to sin daily. Our old man takes time to get out. Old bad habits have to be replaced with new better ones.

When we escape from our prisons of sin by receiving Christ as our Lord and Savior we must remember that your prison guards are still looking for you. They have no more power over you unless you turn yourself in to them and surrender to sin. 2Peter 2:20 states that, "For after they have escaped the pollutions of the world through the knowledge of the Lord and Savior Jesus Christ, they are again entangled therein, and overcome, the latter end is worse with them than the beginning."

Satan's prison guards was looking and waiting on you to return because you had escaped from the power of sin. You were delivered from the powers of darkness. Now you are led by the Spirit of God. You have to remember that you are not a slave to sin anymore instead the angels of the Lord encamps about you and delivers you from every evil work. When blacks were slaves and they were freed some went back or did not leave their slave master. God sentence Satan upon his belly and dust thou shalt eat. We are made from dust and we are the dust that he eats. Satan slithers around our leaders and we should hold them up in prayer at all times.

Some criminals are released from prison and go right back because they have been in bondage to sin so long they don't know how to receive freedom. Jude 1:6 reminds us what God did those rebellious angels from heaven. "And the angels which kept not their first estate, but left their own habitation, he hath reserved in everlasting chains under darkness unto judgement of that great day. Lots wife loved sin so much that she did not want to leave sin and break sins heart. Romans 6:6 say,

"Knowing this, that our old man is crucified with him, that the body of sin might be destroyed, that henceforth we should not serve sin."

Today young blacks love sin so much they can't wait to donate themselves into prisons. This is the new slavery. The crimes that they commit against one another are senseless and they are reporting to courtrooms as to say, I want to enlist in this new slavery. This new generation heard about slavery but do not have an idea of what it is all about. If they did they would not be so eager to donate themselves to work free. Jobs are available all over America but people would rather covet that of another. Companies are hiring all over but they refuse to work.

You don't even have to be smart to understand when you read Deuteronomy 30:19. "I call heaven and earth to record this day against you, that I have set before you life and death, blessing and cursing: there choose life, that both thou and thy seed may live." God set before them life and death and blessing and cursing. Then he told us which one to choose by giving us the answer telling us to choose life that brings the blessing. This generation still failed the test and has chosen death and the curse rather than life and the blessing.

Colossians 1:21-23 "And you, who once were alienated and enemies in your mind by wicked works, yet now He has reconciled --Vs. 22 in the body of His flesh through death, to present you holy, and blameless, and above reproach in His sight—Vs. 23 "if indeed you continue in the faith, grounded and steadfast, and are not moved away from the hope of the gospel which you heard, which was preached to every creature under heaven, of which I, Paul became a minister." The God of peace wants your whole mind, body and soul to be preserved blameless until his return. He wants you set apart unto him.

As men and women change the natural use of their bodies we must continue in the faith. What is being said in the pulpit that makes sin so alluring and church repulsive? Hollywood already has sin flowing from the TV screen into the homes of God's creation that plant seeds in the minds of its viewers about the church. Sin needs no support from the Church. It is a battle for souls and why war against yourself?

There has to be a lack of posterity or the passing down of the love of Jesus Christ from the Church to mothers and fathers to the children. God tells us that all souls are mine. The soul that sinneth it shall die.

In the book of Ezekiel 18:4 tells us "Behold, all souls are mine; as the soul of the father, so also the soul of the son is mine; the soul that sinneth, it shall die." "The soul that sinneth it shall die. "The son shall not bear the iniquity of the father, neither shall the father bear the iniquity of the son: the righteousness of the righteous shall be upon him, and the wickedness of the wicked shall be upon him." So, now you choose.

God said in Ezekiel 18: 21 "But if the wicked will turn from all his sins that he has committed, and keep all my statues, and do that which is lawful and right, he shall surely live, he shall not die." Ezekiel18:24, "But when the righteous turneth away from his righteousness, and committeth iniquity, and do according to all the abominations that the wicked man doeth, shall he live? All his righteousness that he has done shall not be mentioned: in his trespass that he hath trespassed, and in his sin that he hath sinned, in them shall he die."

Times got hard after Covid 19 and the woman went back to prostitution and the preacher was about to lose his church and backslid by burning it down for insurance purposes. The gay man got saved and went back and put his dress and high heels on. 2Peter 2:21, "For it had been better for them not to have known the way of righteousness, than, after they have known it, to turn from the holy commandment delivered unto them." God said in Jeremiah 3:20 "Surely as a wife treacherously departed from her husband, so have ye dealt treacherously with me, O house of Israel, saith the Lord."

Those who turn their back on God resemble the prodigal son going into the slop pen and the dog that returns to his own vomit and eateth it. 2 Peter 2:22 "But it is happened unto them according to the true proverb, "The dog is turned to his own vomit again; and the sow that was washed to her wallowing in the mire." As the dog love filth will return to his vomit and the sow that was washed to her wallowing in the mire." Once the pig is clean he runs right back to the mud. The pig can't seem to stay clean three hours. We should always be mindful of holy things in our minds and our gifts showing Holiness to the Lord.

Look at how you treat God! You get washed in the word of God and go right out and run back to your pigpens of vomit and desecrations. After church just like the pigs you can't stay clean from sin three hours. Your minds are set on mischief. 2 Peter 2:20 warns us, "For if after they have escaped the pollutions of the world through the knowledge of the Lord and Savior Jesus Christ, they are again entangled therein, and overcome, the latter end is worse with them than the beginning."

There is call for repentance that says, "Return, ye backsliding children, and I will heal your backslidings. God is married to the backslider. Come on home where you belong. "Behold, we come unto thee; for thou art the Lord our God" Jeremiah 3:22.

Humankind gets an A+ in doing evil, but to do good they have no knowledge. After they have escaped the pollution of the world our enemy comes on the scene in disguise using his merchandise of deception to get us off track. He comes in a different cloak or mask to conceal his identity or true nature. He has many different looks in appearance or behavior that misleads by presenting a different apparent identity. Women are coming in disguises as a means of hiding their movement and intention. Satan works and comes through a person, group, organization or thing.

Satan comes even quoting the scripture. In (1Kings13:14-32 Paraphrase), There were two sons that came home and told their father about the old prophet in Bethel who did all the miracle works of a man of God that he did to Jeroboam. The man of God had instructions from God not to eat nor drink with anyone. The old prophet lied to the man of God saying an angel spoke to him saying an angel told him to take him home with him. Some people will lead you to hell to satisfy themselves for greedy gain. So the man of God disobeyed God's instructions because the old prophet wanted the pleasure of being in the man of God's presence. We must hear from God and obey.

He came to the man of God in humility and a contrite spirit to talk him out of his destiny and assignment. The old man of God ended up with his carcass on the side of the road eaten by a lion. People passed by and ask who is this? He was the man of God who was disobedient unto the word of God. We must obey and continue to be steadfast and rooted and grounded in the word of God.

When you got saved you were happy in the Lord for a moment and ended up right back eating your own vomit. You love sin so much that you did not want to break sins heart like Lots wife when she turned around and looked back. Those you escaped from in your past would love to have you back.

You go right back into your slop pens, vomit and waddle in filth. Are you a man or woman that became a vomit eater; a vomit lover that love filth? You had a weak foundation where you were taught the scriptures and did not sanctify yourselves unto God. When the storms of life came your spiritual foundation could not hold you up. When life happens to you repent. It was better for you to have not known speaking in tongues having the Holy Spirit being baptized in water than to go back. How did vomit become your daily essentials? Thank God for being married to the backslider.

Churches are becoming movie theaters and night clubs as the lights go down slowly dimming in the church. Sinners love darkness because their deeds were evil. Ask your church leaders why are you dimming the lights and playing with psychedelic lights like night clubs? Next they will be asking the ushers serving at the bar Non-Alcoholic beer because of the weakness of some members and the greed of its leaders.

Is that your way of getting romantic with God? Do the church want to go back to sin that bad? Satan use men and women to play on your needs and wants. Like Lots wife she loved sin so much she wanted to go back in her heart. Do you want slop that bad? Are you slipping into darkness? Repent!

All of God's ministers that are watching over their flock for greedy gain and are not preaching the whole council of God have a need to Repent! Selling out all the souls of the congregation for government money? Isaiah 56:10-11 exposes, "His watchmen are blind: they are ignorant, they are dumb dogs, they cannot bark; sleeping, lying down, loving to slumber. (Vs.11), Yes they are greedy dogs which can never have enough, and they are shepherds that cannot understand: they all look to their own way, every one for his gain, from his quarter."

(Isaiah 28:7-8), "But they have also erred through wine, and through strong drink are out of the way." Wisdom teaches you to see the man that takes a drink and man takes another drink, then the drink takes the man. the priest and the prophet have erred through strong drink, they are swallowed up of wine, they are out of the way through strong drink; they err in vision, they stumble in judgement. (Vs.8), "For all their tables are full of vomit and filthiness so that there is no place clean."

Who is teaching doctrine? New believers are not getting the understanding from those in pulpits. They are drunk with stammering lips and give no understanding. Those who are weary get no rest while the orator thinks he has given line upon line and precept upon precept. All he really is giving is hear a little and there a little. Those who want to escape sin slip right back into darkness and fall back into sin, broken, and snared and taken. "For as many as are led by the Spirit of God, they are the sons of God" Romans 8:14.

Some ministers teach as those from the synagogue of Satan that made lies their refuge under falsehood and they have hid themselves and the truth, End of Paraphrase. Their title D D behind their name becomes Dumb Dog in the Holy Scriptures when they don't all speak the same thing. They all have a different song and different doctrine. They don't have the same mind. There is too much division.

New converts need clarity when being taught the word to agree with that new Holy Spirit that they have just received. Thank God that, "The Spirit itself beareth witness with our spirit, that we are the children of God" Romans 8:16. God searches all hearts and He knows "what is the mind of your spirit." I Corinthians 2:11 "For what man knoweth the things of a man, save the spirit of man which is in him? Even so the things of God knoweth no man, but the Spirit of God."

We all have to experience God's love for ourselves to be filled with the fullness of God. To be saved is a process that we go through in our journey to come out of darkness to the light in order for us to become Christ like. When we are on the battlefield for the Lord we can help reap more souls if we have no darkness at all in us. The labor and specialization are two key means to achieve a larger return in the soul business. Through these two techniques, soul winners would only be able to concentrate on one specific task; soul winning.

Church is a spiritual hospital and a camp for learning to be a soldier for Christ. In time they will be able to improve their skills that are necessary in soul winning. It could be performed better and faster. Hence, through such efficiency, time and money could be saved while production and soul winner's increase and winning souls increase production in the Kingdom of God. We give glory to God because while we were yet sinners he died for us to save us from our sins. He wanted to give us abundantly above all that we can ask or think.

Those who are born once you will die twice. You will die physically and your body will go back to dust and then in damnation you will die spiritually in the lake of fire. John 5:28-29, "Marvel not at this: for the hour is coming in the which all that are in the graves shall hear his voice, And shall come forth: they that have done good unto the resurrection of life: and they that have done evil, unto the resurrection of damnation." When you are born again or twice, you will die once.

Stay rooted and grounded in God's word with one Lord, one faith and one baptism. Stay rooted until you become fully grown in Christ knowing the difference between the truth and a lie. Let your thoughts and attitude change for the better. Forgiveness is necessary because Christ came for the forgiveness of our sin to bring us back into right standing with our creator. Anything that you love more than God is an idol.

Beware of anyone who wants to excuse sin. We have to make the most of every opportunity to be a light in a dark and sinful world. Just let the energy of Jesus Christ work in you to defeat sin. Stay in the word of God to receive your nourishment and strength to grow in the Lord. Then you will be able to give God thanks, and his glory and his praise. Your faith will grow and your love for each other will grow as long as you walk in his love and grace. God is preparing you for his kingdom to come. This is why we have to let his will be done in our life here on earth even as it is in heaven.

God wants his children to be good because he is a good God. He wants to reward your faith with his power, the power of his resurrection. This will result in God getting his glory by people seeing God work thru you. So stand strong in the truth of his word and God will bless you in everything you say and do. When we use our faith and pray believing what God promised helps us daily overcome the enemy. We die to sin daily not all at once. Just keep practicing and working the word and never stop doing the right thing and it will keep your conscious clear. It is never wrong to do the right thing.

Keep check on yourself before you wreck yourself. Think twice and speak once. Remember that we have angels that hear our words. They are spirit messengers to help those who are to receive Jesus as Lord and Savior. The Holy Spirit thoughts are more supreme than your thoughts and we must listen to him. God had patience for forty years as Israel tried his patience but God kept right on being God and doing his miracles.

Whenever you keep looking at circumstances and conditions you are looking the wrong way. You are looking at the problem when you should be looking up to the problem solver. Look up to God because he has the answer in the wisdom of the Holy Scriptures to all our problems.

If you keep looking at the problem you will never find the path that God wants you to follow. Israel was always talking the problem and not the answer. They were murmurers and complainers and God don't like ungratefulness.

God gave us his promises in his word. We must trust in the Lord with our whole heart and lean not to our own understanding. Our own heart is deceitful and it can lead us away from God. Some of the worst thoughts and desires are found in men and women's heart. Jeremiah 17:9, "The heart is deceitful above all things and desperately wicked who can know it?" Only God knows because he know all hearts.

When man and woman rebelled against God in the Garden of Eden it brought the curse on humankind and the earth. This act of disobedience made all men that were born to become inherited sinners that came after them. Humankind had a new master Satan. We were all born into sin. Satan is the prince of the power of the air. He is a liar and the father of lies.

Adam and Eve was not the first to sin but it was Satan in heaven who rebelled against God with pride. Now sin is working in the hearts of humankind when they are born. We are born into sin and we now have a need to be born again. We are born of a woman and then we must be born of the spirit to be in good standing with God. Thank God for his mercy that endureth forever.

Before we are born again of the Spirit our life only express the evil that is within us. God had given man and woman the ability to choose. In the book of Deuteronomy 30:19 KJV "I call heaven and earth to record this day against you that I have set before you, life and death, blessing and cursing: therefore choose life, that both thou and thy seed may live."

We are God's property but through the disobedience of one man Adam; death came upon all man-kind. God's creation became lying, hardheaded, rebellious and disobedient people now living under a curse that we received from our new father, Satan! We must be born again to return to our rightful Father God Jehovah.

I want you to please be advised that we can now share in the goodness of God once again. Mankind was created to live forever with God depending on their obedience but they were kicked out of the Garden because of their disobedience. God sent prophets, judges, all kinds of men and women to deliver his chosen people all through the Old Testament with no success.

God went to plan B and sent Jesus Christ to be our deliverer from sin. This was God's next step as soon as Adam and Eve sinned to bring his creation back to himself. Now all we have to do is repent and confess Jesus Christ as Lord and Savior and be baptized in the name of Jesus Christ and receive the gift of the Holy Spirit with obedience until the end.

This became God's perfect plan for imperfect people. God placed his power within believers. Now we must believe in our hearts and confess with our mouth that Jesus Christ is Lord over our life. Christ was with them in the Old Testament and was even with Moses. Jesus Christ has always been even before the earth was created. He is the one who said "Let there be light."

Jehovah gave us his word to communicate with him. God's perfect plan was the Holy Spirit inside every believer. Instead of going to the Temple we became a Temple and we still have the right to choose. God placed the power of his spirit inside every believer. He also gave every believer special abilities and strength to bind and lose in Mathew 16:19.

We have the keys of the Kingdom. God's spirit gives us power to tell and bring others into the kingdom of God. All his believers became recruiters. God's wisdom brought the just and the unjust together making both one in him when the unjust receive Christ Jesus as Lord and Savior.

Remember in the Garden Adam and Eve was kicked out for their disobedience away from his presence. Satan who was the father of lies was also kicked out of heaven like a lightning bolt by the angel Michael because of his pride and disobedience. Now when we get saved we are in right standing with Jehovah and we are invited back into his presence.

We can return back into his peace and all our needs are met according to his riches and glory by Christ Jesus. We don't have to run, duck, hide and cover-up from God when we sin. Like when Adam and Eve hid them-selves, instead we run to him and not be ashamed by repenting asking for the forgiveness of our sins. Jesus Christ became our antidote when we are bitten by Satan to sin. The poisonous venom of sin brought death to all mankind that inflicts pain or illness. Instead of looking up to the brass pole we look up to Jesus Christ who is our healer and deliverer.

The sin of disobedience is the spirit from Satan that causes illness, injury or spiritual death and sometimes physical death. Jesus Christ took all the poison of sin for us on the cross becoming sin for us as a scape goat that carried all the poisonous venom or sting of sin away from us out of the camp away from us. God also told Moses in Numbers 21 when Israel was wandering in the Wilderness became rebellious against Moses murmuring and complaining.

They were ungrateful despite all that God had done for them by bringing them out of Egypt showing them mighty miracles. They fell in a state of unbelief. In Numbers 21:6 says, "And the Lord sent fiery serpents among the people, and they bit the people, and much people of Israel died. After they realized their sin of mumbling and grumbling toward God being ungrateful they repented. The Lord told Moses to make a fiery serpent of brass and set it on a pole and everyone that was bitten when they look upon the serpent of brass shall live.

The feet of Jesus was the feet like unto brass as the serpent was made of brass on the pole in Revelation 1:15. It was healing in Numbers 21 when Moses lifted up the brass serpent on the pole and Jesus was also lifted up on a pole at the Cross. Jesus told his disciples also if I be lifted up I will draw all men unto me. The brass serpent on the pole is seen today on the shoulders of Doctors and those in the medical field today representing healing.

Cowards run, duck and hide. It was said in the book of Judges that 8:21, "As a man is, so is his strength. "We must have the power of God as our strength. We have faith in God to deliver us. Instead of running from him we can just run to him and "Repent" and receive his forgiveness. "If we confess our sins he is faithful and just to forgive us of our sins and to cleanse us from all unrighteousness through Jesus Christ."

When God created man he was created part heaven and part earth. The Garden of Eden was paradise and man was made from paradise dust. God formed man from the dust of the earth and breathe the breath of life into man and he became a living soul. God who is spirit breathe a part of his eternal self into man.

Malachi 3:15-18Paraphrase, Those who are evil have become proud and arrogant and will not submit to God to rule over them. They shake their fist at God thinking he won't punish them. In Malachi 3:16, God has a Book of Remembrance taking notes about those who speak often of him and love him. When you repent God's soul is grieved toward you because of your misery in the book of Judges 10:16 KJV. "And they put away the strange gods from among them, and served the Lord: and his soul was grieved for the misery of Israel."

God will show different treatments of those who love him and those who are proud of their sin. On that day of judgement the proud and arrogant will burn to the ground completely. Proud people think they can do anything in their hearts desire because it is their heart. Man has a heart problem. God searches the heart. Mathew 5;28 says, "But I say unto you, That whosoever looketh, on a woman to lust after her hath committed adultery with her already in his heart."

Take those men and women who lust in their hearts in Ezekiel 16:17 that make God angry see what He says about the Dildo or toy that women and some men play with, "Thou hast also taken thy fair jewels of my gold and of my silver, which I had given thee, and madest to thyself images of men (Dildo), and didst commit whoredom with them." Satan duplicates everything that God created. Satan has counterfeit men and women but with Dildos he cannot duplicate the seed that God gave to all male species. This leaves those who use them with lust of the mind and heart. Lust is from Satan's devices and lust is one of his merchandise.

Satan wants to destroy the woman because without the woman today there will be no man. He wants to destroy the young women's health. Satan uses drugs, men and other women to accomplish his mission. Satan is wrapping around men and women like a snake and the first thing he wants to consume is your head. He wants to "Mentally Kidnap" you. His first target is your thoughts. Satan destroys the mind of Christ that is in you. He wants to twist your thoughts. He wants to take away your sound mind.

Our government and the parents give the young woman too much privilege. The Holy Scriptures tells us that mothers should not prostitute their daughters by letting them become a woman too soon. They have to be slowed down before they abuse themselves. Teach them to be stable minded.

In Ecclesiasticus 26:25 says, "A shameless woman shall be counted as a dog; but she that is shamed faced will fear the Lord." A reprobate is those whom God has rejected as godless and wicked. A reprobate mind has no conviction. A reprobate is an unbaptized, unprincipled, or depraved person. Those who die with a reprobate mind is damned. But if you live with any kind of sin it is always forgivable when you repent of it. Sins against the Holy Spirit is the only unforgivable sin.

Cemeteries use to bury these types of people (criminals) separate from those who were baptized. Example; take for instance boot hill for outlaws was separate. They lived contrary to God and were buried in separate graveyards. Not today because of equality sinners are buried with saints even though they did not live the same. Jesus wants the wheat and the tares to grow up together where he will do the separating.

The portrait of a wicked man goes around as a scoundrel and a villain a worthless person. Proverbs 6:12-15 shows his wisdom, character, and consequences. Vs.12), "A worthless person, a wicked man, goes about with crooked speech, (Vs.13), "winks with his eyes, signals with his feet, points with his finger, (Vs.14), with a perverted heart devises evil, continually sowing discord; (Vs.15), therefore calamity will come upon him suddenly; in a moment he will be broken beyond healing."

There are some who believe there is no resurrection and judgement of God. "Be not deceived: evil communication corrupts good manner" 1 Corinthians 15:33. "Wherefore let him that thinketh he standeth take heed lest he fall 1 Corinthians 10:12." We must be addicted to the ministry of the saints and serve the Lord in sincerity and truth. "But as for me and my house, we will serve the Lord." Joshua was telling the children of Israel in Joshua 24:20, "If ye forsake the Lord, and serve strange gods, then he will turn and do you hurt, and consume you, after that he hath done you good."

Now! This is going to hurt me as much as it is going to hurt you if there is no resurrection. There are even disputes about Jesus Christ being from heaven. God made a body in Mary and got in that body when the Holy Spirit fell on him like a dove that gave Jesus Christ the power from on high power. The Holy Scriptures tells us that in 1 Corinthians 15:47 "The first man is of the earth, earthy: the second man is the Lord from heaven."

1Corinthians 15:13-14 says that, "For if there is no resurrection of the dead, then Christ must still be dead. And if he is still dead , then all our preaching is useless and your trust in God is empty, worthless, hopeless; (Vs15), and we apostles are all liars because we have said that God raised Christ from the grave, and of course that isn't true if the dead do not come back to life again."

So we as followers of Christ let that thought pass. It hurt for a moment just to think about it. We rebuke and wave that thought away. "Knowing that he which raised up the Lord Jesus shall raise up us also by Jesus, and shall present us with you" 2 Corinthians 4:14 KJV. I want to say things to you that are joyous, not sad because the joy of the Lord is our strength.

Since Christ love controls us we should encourage, up-lift and motivate one another. We know Christ died for all of us who live no longer to just please themselves. So we should be excited about the one who died and rose again for us. Satan, the Lord rebukes you, because we are God's property and we obey the commands of God.

God brought us back to himself through what Jesus Christ did for us. God placed his spirit into an undefiled body to be a sacrifice once and for all humankind. Through Christ Jesus who received God's spirit is restoring the world back to himself by forgiving us of our sins when we repent of them.

God got in Jesus a lamb without spot or blemish as our sacrifice for our sin and gave us his goodness in return. God will use sorrow to turn us away from our sin so we can have eternal life. God chose us before the earth was formed. Romans 8:31 speaks loud to us confirming that, "What shall we then say to these things? "If God be for us, who can be against us?

When sin came into the world Jesus Christ was God's plan to make us holy in his eyes without a single fault we are covered by the blood of Jesus and his love for us. Jesus Christ was the ram in the bush that God prepared for us before the foundation of world. He prepared it for Abraham and it was only a test for Abraham. Adam and Eve were created without any faults but God had given them a choice and they made the wrong one.

Even in today's world we still make wrong choices if we don't keep God's word first place in our life. 2 Corinthians 5:11tells us, "Knowing therefore the terror of the Lord, we persuade men; but we are made manifest unto God; and I trust also are made manifest in your consciences." The terror of the Lord is something we all will have to endure when we go before the Judgement Seat of God.

So we want everybody who will receive him to be right with God upon his return. 2 Corinthians 5:10 warns us, "For we must all appear before the judgement seat of Christ; that everyone may receive the things do ne in his body, according to that he hath done, whether it be good or bad." We must have an answer to religions those who glory in appearance and not in heart. God is not black or white but God is spirit and those who worship him must worship him in Spirit and in Truth. "God is not a man that he should lie" Numbers 23:19.

God wanted to make us stronger by putting his spirit in us. We are similar to the Ark of the Covenant carrying the Holy Spirit inside us. God was in the flesh but he was not that flesh that he was in. The nature of God is spirit. Inside the Ark was all God. Also, "To wit, that God was in Christ, reconciling the world unto himself, not imputing their trespasses unto them; and hath committed unto us the word of reconciliation" 2 Corinthians 5:19.

He was the shepherd. Jesus Christ was made sin for our sake so that we might be made righteous. He was the Lamb of God. Jesus Christ was crucified through weakness of the flesh, yet he had the power of God in him. We are strong in him and live with him by the power of God's spirit. Remember God is spirit.

Each individual need to examine themselves through the mirror of the word of God whether they be in the faith. Without faith it is impossible to please God. Don't you know of yourselves that Jesus Christ is in you by his spirit. The world can do nothing against the Truth of God but for the Truth. We are in a spiritual battle and we should use the sharpness of the sword of the word of God that he has given us.

I don't mean to sound like I am all that, but I keep working toward that day when I will finally become all that Christ saved me for and wants me to be. This will be according to the power that worketh in me. I am in the spirit world. My communion is with the unseen and that is with the Holy Ghost in me. We are not wrestling with flesh and blood. "While we look not at the things that are seen, but at the things which are not seen: for the things that are seen are temporal; but the things which are not seen are eternal" 2 Corinthians 4:18.

CHAPTER 8

TRUST GOD

B rothers and sisters my heart's desire and prayers to God for the people of the world is that they might be saved. I pray that they put their faith, trust and confidence in Jehovah and not mere men and women who can't even save themselves. The wages of sin is still death. Paul said in Galatians 3:1, "O foolish Galatians, who hath bewitched you, that ye should not obey the truth, before whose eyes Jesus Christ hath been evidently set forth, crucified among you? After being saved by the spirit of God how can you continue to believe in the flesh? "The just shall live by faith."

We receive the promise of the spirit through faith in Jesus Christ to those that believe. This makes us children of God by faith in Christ Jesus as we trust and obey Him. When we put on Christ you will become one in and with Christ Jesus. Churches are caught up in the traditions of their fathers who passed wrong teaching down thru generations and they were not teaching the Gospel of Jesus Christ that save the souls of men. People are not being taught the dangers of hell. Services at some churches are showing a sinner the same life they are trying to flee from as believers are showing their minds have not been renewed.

Galatians 4:9 says, "But now, after that ye have known God, or rather are known of God, how turn ye again to weak and beggarly elements, whereunto ye desire again to be in bondage? The book of Romans 10:9 reminds us, "That if thou shalt confess with thy mouth the Lord Jesus, and shalt believe in thine heart that God hath raised him from the dead, thou shalt be saved."

We should repent and turn to God, and do works meet for repentance. After you repent you must be baptized in the name of Jesus Christ for the remission of sins and receive the gift of the Holy Spirit. To be of God you must have his Holy Spirit not the spirit of the world. "Be ye holy for I am holy" The Holy Spirit will be the one that marks us present in heaven.

Satan is the God of this world who has the spirit we were born with into sin. Satan will remind you after you are saved by making you feel like you are the enemy because you tell the truth. He is the father of lies. To prick a sinner's heart we must make manifest the secrets of the unbeliever's heart unto repentance. Feeling sorry for his sin he or she will fall down on their face to worship God taking away their doubts that God is in you. We must watch how we present ourselves around unbelievers.

Since the fall of couple #1 Adam and Eve in the Garden of Eden God requires us to be Born Again. We were born from our mother from the flesh and now we must be born of the spirit by "Repenting," and being baptized symbolizing with the death, burial and resurrection of Jesus Christ for the remission or forgiveness of our sins, and receive the gift of the Holy Spirit....Acts 2:38. We must ask God and sometimes tarry and wait until we receive the Holy Spirit. Some receive it at baptism.

To be in good standing with God we must be born of the water and of the spirit. We must receive the Spirit of God and hang in there until Christ is formed in us because salvation is a process. Galatians 5:13 tells us that, "For brethren ye have been called unto liberty; only use not liberty for an occasion to the flesh, but by love serve one another." Jesus sent us his Spirit called the Holy Spirit to receive God's salvation that makes us his.

Continue: Romans 10:12-13, "For there is no difference between Jew and the Greek: for the same Lord over all is rich unto all that call upon him." (Vs.13), "For whosoever shall call upon the name of the Lord shall be saved." People need to stop believing that God is just for their race. "For whosoever shall call upon the name of the Lord shall be saved" Romans10:13. You are that whosoever.

Whatever race you may be or whatever you have done in sin makes you that whosoever. Don't let guilt, shame and condemnation keep you from repenting and being baptized. Galatians 5:14 "For all the law is fulfilled in one word, Thou shalt love our neighbor as thyself, (Vs.15), But if ye bite and devour one another, take heed that ye be not consumed one of another." The Apostle Paul reminds us not to self-destruct.

You can well see how people are destroying one another in our world today for coveting that of another. They don't see you; they only see what you got and anything more that you have they unfortunately kill for it. For Christ sake we must be ready to face death at every moment of the day. We magnify Christ in our living and if need be dying also. The war is between the Spirit and the flesh. When you are in warfare with doubt and unbelief can and will keep us from our destiny. We must keep our mind on Jesus Christ who gives us that perfect peace into our victory.

In Christ we have that peace that surpasses all understanding. Remember, "For our conversation is in heaven, from whence also we look for the Saviour, the Lord Jesus Christ" Philippians 3:20. We look up to the hills from which comes our help. Those of the world mind the things of the flesh. Those who worship Jesus Christ mind the things of the spirit because the things that are not seen are eternal.

God is spirit and he is an eternal, everlasting God. We mind the things above because our conversation is in heaven. Be careful not to walk in misdirected zeal because God has mercy on those on whom he will have mercy and harden those whom he will harden. Let the peace of Christ rule in your heart.

Sometimes we wonder why some people don't come to God no matter what happens to them. Like the Pharaoh of Egypt God hardened their heart. Zeal for the kingdom of God must be put into you for the word and will of God. They have the zeal of God but not according to the knowledge. Romans 11:33 tells us that, "O depth of the riches both of wisdom and knowledge of God! How unsearchable are his judgements, and his ways past finding out."

God's knowledge and wisdom is unsearchable are his judgments and his ways past finding out. Romans 11:34, "For who hath known the mind of the Lord? or who has been his counsellor?" Malachi 3:6 says "I am the Lord, I change not; therefore ye sons of Jacob are not consumed."

Sinners keep sinning because God has not punished them for their sins yet. Galatians 6:7-10, "Be not deceived; God is not mocked: for whatsoever a man soweth, that shall he also reap. (Vs.8), "For he that soweth to his flesh shall of the flesh reap corruption; but he that soweth to the Spirit shall of the Spirit reap life everlasting." He is not just talking about money. Get God out of your little box.

Continue: (Vs.9), "And let us not be weary in well doing: for in due season we shall reap, if we faint not. (Vs.10), "As we have therefore opportunity, let us do good unto all men, especially unto them who are of the household of faith." Romans 11:36, "For of him, and through him, and to him, are all things: to whom be glory for-ever. Amen." Sinner's sin until their cup is full and brings with it judgement.

They don't understand that Christ died to make them right with God when they choose to come to him. Jehovah has given us grace and he is slow to get angry and plenteous in mercy. God wish that all should be saved and come to repentance for their sins. If you return to Jehovah he will return to you. Malachi 3:7 invites us, "Even from the days of your fathers ye are gone away from mine ordinances, and have not kept them. "Return unto me, and I will return unto you, saith the Lord of host. But ye said, wherein shall we return? Some people won't come to church because they want to get themselves right first. They want to make them-selves good enough to gain God's favor. That's not God's way of salvation.

God has all our little problems worked out when we come back to live in him. We should be saying, Ephesians 1:3-12, "Blessed be the God and Father of our Lord Jesus Christ who hath blessed us with all spiritual blessings in heavenly places in Christ: (Vs.4), "According as he hath chosen us in him before the foundation of the world, that we should be holy and without blame before him in love:

Continue; (Vs.5), "Having predestined us unto the adoption of children by Jesus Christ to himself, according to the good pleasure of his will, (Vs.6), "To praise of the glory of his grace, wherein he hath made us accepted in the beloved. (Vs.7), "In whom we have redemption through his blood, the forgiveness of sins, according to the riches of his grace; (Vs.8), "Wherein he hath abounded towards us in all wisdom and prudence." (Vs.9),"Having made known unto us the mystery of his will; according to his good pleasure which he hath purposed in himself:"

Continue; (Vs.10), "That in the dispensation of the fullness of times he might gather together in one all things in Christ, both by which are in heaven, and which are in earth; even in him: (Vs.11),"In whom also we have obtained an inheritance, being predestined according to the purpose of him who worketh all things after the counsel of his own will: (Vs.12), "That we should be to the praise of his glory, who first trusted in Christ." Read and meditate on all Ephesians chapter 1.

After we repent and be baptized and receive God's spirit we become children of God. God want to supply all your needs but you will be trying to be your own god by scuffling doing everything yourself. Salvation comes from trusting Christ. It is closer than you think. Salvation is confessing with your mouth and believing in your heart that Jesus is Lord. Put all your confidence, trust and reliance in Him.

Romans 10:13, "For whosoever shall call upon the name of the Lord, shall be saved." Remember it said "shall'---- be saved because salvation is a process. There are people who are finding Christ without looking for him because you spoke the Gospel of Christ to them.

God blinded the eyes of some by shutting their eyes and ears so they don't understand what we are talking about. These otherwise minded men have left the teaching of the cross. There are some hardhearted people that want God's salvation but they just don't understand, and they are the walking dead. God loves to see the dead come back to life and so should we. We should be saying, "Can these dry bones live? As soon as those who sin humble themselves and become grateful they will be on their way to God's goodness.

There are some people who think that they are smarter than God and others who think that they can pay him off. Romans 11:16 says "For everything comes from God alone. Everything lives by his power and everything is for his glory. To him be the glory forevermore."

Jehovah will let criminals go free when they repent of their sins and believe and confess with a sincere heart that Jesus Christ is Lord who takes away sin. He is the Father of mercies and the God of all comforts. We should not trust in ourselves, but in God who raised the dead.

So, Romans 13:1-2 states, "Let every soul be subject unto the higher powers. For there is no power but of God: the powers that be are ordained of God. (Vs. 2), "Whosoever therefore resisteth the power resisteth the ordinance of God: and they that resist shall receive to themselves damnation."

God declares sinners to be good in his sight if they have faith in Christ to save them from God's wrath Romans 4:5. It is a free gift that cannot be earned but we receive it by faith only. Humankind was unable to keep God's laws without breaking them. God saw the condition of his creation and sent Jesus to be a sacrifice to put us in right standing with Jehovah.

God quickened or gave life to those who were dead in their sins who walked according to the prince of the power of the air that now work in the children of disobedience. Punishment was sufficient for all who walked in disobedience, but God forgives and comfort them instead of leaving them in sorrow and letting Satan get an advantage. God wants to snatch you out of the clutches of Satan before the poison or venom of sin kills you.

God has benefits for holiness and he gives everlasting life. Psalms 103:3-5 shows us our benefits. (Vs.3), "Who forgiveth all thine iniquities; who healeth all thy diseases; (Vs.4), "Who redeemeth thy life from destruction; who crowneth thee with lovingkindness and tender mercies; (Vs.5), Who satisfieth thy mouth with good things; so that thy youth is renewed like the eagle's. Life and death are in the power of the tongue. We also speak life and health.

We have a brand new conversation when we follow God. We call it the Truth. We serve God in a new way and not with a set of rules and that new way is obedience with our mind and heart. Romans7:7 LB), "Well then, am I suggesting that these laws of God are evil? Of course not! "No, the law is not sinful but it was the law that showed me my sin. "I would never have known the sin in my heart – the evil desires that are hidden there—if the law had not said, you must not have evil desires in your heart. (Vs 8), "But sin used this law against evil desires by reminding me that such desires are wrong and arousing all kinds of forbidden desires within me! "Only, if there were no laws to break would there be no sinning."

This shows us that people that do wrong feel that they are doing right until they learn God's truth. Our laws in government today are supposed to be good for the people until the laws become contrary to the word of God. There are some laws today that support sin. Perverseness and drugs are being tolerated to make money. Money has become their god. Sin is advancing for money sake.

We are being "Mentally Kidnapped" and sold into sin by passing laws against the Holy Scriptures. These laws are passed and must be obeyed even if we disagree. Our government is spitting in our hands and telling us that it is raining. "What profit is there if you gain the whole world—and lose eternal life? What can be compared with the value of eternal life? 11 Corinthians 5:10 warns us that, "For we must all appear before the judgment seat of Christ; that every one may receive the things done in his body, according to that he hath done, whether it be good or bad."

Worth is what you think it is worth. Weigh all the money and fame on one side and put your soul on the other side of the scale and your soul will outweigh all that. A soul is worth more than all the silver and gold on earth. Mark 8:36 says, "For what shall it profit a man, if he shall gain the whole world, and lose his own soul." Christ died for all because after Adams and Eve's sinned all were born dead in sin.

Those following Christ have a concern about laws being passed toward Socialism and the New World Order. Humankind's hand is too short to box with God and mankind weighs less than air compared to God. The answer is in Romans 13:14 that says, "But put ye on the Lord Jesus Christ, and make no provisions for the flesh." Every morning when you wake up dress up by putting on the whole armor of God before you start your day. Dress up by confessing, declaring and decreeing you're victory through prayer and God's word for that day. Pray Psalms 35 and 91 for protection. Then you will be able to quench all the fiery darts that the enemy throws act you.

The Holy Bible says, "If a man don't work he shouldn't eat." The laws today are wrong and in a way sinful because a mind is a terrible thing to waste. Men and women getting paid before they do any work will make a lazy man and woman. Our nation wants to make sup lines acceptable to all. Think about a whole nation laying around idle getting high on weed plotting like drug addicts on how to rob and steal for their next meal and temporary fix. People just lay around coveting that of another.

The door that is about to open from this new normal will never be enough for the greedy. It will only enable an able body human and make him or her non -productive in our society. You can't issue a set amount to greedy people. That's why they are called "Greedy." They don't know anything about Philippian 4:11-13 that says "whatsoever state I am, therewith to be content." We must put our faith and trust in God. "Without faith it is impossible to please him and "for whatsoever is not of faith is sin."

These laws only help strengthen sin. They strengthen the hand of evil doers. Idle minds are the devils workshop. We know that there is no man without sin. The laws now being passed are from a group that is full of lust. They try to do right, but do wrong anyway. They are experts at doing wrong.

When I look at the internet and see government official's family members caught up in incest on the screen having sex with children shows a lack of self- control. High ranking officials stealing each other lap tops to expose each other's wrong doings. There is no honor among thieves. Their position is too high in government for them not to be able to control their lower nature between their legs.

When humankinds lower nature rule it bring about all sorts of evil. The lower life put chains on those in sin and keeps them in sin slavery. They are in chains and bondage to do the same sins every day. There are many top churches being run by chains in the bedroom of the Pastor causing the flock to sin also. Is the bedroom of the Pastor running the church?

Jesus Christ came to break the chains so that humankind can be set free. Jesus brought forgiveness of sin to us to free us from condemnation from the guilt of sin. Jesus came to deliver us from the powers of darkness so that we can walk in the light and be led by the spirit of God. If you don't have the spirit of Christ you are not his Son. You may be his creation but not in good standing with God because you have not repented of your sins and baptized in the name of Jesus Christ and ask for his Holy Ghost.

You must put on the new man in Christ Jesus when you receive him. The old man that is ruled by sin will never obey God and it never will.

When you get saved and stop reacting to fleshly things of lust, the lust of the eye, the lust of the flesh, and the pride of life means that your body is dead to sin. Only the power of the Spirit of God can deliver us from the bondage of sin.

The spirit of God will begin to dominate you and you will be led by the spirit of God and that will make you a son of God. That means that everything that Jesus the Son of God has belongs to you. We will be heirs of God and joint heirs with Jesus. We will also become heirs to the blessing of Abraham. All our needs are met according to his riches and glory by Christ Jesus.

11 Corinthians 5:17-19 "Therefore if any man be in Christ, he is a new creature: old things are passed away; behold all things are become new." (Vs.18), "And all things are of God, who hath reconciled us to himself by Jesus Christ, and hath given to us the ministry of reconciliation; (Vs.19), "To wit, that God was in Christ reconciling the world unto himself, not imputing their trespasses unto them; and hath committed unto us the word of reconciliation.

When humankind can see their sins in the mirror of the Word of God they have no more excuse for their sin. We need to search the scriptures and find our- selves in the Holy Scriptures and obey what we find to change our life. The Truth of God came on the scene and it is the supreme reality, the ultimate meaning and value of existence.

John 17;17 says "Sanctify them thru thy Truth thy word is Truth" A lie cannot stand next to the truth long at all no more could Baal the idol god stand next to the Ark of God. A lie is the way things are situated and arranged to give a false impression. Our world is full of unbelief. That unbelief is, not believing that Jesus Christ is the Son of God.

God's word is the only thing that can make us pure and holy. Believing in Jesus Christ is the beginning of our becoming consecrated into truth and holiness. 11 Corinthians 5:21 gives us sure words that says, "For he hath made him (Jesus) to be sin for us, who knew no sin; that we might be made the righteousness of God in him."

Our government is making laws that offend God and they are contrary to the Word of God. They support evil thinking that destroy men and women souls. Romans 16:18 tells us, "For they that are such serve not our Lord Jesus Christ, but their own belly; and by good words and fair speeches deceive the hearts of the simple."

This is why we must stand firm in the Spirit of God centering in on the Gospel's work. We must put on the hold amour of God and the mind of Christ and hold the thoughts, feelings and purposes of his heart. We must stay connected to the vine by being of one mind and heart with Jesus Christ our Lord. God in Jesus Christ by the Spirit that was in Jesus Christ in us is the vine.

Without the Spirit of God we can do nothing. Wait a minute, yes you can you can sin and go to hell. The same love that God has for Jesus Christ he also has for us. All who love and follow truth follow Jesus Christ. Rebellious people try on purpose to misunderstand and are disobedient to God knowing the penalty of sin.

They want to move God and his laws off the set or church. They say that it is hard to live Holy. They say I got to have Big Booty Susie or Hanging John. I got to have my Weed. I don't drink but a little only for my stomach sake. God told Isaiah in 30:8-13 to, (Vs.8), "Now go and write down these words. Write them in a book. They will stand until the end of the time as a witness." (Vs.9), "that these people are stubborn rebels who refuse to pay attention to the Lord's instruction."

They don't want to hear what God said, but they tell the preacher, (Vs.10), "They tell the seers, "Stop seeing vision!" They tell the prophets, "Don't tell us what is right. "Prophecy not unto us right things, speak unto us smooth things." In other words lie to us. They tell God who is the head of the church to, (Vs.11), "Get you out of the way, turn aside out of the path, cause the Holy One of Israel to cease from before us." They want no part of God but want only gospel comedians. They want pole dancers in the church. They say they are tired of all this obedience to God and for money sake and the preacher complies.

Continue (Vs.12), "Wherefore thus saith the Holy One of Israel, "Because ye despise this word, and trust in oppression and perverseness, and stay thereon." God has taken all he can stand and he can't stand no more. (Vs.13), "Therefore this iniquity shall be to you a breach ready to fall, swelling out in a high wall, whose breaking cometh suddenly at an instant."

No man will know the day or the hour. If you are rich your riches will not be able to save you from the wrath of God. You can't buy your way out. Movie stars look out because is not recognizing Grammy Awards on Judgement Day, False prophets that preach for money sake who take the souls of its members to hell with them will be in hell fire burning. The lake of Fire is always, never ending, always falling. They will be cursing God who they rebelled against. All the blood of the souls of this people will be on your head false prophet. There is a need for Repentance.

God punishes sin no matter who you are because "God is no respecter of persons." God gives everybody to receive the plan of salvation. People know right from wrong and their conscious excuses and accuse them. They care less what you think and what God thinks even though the word shows them their sin and faults. Criminals today care less about being caught on camera participating in a crime. The simple ones thrive for internet fame throwing away their life for nothing.

Jesus wish is that all should be saved and come to repentance. Jesus Christ came to help us defeat sin and make us sinless by taking our sins by the shedding of his blood. The glory of Jesus Christ declares us not guilty if we repent, confess our sin and be baptized in His name (Jesus Christ) and receive His spirit. This will make us right with God.

God prophesied all through the Old Testament about Jesus coming. Jesus was here before the earth was formed. Colossians 1:16 reveals, "For by him were all things created, that are in heaven, and that are in earth, visible and invisible, whether they be thrones, or dominions, or principalities, or powers: all things were created by him, and for him."

Prophecy is spoken all through the Holy Scriptures. In Revelation chapter 5&6 is when God searched heaven, earth and under the earth for someone worthy to open the seven seals. Genesis 12:3 tells how the nations will be blessed through Abraham's lineage. "I will bless those who bless you, and whoever curses you I will curse, and all people on the earth will be blessed through you." Jacob was part of Jesus genealogy in Genesis 28:14 when prophecy was spoken by the Lord, Your descendants will be like the dust of the earth. Words were being spoken all through the Old Testament.

Words was being spoken (prophesying) when God told David in 2 Samuel 7:12-13 that his son shall build him a house instead of him. God said "He is the one who will build a house for my Name, and I will establish the throne of his kingdom forever." Isaiah 7:14, "Therefore the Lord himself will give a sign: The virgin will conceive and give birth to a son, and will call his name Immanuel." Immanuel means God with us.

Words were being spoken prophesying Jesus birth. In Micah 5:2, But you, Bethlehem Ephrathah, though you are small among the clans of Judah, out of you will come for me one who will be ruler over Israel, whose origins are from of old, from ancient times."

Prophesying words was being spoken when Israel was blessing his sons in Genesis 49:10 telling how "The sceptre shall not depart from Judah. Words were spoken prophesying the coming of Jesus Christ. Jesus the spotless Lamb prevailed to open the book and loose the seven seals. Revelation 5:12 tells us what happened on earth Saying with a loud voice, Worthy is the Lamb that was slain to receive power, and riches, and wisdom, and strength, and honor, and glory, and blessing.

God is spirit and He always was in Colossians 1:16 Abbreviated Version, "For by him all things were created." Words were spoken prophesying his coming. The body of Jesus Christ was prophesied in Isaiah 9:6 that says even before Jesus parents Mary and Joseph was born, "For unto us a child is born, unto us a son is given: and the government shall be upon his shoulder: and his name shall be called Wonderful,

Counsellor, The Mighty God, The everlasting Father, The Prince of Peace. Jesus physical body came from the Lion of the tribe of Juda, the Root of David.

Words were spoken in the prophecy before Jesus was born of Mary in Isaiah 11:1-2, "And there come forth a rod out of the stem of Jesse, and a Branch shall grow out of his roots. (Vs.2), "And the spirit of the Lord shall rest upon him, the spirit of wisdom and understanding, the spirit of counsel and might, the spirit of knowledge and of the fear of the Lord."

The Spirit that got into the body of the man Jesus Christ fell on him like a dove and gave that man the anointing called Christ. The Spirit of God who fell on Jesus Christ after his baptism is the God of all Spirits. He was the messenger from heaven sent to heal and deliver humankind from the curse that we received from Adam and Eve's disobedience in the Garden of Eden.

God is not a man in Numbers 23:19. "God is Spirit: and His worshipers must worship him in spirit and in truth" John 4:24. God is not flesh and blood. Jesus the man died but God who is spirit never die. Spirits don't die. Spirit is eternal, always, never ending. God is spirit and God made Jesus in Mary to come and show us how to walk in his spirit on earth in the flesh

. Jesus Christ was that expressed image of God. God revealed himself through Jesus Christ. Jesus said the Father in me he do the works. Believe me that I am in the Father, and the Father in me or else believe me for the very works sake" John14:11. He always gave his Father the credit. In John 10:30 He also said, "I and the Father are one" and he invited the Apostles to the Promise of the Spirit in John chapter 14.

God put restraints on Adam and Eve so that He could check the desires of their flesh and the mind. The flesh and mind are the two great fountains of sin that are the corrupt nature of man. They became cowards after they sinned after knowing good and evil. Even though God gave us a choice men began to love darkness more than light because their deeds were evil.

They hated the light because it exposed their evil deeds. This is why women and men run, duck and hide from the presence of God and the police after they sin. They run, duck and hide because sin or crime is contrary to man's law and God's law. They can't stand to be in the presence of man because they are afraid to be seen and caught. They can't face God because sin is separation from God. They do this because there will be punishment.

How long will you imagine mischief against God and man? You should expect your needs to be met from God, not man, but God do work through the love in people that love their neighbor as they love themselves. "Trust in him at all times; ye people, pour out your heart before him; God is a refuge for us Selah Psalms 61:8. "Trust not in oppression, and become not vain in robbery: if riches increase, set not your heart upon them" Psalms 61:10. All power belongs to God. God also gives his mercy to every man according to his work.

Sin only bring God's wrath upon those who transgress if not repented of quickly, and eventually even the police will soon find you out. These are the ones who are afraid to come to church. They claim they can have a relationship with God at home. It could be true if they have the help of the Holy Spirit in them. God is spirit and those who worship him must worship him in spirit and truth.

Some of the people of the people in the church and the world are ignorant about who God is. How can you worship God not knowing who he is? We find out who God is from His church. We read his word by the power of the Holy Spirit and the teachings in Gods church. Jesus said to Peter upon this rock I build my church and the gates of hell will not prevail against it.

The world is afraid to eat that true bread from heaven and live forever. Reading God's word is how you receive the spiritual life to walk in God's ways. All sinners do is run, duck and hide from the only one who has the power of eternal life to save them. Scientist searched the galaxies trying to find eternal life when all they have to do is confess Jesus Christ as Lord.

When they open their Holy Bibles the Truth is starring them in the face. The Truth convicts them of their sins and they run and cover up and make excuses. You can tell sometimes even in your own household how people throw the cover over their head when you say get up and lets go to church to honor and thank God.

The world likes to listen to men who speak their own worldly thoughts by measuring and comparing themselves among themselves. They find those who will agree so they don't have to change. There are many that speak their own thoughts to get the praise of men and will not honor God. When the blind leads the blind they stumble and both fall in the traps and snares of the devil.

They deny themselves the Light that we get from God. Some will even die still evading the love of God. They wake-up day after day and commit the same sin until it catches up with them. Some deny themselves "Truth" because of false churches that hide the truth for fleshly gain. 11 Corinthians 6:17 that says, "Wherefore come out from among them, and be ye separate, saith the Lord, and touch not the unclean thing; and I will receive you."

Children of the devil love to do evil. Their father Satan is the father of lies. When God shows up the devil got to flee. Sometimes it may take fasting and prayer to get delivered from some demons. In Psalms 77:16 "The waters saw thee, O God, the waters saw thee; they were afraid: the depths also were troubled." Those who worship God do not fear God as they should. The Old Testament Scriptures was put here to show us how God is displeased with all disobedience. If what happened to them back then would happen to us today we would have the fear of God in us. If people of today did fear God they would obey God's word.

When a man and woman preach truth to them they naturally don't believe them because lies are normal to them. Lies make people comfortable in their sins. God is able to send a lying spirit to the evil man. 1 Kings22:22 God sends a lying spirit in the mouth of the prophets. Two verses before the Lord said who shall persuade Ahab? In verse 21 a spirit step up and said I will persuade him. Remember God don't lie. The spirit (became) as a lying spirit. In Egypt God sends evil death angels to accomplish his mission. He "And smote all the firstborn of Egypt; the chief of their strength in the tabernacle of Ham."

How can any person that breathes God fresh air not want to say thank you Lord. They are spiritually blind, but if you let them tell you they know what they are doing and where they are going. Do that sound familiar to you? They know everything and can't even tell you how breath got in their own nostrils, but they know how to kill and stop another from breathing. There is a need to cleanse ourselves from all filthiness of the flesh and spirit, perfecting holiness in the fear of the God.

CHAPTER 9

A MURDEROUS SPIRIT

Our world has voted to release Barabbas a murderer at their own request instead of Jesus Christ. Murders are running rampant in our world. The world is being distracted because it loves darkness more than the Light of Jehovah. Are you carrying your own cross? The leaders, false prophets and the Pharisees leading the social movement of 2021 have "Mentally Kidnapped" the world into their school of thought. This war for souls calls for the pulling down of strongholds and casting down the imaginations of every high thing that exalted itself against the knowledge of God, by bringing every thought into captivity to the obedience of Christ. The world's disobedience towards God is intensifying.

They are validating their own oral traditions concerning man's law, not Gods. They have gone beyond shame boasting and celebrating with a haughty spirit in the month for their gay pride. I don't know if Lucifer was kicked out of heaven in gay pride month for rebelling against God because of his pride. Pride comes before destruction and a haughty spirit before a fall. This group will not fear God even on their dying bed. God gave us freedom not to self- destruct. They are measuring and comparing themselves among themselves instead of the measure of the rule which God through his word has distributed to us.

Sinners are lawbreakers. Jesus Christ did no sin but went to the cross with two criminals. One of the criminals scoffed at Jesus telling him to come down off the cross and save himself. Our leaders are scoffing at God when they pass laws contrary to his Word. Just as Eve reasoned in her mind was beguiled by the devil through his subtle ways. The devil is crafty and he tells truth intertwined with a lie. The mind of the world is corrupted from the simplicity of who Christ is. There are followers who really don't know who God is in the Holy Scriptures.

They are preaching another Jesus with another spirit and another gospel that we have not accepted. Satan is transforming himself into an angel of light and his ministers are also being transformed as ministers of righteousness 11 Corinthians 11:13-15 paraphrase. Men are exalting themselves putting many into spiritual bondage among false brethren. Jesus Christ is coming back and we should make sure we do not have un-repented sin from uncleanness, lasciviousness and fornication.

So we must examine ourselves often. 11Corinthians 13:5 says, "Examine yourselves, whether ye be in the faith; prove your own selves. Know ye not your own selves, how that Jesus Christ is in you, except ye be reprobates? (Vs.8), "For we do nothing against the truth, but for the truth." We should all be of one mind and that mind is to have the mind of Christ and hold the thoughts, feelings and purposes of his heart. Then we will have the grace of the Lord Jesus Christ, and the love of God and communion of the Holy Ghost will be with us.

Criminals symbolize the world. Who's on the Lords side? Who will the chief priest and leaders try to hand over to the world this time to condemn to death. The world laws against Jehovah reveal to us that we must be delivered from this present evil generation. When Jesus ascended to heaven he left us repentance to remove sin if we have a sincere and willing mind.

We receive Jesus Christ as Lord and Savior with a ready mind. Remember, "Before anything else existed, there was Christ with God, and we were made in the image of God. Christ always loved us because there is nothing that exist that he did not make; that mean you too. When he made man and woman they were intended to have eternal life in and with him. The disciples of Jesus Christ were left to be a light that shined in darkness to spread the Gospel of Christ throughout the earth. God's light is still shining through us today delivering us from this present evil world that wants to pervert the gospel of Jesus Christ.

Humankind sinned by rebellion and began to live in that darkness and it became man and woman's new norm. We must remember that God will deliver his strength into captivity and his glory over into the enemies hand because of disobedience. God will turn you over to your enemies and let them spank you for him. Sin and darkness was so normal that the world did not recognize the True Light when he came into the world. To get that True Light you must be born again.

No, you don't have to spend nine more months in the womb of a woman, but to be born of water and of the spirit. He came "Who gave himself for our sins, that he might deliver us from this present evil world, according to the will of God, and our Father. "To whom be the glory forever and ever. Amen." (Galatians 1:4-5).

After Jesus Christ was born in the flesh the Spirit of God fell upon him in the form of a dove after his baptism. God came to us in the spirit in Jesus Christ clothed in an earth suit to take us to class on how to walk in the spirit in our flesh. He was born from the flesh that made him man and he was baptized and filled with the Holy Spirit. God's Spirit came into Jesus when he was baptized by John the Baptist. God cannot be born of a woman. Man is born of a woman but to be born again he must be born of water and the spirit of God called the Holy Spirit. God has always been he is from everlasting to everlasting thou art God.

Our class began when we began to walk in the Spirit. When God shines in us we win by the power of the Holy Spirit. This was God's perfect plan for imperfect people by placing his Spirit in humankind to help us get the victory over all the powers of Satan. This is God inside of us because God is spirit and he gives us a piece of himself. He made man part heaven and part earth. When we speak God's word God becomes alive and working in us. 1 Corinthians 2:7, "But we speak the wisdom of God in a mystery, even the hidden wisdom, which God ordained before the world unto our glory." God spoke this world into existence.

When we speak God's word our words become words of power, love and words of life that produce good things into our lives and into the lives of others. When we choose God's word for our lips we choose God's will for our life. We become a vessel that he works through. When he created man from the dust he breathed a piece of himself into man and he became a living soul or being. This made man part heaven and part earth being formed from the dust of the ground. God breathed the breath of life into that dust making it animated and alive by giving us a soul, (a mind, will and emotion).

The real you is your spirit. Man is a spirit and he lives in a body and he has a soul. The soul consists of your mind, will and emotion. Humankind is still looking for a new life on Mars, but that new life can only be found through Christ Jesus. Men and women have lying spirits inside them that makes them forgers of lies.

We must present our bodies to be a living sacrifice and stop crawling off the altar when times get tough and the going get rough. When we are born again all things become new. When the going gets tough, the tough get going. We are like the palm tree we will bend but we will not break. We already know that there is sunshine after the storms of life. If you are still breathing you have another opportunity to get it right.

Jesus Christ breathed the breath of life into man and he came to show us the power that we possess as children and sons of God. He put on an earth suit and showed us how to fight evil and walk in victory in our bodies. Our class was cut short by the devil because of our disobedience in the Garden of Eden. After man's disobedience we needed new life from heaven.

So God revealed himself through Jesus Christ to give us an up close and personal example of how we should walk with his spirit in us. Man was formed from the dust of the ground and God made woman from the rib of man. Every since then man was born of woman because God commanded Adam and Eve to be fruitful and multiply. Jesus Christ became the antidote for mankind's sins.

Jesus Christ revealed the name of God in John 17:6, "I have manifested thy name. The name Jesus was from the beginning. His body was born of a woman named Mary in the flesh. God manifested himself in Jesus Christ in the flesh when he was baptized in water by John the Baptist and the Spirit of God fell upon him like a dove.

Just like in Acts 1:5 says, "For John truly baptized with water, but ye shall be baptized with the Holy Ghost not many days hence." In Acts 2;4, "And they were all filled with the Holy Ghost, and began to speak with other tongues, as the Spirit gave them utterance." He showed us the same thing we must do to receive God's character. God is spirit but holiness is his character. "Be ye holy for I am holy."

God commands a separation for himself. "Now this I say brethren, that flesh and blood cannot inherit the kingdom of God; neither doth corruption inherit incorruption." There are also celestial bodies, and bodies terrestrial: but the glory of the celestial is one, and the glory of the terrestrial is another 1 Corinthians 15:40.

Jesus Christ flesh came from earth and the spirit from heaven. The first man Adam is of the earth and the second man Jesus is the Lord from heaven. We have borne the image of the earthy and through Jesus Christ we will also bear the image of the heavenly. This is when we will see the mystery of being changed in a moment, in the twinkling of an eye when we hear the voice of Jesus or at the last trump when Jesus comes in on a cloud.

Luke 3:22 tells us "And the Holy Ghost descended in a bodily shape like a dove upon him. This was God in similitude as a dove. " Luke 9:35 says, "And a voice from heaven said, "This is my beloved son in whom I am well pleased." The flesh of Jesus was called Son of God and Adam was also called the son of God. In Luke 3:38, "Which was the son of

E-nos, which was the son of Seth, which was the son Adam, which was the son of God." There was one from earth and the other from heaven. Man made in the image of God is a mystery.

God manifest himself in similar-tude in shapes, in forms, in people and in things. The angel of the Lord told Joseph who was the son of David to take Mary as thy wife. That holy thing which is conceived in her is of the Holy Ghost. Jesus had his name before he came out of the womb of Mary. Jesus is God's name from eternity before the earth was. His name was inherited. They called him Emanuel meaning God with us. God set the stage all through the Old Testament talking about his coming.

Herod tried to take Jesus the Christ out or kill him but was unsuccessful. The Holy Spirit convicts us and it lets us know we have done wrong. When you reject the Holy Spirit God will give you up unto your own hearts lust: and let you walk in your own counsel. Haters of the Lord will not submit themselves to him when they could have had a chance to live forever with him.

Today those who will not submit to God will not seek him or come into his presence. Jesus came to save his creation from their sins. We are all God's creation but you belong to Jesus Christ only if you have his spirit and obey him. When the Holy Spirit is not present in people think that their wrong is right. They have no one to convict them and their heart becomes hard towards God.

Satan can show you lustful thoughts and all the kingdoms of the world in a flash in your mind. Thoughts come through our minds like a kaleidoscope flickering different thoughts and images in our mind. Humankind wants to live at the speed of thought and some can't even remember what day it is. They need to sit down somewhere.

Scientist are still trying to fix the brain of Alzheimer's. The best that they can come up with is hooking your brain up to a computer and here comes the Covid 19 process. Now the medical field is looking at a gold mine. This is the best scheme going since the fountain of youth, the gold rush and fools gold. Hopeful products are jumping up all over the place. Putting your thoughts and personality into a computer file is the best thing yet.

The earth is the Lord's and the fullness thereof and all that dwell there-in. "All the foundations of the earth are out of course." Satan wants humankind to worship him but our worship belongs to Jehovah who created us. When you get saved Jesus will give you the keys of the kingdom. He does this so you can rule and reign in your new body or clean vessel free from sin.

God works in thick darkness and will clean you up and make you a clean vessel. He will also work or heal in a unclean vessel. If you were clean before you got saved you would not need God to save you. All was born into sin and need to be born again and we also need the spirit of God to save us as we obey.

God has given us dominion so we can defeat the enemy that brings traps and snares in our life and from those who come for greedy gain. God's Holy Spirit strengthens us giving us power to spread the Gospel of Christ and to discern evil spirits. We have to let people know that God is ready to bless those whose heart have been broken and the poor. We need the power of God to defeat our enemy called Satan that comes to steal, kill, and to destroy. It is written gives us the victory.

When Jesus shows up demons must go because Satan, the Lord rebukes you. The devil only comes to steal, kill and to destroy. God formed and made male and female for his good pleasure. Jesus Christ the rightful owner has shown up and demons or squatters must leave the premises. Devil, get out of here now, in the mighty name of Jesus Christ. Your delight should be for the souls of men and all demons must flee. Evil men and women only produce evil deeds from their hidden wickedness. There is a call for "Repentance".

Humankind is transgressing the covenant because they love darkness more than they love the light of God. Thank God that he will dwell in thick darkness and bring us out. God kicked rebellion, evil and uncleanness out of heaven and sent it down to the earth. Isaiah 14:12 says, How art thou fallen from heaven, O Lucifer son of the morning!

You know what you do wrong against God. You need to stop lying to yourself first of all and repent. Before the earth was formed he knew your lying, hardheaded, rebellious disobedient self. By one man sin death came into the world and by one man's obedience all can be saved.

I don't care how tough, pretty or smart you think you are when death comes your way you got to give up the ghost. Have you ever stumbled upon a dead body where maggots were all in the body? In Ecclesiastes 8:8 says, "There is no man that hath power over the spirit to retain the spirit, neither hath he power in the day of death: and there is no discharge in that war; neither shall wickedness deliver those that are given to it."

Moses smote the dust of the land and it became lites in man in Exodus 8. Man is going to turn into worms, maggots and lites because he came from the dust of the earth and will return to the dust. Man goes back to the earth where the worm dieth not. There are many young men that died too soon. They don't think about that they only have one dance and one chance for life. It would be better if they die serving in the Army, Navy, Marines or Airforce. When they get out in 3 or four years they could buy a home and have benefits for their family if they were killed in war.

The spirit of whoredom is in the mist of our country and there are many who do not know the Lord. "And as troops of robbers wait for a man, so the company of priest murder in the way by consent: for they commit lewdness" Hosea 6:9. They have deeply corrupted themselves as in the days of Gibeah in the book of Judges.

God brings judgement on those who are rebellious. We find this in Hosea 9:14, "Give them, O Lord: what wilt thou give? Give them miscarrying womb and dry breast." This is breast cancer that we see from abortions throughout the world where over one million babies were aborted in the 1st ten days of 2021.

If you are still breathing God's fresh air; He is warning you backsliding church. It is revealed by the overflow of their wicked mouth that comes from their wicked heart. Hosea 4:9 states, "And there shall be, like people, like priest: and I will punish them for their ways, and reward them their doings."

This will cause the new converts who do not understand to fall. Hosea 10:12 reveals, "Sow to yourselves righteousness, reap in mercy; break up your fallow ground: for it is time to seek the Lord till he come and rain righteousness upon you." Hosea 14:9 in my words says, "Those who have wisdom and understanding know the ways of the Lord is right and just men walk in them, but transgressors shall fall therein.

Evil men and women are walking in quick sand and the more they move around in sin it will slowly take them under. They refuse God's plan for their lives. Jesus shed his blood for us sealing the New Covenant that brings us back into right standings with our creator. Some people bring tears to my eyes when I see how close to being saved they came, and they turn around and turned God down.

They came so close but Satan the god of this world their father cut them off before their time. They seem to be insisting and demanding to die in their sin. They want to impress man and they want to receive the praise of man rather than to obey God their creator who made the heavens and the earth. They are ignorant to the choice they made because they chose death, but their life could have been more abundantly.

Jesus was subject to Satan in the wilderness for forty days. Resist the devil and he will flee from you. The thing is people are not resisting but they are giving into their fleshly desires. Jesus resisted and the angels came and cared for him.

The more you resist and practice what you read and hear the more you will understand. Our souls are harmed by what we think and say. When your thoughts and words get polluted it will make you unfit for God. We must cast down all vain imaginations and every proud thought that come against the true knowledge of God. God who is our boss gives us power to send them back down to the pits of hell where they belong in the mighty name of Jesus Christ.

CHAPTER 10

WHERE ARE GOD'S BATTLE AXES?

God sends deliverers to break the nations in pieces and cry out for the sins of the world. When the word is preached something has to die. For our own sake we are killed all the day long. 1 John 4:4 tells us that we are "Daily overcoming the devil. Our hard heart has to be broken into pieces.

In 2 Kings 9:1, Jehu was anointed to smite the house of Ahab. God sent Jehu to murder physically. Today God send men with a Battle Axe to break in pieces and a hammer to beat, break and cut with the word to convict and kill your will. For your sake we are killed all the day long. When the word is planted through preaching it shows up in your spirit when you are about to sin and you must choose to obey or be drawn away by your own lust.

God wants us to come to the table and eat his word. The Church has to be careful about what she eats. We must keep doing things through Christ who strengthens us. Be careful who you listen too. Remember in Colossians 3:13 "We have been delivered from the powers of darkness." The Church even has to beware of fornication and adultery in their dreams.

You can be praying and the devil will send lustful thoughts like a naked man or woman's picture in your mind. We must walk by faith and not by sight in 2 Corinthians 5:7. We have to cast down vain imaginations in 2 Corinthians, 10:4-5, because we are not moved by what we see 2 Cor.5:7. When we are being transformed by the renewing of our mind from sin into righteousness in Romans 12:1-2, we have to bring every thought into captivity into the obedience of Christ" 2 Cor.10:5.

We must repent about Jude 1:8, Likewise also these filthy dreamers defile the flesh, despise dominion, and speak evil of dignities." There are holy dreamers whose dreams defile the flesh and you know it's true. The devil is in the preaching business and some preachers have become forgers of lies and are physicians of no value. James 3:1 warns us and says, "Dear brothers and sisters, not many of you should become teachers in the church, for we who teach will be judged more strickly."

Thinking more of our own mistakes and offences we should be less apt to judge other people. When you teach your own mouth condemns you. We should be more in agreement with the word that judge righteously. Self- deceivers and self-justifiers can prove worse than any faults they condemn in others.

Jesus said, "If I be lifted up I will draw all men unto me." God is being moved to jealousy. Gods wish is that men should hold their peace and let that be their wisdom. Men and women need more healing than judgement. Today it seems that those in sin resent hell fire preaching and don't believe in the judgement of God.

The dragon is attacking the minds of God's people. They are afraid to look in the mirror of the word of God and see themselves like the Madusa. They let the ways of the world reflect to what the church should look like. Sin pollutions from the world are coming into the church influencing weak preachers who still have the world in them.

Adam is in the pulpit not Jesus. Adam fell in the Garden of Eden and the congregations are falling like Adam to disobedience. Money is taking the place of God because churches have become strictly business and have put souls on the back burner. Satan is still telling God's creation "did God actually say?

Satan is telling preachers to teach in different ways instead of preaching the Gospel or the message of deliverance. Their eyes are being opened and money becomes their god and their teachings are contrary to the word of God. Like Eve thought God was holding out on her when he said, "don't eat of the Tree." Women that preach still think that God is holding out on them, so they preach anyway.

Celebrities are mocking God and man in his image. Education is good when used properly. Churches have even begun to have comedy shows in the church. Job 13:7 says, "Will ye speak wickedly for God? And talk deceitfully for him? (Vs.8), Will ye except his persons? Will ye contend for God? (Vs.9), "Is it good that he should search you out? Or as one man mocketh another, do ye so mock him? (Vs.10), He will surely reprove you, if ye do secretly except persons." Their own mouth condemns them and their own lips testify against them.

The lack of fear of God does not make them afraid that God will fall on them. They say let me alone like the demons told Jesus Christ. They say let me speak, and let come on me what will. Jesus is our salvation and we must maintain our ways before him. Some say God's word is outdated. God's word was here before paper or ink. His word is the same yesterday, today and forever more and it don't change for the young or old generation. It is always the same.

God wants skillful men of understanding to convey his word. God do not want us to be afraid of their faces. God wants us to speak unto them all that he has commanded. Here comes a generation who know not the Lord. Jeremiah 2:8 reveals, "The priests said not, Where is the Lord? and they that handle the law knew me not: the pastors also transgressed against me, and the prophets prophesied by Baal, and walked after things that do not profit."

God told Jeremiah in 2:9 saying, "Wherefore I will plead with you, saith the Lord, and with your children's children will I plead." Jeremiah 2:19 tells you, "Thine own wickedness shall correct thee, and thy backsliding shall reprove thee: know therefore and see that it is an evil thing and bitter, that thou hast forsaken the Lord thy God, and that my fear is not in thee, saith the Lord God of host."

They don't know the secrets of God and they have the nerve to put their folly next to God like the Ark was set next to Dagon who falls on his face. Jeremiah 2:8 says, "The priest said not, Where is the Lord? and they that handle the law knew me not: the pastors also transgressed against me, and the prophets prophesied by Baal, and walked after things that do not profit."

In Jeremiah 3:3 tells how rebellious man has become, "Therefore the showers have been with-holden, and there hath been no latter rain; and thou have a whore's forehead, thou refusedst to be ashamed." They justify themselves. They have turned their back unto God, and not their face serving other gods. When trouble come, God save us is the first thing come out of their mouth.

These men speak vain knowledge and they reason with unprofitable talk while they cast away their fear and drink iniquity like water. The saving of your soul has become a joke to them. The Holy Scriptures warns us about the talebearer revealeth secrets in Proverbs 11:13. Deuteronomy 29:29 says, "The secret things belong unto the Lord our God; but those things which are revealed belong unto us and to our children forever, that we may do all the words of this law."

Satan manipulates by lying and deceiving. Their hard heart carries them away from God as they flirt with sin by winking and flirting with temptations and sin. Lucifer slithered, con and manipulated a 3rd part of heaven. In Revelation 12 the dragon was wroth with the woman. How did the church end fighting against those who keep the commandments of God. They are fighting against those who are holding on to the "Truth" and those who have the testimony of Jesus

Christ. People of today have the nature of a beast and live in their own wicked imagination.

These battle axes were put here to help God's people understand his knowledge of the mystery of Jesus Christ. As the priest try to keep up with the styles of religion they turn their spirits against God and let wrong words come out of their mouth. Job 13:4, "But ye are forgers of lies, ye are all Physicians of no value, O that ye would altogether hold your peace and it shall be your wisdom." In their prosperity the destroyer shall come upon them. The Church needs a recall to get the bugs out of religion. Job 15:34 says, "For the congregation of the hypocrite shall be desolate, and fire shall consume the tabernacle of bribery."

The Holy Scriptures in Ephesians 3:9-12 says, "And to make all men see what is the fellowship of the mystery, which from the beginning of the world hath been hid in God, who created all things by Jesus Christ: (Vs.10), "To the intent that now unto principalities and powers in heavenly places might be known by the church the manifold wisdom of God, (Vs.11), "According to the eternal purpose which he purposed in Christ Jesus our Lord: (Vs.12), "In whom we have boldness and access with confidence by the faith in him."

Paul says, "For I determined not to know anything among you, saved Jesus Christ and him crucified" 1 Corinthians 2:2. Our world needs ministers that know how to sling the axes that Jesus Christ has prepared for them to sling at his people. Those who can sling the Old Testament as well as the New Testament to make them harmonize with each other to bring clarity of his word to the surface for understanding. The classes that I took in the university that pertain to the bible had not the spirit of God, but were dead courses in philosophy. I could hardly tell if we were talking about the same God.

They were enticing words of man's wisdom and not of the Spirit and power of God. People are tired of being lied to and played with about money. They were past down history lessons. Having been born again and filled with the spirit of God made me feel that I was in cemetery school being taught by instructors who had not the Holy Spirit but was the walking dead with no knowledge of the spirit of God.

1 Corinthians 1:18-21 proclaims that, "For the preaching of the cross is to them that perish foolishness; but unto us which are saved it is the power of God." (Vs.19), "For it is written, I will destroy the wisdom of the wise, and will bring to nothing the understanding of the prudent. (Vs.20), "Where is the wise? Where is the scribe? Where is the disputer of this world? "hath not God made foolish the wisdom of this world? (Vs.21), "For after that in the wisdom of God the world by wisdom knew not God, it pleased God by the foolishness of preaching to save them that believe."

Paul preached a crucified Jesus Christ plain and simple. The Truth don't need to be dressed up it stands out on its own. All should be saved and repent of their sins be baptized in the name of Jesus Christ and ye shall receive the gift of the Holy Spirit for the remission of sins need no human help. The plain preaching of a crucified Jesus Christ is more powerful than all the preachers styling and profiling across the pulpit with philosophy taught in heathen cemetery schools of the world. This is flesh trying to glory in God's presence.

Only Jesus Christ can make unto us wisdom, righteousness, sanctification, and redemption. Paul said in the book of 1 Corinthians, "We preach Christ crucified." He said that this is all he really wanted to know is Jesus Christ and him crucified called the soul business. In this he demonstrated the Spirit of God and the power of God so our faith would not stand in the wisdom of men, but in the power of God.

In 1 Corinthians 2:7 he said, "But we speak the wisdom of God in a mystery, even the hidden wisdom, which God ordained before the world unto our glory." If you get lost always go back before the earth was formed or in the beginning or before the world was. Satan likes to play with scripture but this will jump over the wisdom of humankind.

We must keep the mind of Christ and hold the thoughts feelings and purpose of his heart. Are you believing in the most popular bishop or apostle, pastor preacher, teacher or Jehovah your God? Who are you bowing down to giving away God's glory? The word of God should be the center of our being. There is no other foundation that men or women can lay than that which has already been laid and that is Jesus Christ. No matter who you are your work will be tried by fire of what sort it is.

Let no man glory in men because they are only stewards of the mysteries of God. 1 Corinthians 10:1-4 says, "Moreover, brethren, I would not that ye should be ignorant, how that all our fathers were under the cloud, and all passed through the sea; (Vs.2), "And were all baptized unto Moses in the cloud and in the sea; (Vs.3), "And did all eat the same spiritual meat; (Vs.4) "And did all drink the same spiritual drink, for they drank of that spiritual Rock that followed them: and that Rock was Christ."

Christ was here before Mary or Joseph was even born. God will judge all the hidden things of darkness and manifest the counsels of the heart. "I can do all things through Christ which strengthens me." God needs those who can sling the Old Testament in their left hand and the New Testament in their right to make his word fall into place. God's doctrine or rules are already written.

The wisdom of men contradicts the wisdom of God. 1 Corinthians 2:13 says, "Which things also we speak, not the words which man wisdom teacheth, but which the Holy Ghost teacheth; comparing spiritual things with spiritual." Students of bad teaching is past down. Gabriel won't come blowing a trumpet but1 Thessalonians 4:16 states, "For the Lord himself shall descend from heaven with a shout, with the voice of the archangel, and with the trump of God: and the dead in Christ shall rise first."

We need the whole council of God the Old and the New Testament for our understanding. These two battle axes or the use of the word of God will cut to the heart and bring repentance. If they are really crucified with Christ and it is no longer them that live but Christ lives in them should get out of the Holy Spirit's way.

Hebrews 4:12-13 says, "For the word of God is quick or (living), and powerful, and sharper than any two edged sword, piercing even to the dividing asunder of soul and spirit, and of the joints and marrow, and is a discerner of the thoughts and intents of the heart. (Vs.13), "Neither is there any creature that is not manifest in his sight: but all things are naked and open unto the eyes of him with whom we have to do."

God's ministers that received of the Lord Jesus should testify the gospel of the grace of God and declare all the council of God; Old and New Testament. We should want to be pure away from the blood of all men. I don't want anyone's blood on my head. Jesus Christ has given his ministers the Holy Ghost and made them overseers to feed the church of God that he bought back with his own blood.

Man is trying to kick the order of God out the church and want members to believe whatever they believe leaving the bible out. Keep your eye on the Holy Scriptures and see how often it is used. Church is slowly getting the word off the set. Lights are getting dimmer and notice those Big Screen T V's are not in there for nothing. It's show time.

The word cuts like a knife and people come out of Churches bleeding after sermons delivered by the Holy Spirit. Most pastors just want to tell and let the people hear some new worldly thing instead of the Gospel. God wants all men everywhere to "Repent." Jesus is coming back to judge the world in righteousness.

There are those who believed that he (Jesus Christ) was raised from the dead and those who believe in the resurrection of the dead. Those testifying that Jesus is Christ to those who will receive is the Gospel. Some leaders have not agreed with Jesus Christ and follow wrong and wicked lewdness. There are wolves wearing sheep clothing that has come in the church not sparing the flock.

Our conversation is now settled in heaven where we look for our Lord Jesus Christ. Those who oversee the flock should want the flock,

"And to know the love of Christ which passes knowledge, that ye may be filled with all the fullness of God" Ephesians 3:19.

There are ministers that are called cussing preachers that speak perverse things to draw away believers after them instead of leading them to Christ Jesus. They are responsible for what they teach and that teaching should be God's word of righteousness. God said in Jeremiah 3:15, "And I will give you pastors according to mine heart, which shall feed you with knowledge and understanding."

The multitude must needs to come together. The times have come when humankind must save them-selves and work out their own salvation with fear and trembling. They should read the word of God for themselves to know what is on their spiritual plate on Sunday. Part of our world is losing its conscience and are offending God and man. Our government has chosen Barabbas a murderous spirit and Judas Iscariot the cross-out artist.

We all make choices in life but we must learn how to manage our souls or our minds, will and emotions. After Jesus finished crying when telling his disciples about the parable about him who sowed his seed in Luke chapter 8 he explained the mystery of parables. We need more revelation that leads us into transformation. In verse 10 in Chapter 8, "And he said, "Unto you it is given to know the mysteries of the kingdom of God: but to others in parables; that seeing they might not see, and hearing they might not understand." (Vs11), "Now, the parable is this; "The seed is the word of God."

There is a lack of conveying the fear of God to their flocks. The choice is heaven or hell and they should not take it lightly. As Jesus expounded to his disciples in Luke 24:27,31 "And beginning at Moses and all the prophets, he expounded unto them in all the scriptures the things concerning himself." He opened their eyes inVs.31, "And their eyes were opened, and they knew him; and he vanished out of their sight." If he that gives the revelation does not give the understanding we are still in the dark still.

The laws of Moses, the Prophets and the Psalms God revealed his will through the writings of the Old Testament. It shows how God spanks disobedience or even use your enemies to spank you as he wait on you to cry to him for help. God then sent his word and healed them. Then God opened their understanding in Luke 24:45. In Vs.9 told them to stay until they receive power from on high. Jesus said to preach repentance and remission of sins in his name to all nations.

Their flocks receive the word with joy but the cares and riches and pleasures of this life make them bring no fruit to perfection. When temptation comes they fall away. Others hear the word and the devil takes away the word out of their hearts lest they should believe and be saved. Some church organizations contradict the word of God.

Jeremiah 51:20 states, "Thou art my battle axe and weapons of war: for with thee will I break in pieces the nations, and with thee will I destroy kingdoms." God's man in the center of God's will is immortal until God is finished with him. God want his ministers to set up a standard in the land and blow the trumpet among the nations. It is either heaven or hell and the people must choose. (Vs.22) "With thee also will break in pieces man and woman; and with thee will I break in pieces old and young; and with thee will I break in pieces the young man and the maid."

Pulpits are full of watered down preaching and preaching that cater to please the world. In Isaiah 28, "Woe to the crown of pride who staggered in the operation of his mind and the table where he eats his meat is filthily stained." There are sins of the people that were supposed to be kept at an utmost distance they find themselves ensnared.

Isaiah 28:7-9 informs us of those who lead us, "But they also have erred through wine, and through strong drink are out of our way; the priest and the prophet have erred through strong drink, they are swallowed up of wine, they are out of the way through strong drink; they err in vision, they stumble in judgement." (Vs.8), "For all tables are full of vomit and filthiness, so that there is no place clean. The table is where you go eat and preachers are throwing up vomit from the pulpits. (Vs.9), "Whom shall he teach knowledge? And whom shall he make to understand doctrine? "But ye are forgers of lies, ye are all physicians of no value" Job 13:4.

Everything God wants us to know is in his word. "Them that are wean from the milk, and drawn from the breast." The nations have been "Mentally Kidnapped" and being brainwashed because they are Bible illiterate. God desires obedience from his creation. They are not obeying the Holy Scriptures. They are not denying themselves by not taking up their cross daily to follow God's Word. You may be a fool that is stubborn making it similar to a dog that returns and eats its own vomit again, even though the vomit maybe poisonous. Take time and look now and read 2 Peter 2 about the false prophets and Proverb26:11-12.

This is not the American dream. This is the American nightmare. The Church is overlooking the deeds of the wicked. They throw up lies and you can't tell the difference between food from God and vomit. God's food is his Word and we should be able to find what is being preached in the Holy Bible. The worst place to be in life is to die without Jesus Christ.

D D does not mean Doctor of Divinity in the Holy Bible. Many have degrees and have DD behind their name and the Holy Bible gives the meaning in Isaiah 56:10, "His watchman are blind : they all are ignorant, they are all dumb dogs, they cannot bark; sleeping, lying down, loving to slumber." "Yea, they are greedy dogs which can never have enough, and they are shepherds that cannot understand: they all look to their own way, every one for his gain, from his quarter.

They only bark when money is involved. They don't make believers see the fellowship of the mystery. Members don't want the preacher to talk about their sin. They say tell us nice things. Churches are full of vomit believers who are saying Amen to vomit and that makes them vomit lovers.

We must open up our Bibles and stand on God's word. There is no place clean. "God forbid: yea, let God be true, but every man a liar; as it is written, "That thou mightiest be justified in thy saying, and mightiest overcome when thou art judged." The pulpit is full of vomit that flows through the church. Some congregations are slurping vomit and it has become their favorite drink.

Vomit lovers may get offended but God said "Be ye holy for I am holy." The church has been so use to eating vomit they can't tell real food from vomit. They can't handle sound doctrine which is the unadulterated or pure, uncompromising or inflexible and unyielding, unchanging and staying the same word of the Living God. Hosea 4:8-9) tells us "Like people like priest." They both are trying to gain the whole world therefore loosing themselves and most of all their souls.

They know not what manner of spirit they are of. My people are destroyed for lack of knowledge, because they have rejected knowledge." (Vs.8), "They eat up the sin of my people and they set their heart on their iniquity." (Vs.9), "And there shall be, like people, like priest: and I will punish them for their ways, and reward them their doings." They know the truth but will not preach it. God said don't strengthen the hand of evil doers. The spirit of whoredom has caused them to err. Thou art my battle axe. They are afraid and silent to mention the devil and stand against sin. They won't cry out to the sins of the world.

Instead of bringing the Old Testament and slinging the New Testament they tell the congregation to follow the world. Friendship with the world is an enemy of God. The Holy Scriptures say preach the word. Preach God's kingdom but it takes a King to preach in God's kingdom. The head on our body is our dome and Jesus is the head of the Church his king-dome. Jesus was before all things and by him all things consist." His word is a decree.

The Holy Scriptures are the thoughts of God of the things concerning man giving him a map thru life. It is an instruction book. We are here for God's glory not to be a fund raiser for an organization.

The church is where the "The Battle for Souls" is taking place. Those who do not sling the axe have the congregation slurping and drinking vomit. Some preachers act like they are afraid to preach hell. Most are men pleasers.

Jesus preached hell more than the bliss of heaven. Why won't preachers sling the Axe? The people need the word to renew and rebuild their mind. Jeremiah 4:22 says, "For my people is foolish, they have not known me; they are sottish children, and they have none understanding: they are wise to do evil, but to do good they have no knowledge." Sottish means drunkard and stupid.

No man knows the day or the hour when the Lord comes back. Jesus Christ was taken up and "a cloud received Him out of their sight" in the book of Acts 1:9 and He will return with the clouds in Revelation. Mathew 26:64Abreviated, when he said; coming in the clouds of heaven. Revelation 1:7 says, "Behold he is coming with clouds." Luke 12:40 says, "Be ye therefore ready also: for the Son of man cometh at an hour when ye think not."

Don't get caught playing church. "Blessed is that servant, whom his lord when he cometh shall find so doing" Luke12:43. If you are caught in your sin when the Lord returns you will have your part with the unbelievers. You prepared not yourself or did according to God's will and will be beaten with many stripes. Jesus Christ was a hell fire preacher. He warned people about hell more than he did the bliss of heaven.

People do not fear God because they have not heard about the dangers of hell fire burning. It is a shame even to speak about some of the things that they do in darkness. Light is the only thing that can make manifest things in darkness. They have not heard because those in the pulpit are not preaching it. Can you imagine a person being so greedy that they would let the flock or whole congregation go to hell because of their greed. They are hirelings not priests.

God made the Church to keep us from hell. Colossians 1:26-27 states, "Even the mystery which hath been hid from ages and from generations, but now is made manifest to his saints: (Vs.1:27, "To whom God would make known what is the riches of the glory of this mystery among the Gentiles, which is Christ in you, the hope of glory." Life is short and we must be sure that we are working out our own salvation with fear and trembling. God wants his creation back. He is reconciling all things unto himself in heaven and earth.

Continue, "Whom we preach, warning every man, and teaching every man in all wisdom; that we may present every man perfect in Christ Jesus" Colossians 1:28. When I first got saved my Pastor pulled me aside years ago and told me that some preachers will lead you to hell. It will be the one that stand out the most that you would not even expect.

This is why God said "My people are destroyed for lack of knowledge. Being a pastor must have been hard for a preacher to tell me that. I'm glad that the pastor saw my sincerity in serving God to tell me the truth. God send stars that shine in a dark place and that place is into the souls of men.

Many people are being beguiled with enticing words and still can't explain the scripture. There is a lack of acknowledgement of the mystery of God, and the Father, and of Christ. Colossians 2:3, "In whom are hid all the treasures of wisdom and knowledge." It is good to have proper knowledge because false prophets are ready to make you out of a fool.

False prophets will lead you straight to hell because of self-preservation and tradition. When I listen to a sermon and the preacher leave hell out makes me wonder what kind of church is this? Hell is not full but has enlarged herself. Hell fire burning is calling for the disobedient saying room for one more.

If they are not trying to lead us away from hell; then what is their agenda? We are warned in Colossians 2:7-8, "Beware lest any man spoil you through philosophy and vain deceit, after the tradition of men, after the rudiments of the world, and not after Christ. (Vs.9),"For in him dwelleth all the fullness of the Godhead bodily."

Are you crucified with Christ? Are your hands and feet nailed? If we are crucified with Christ we are nailed to the cross to keep you from sin. Colossians 2:21-23 "Touch not; taste not; handle not; (Vs.22),"Which all are to perish with the using; after the commandments and doctrines of men? (Vs.23), "Which things have indeed a shew of wisdom in will-worship, and humility, and neglecting of the body; not in any honour to the satisfying of the flesh."

Because of the struggle that blacks went through women and gays feel they have a right to not obey the word of God. They say the church would have gone under if it was not for them. That is no reason to disobey the word of God. Their agenda is not greater than God's agenda for our life. God demands obedience and a sinless church from his creation. God wish that all should be saved and come to repentance. No matter who and where you are in your sin is still separation from God.

God set the standards in his word and his word is settled in heaven. The way you feel don't mean a thing to God. Either you are going to obey God or to hell you will be going. Humankind is caught up in these different groups and they are not in line with the word of God. Every struggle that comes along not in line with God's word is sending people to hell when they put their wants, needs and struggle before his written word.

Satan wants your soul. There is not a woman, man or group that I would like to go to hell with. I have not found anyone that cool with me that I want to go to hell with. Have you? People would rather have their rights today rather than to fear God their creator. The devil shows you the beginning but he never shows you the end.

They are caught up in the things of the world and not the word of God. Your focus should be on where you are headed to and that is eternity. This world is temporary and so are we. We are here for a moment and then we disappear. Where do we disappear to? Our body goes back to the ground and our spirits go back to God who gave it in Ecclesiastes 12:7 paraphrase. So get your priorities in order and make obedience to God your first priority. Don't let your twisted thoughts of how you think your life should be send you to hell. Your life was planned by God before the earth was formed.

Pride is at the root of many errors and corruptions of evil practices that have a great show of humility. They let Christ go and begin living in ordinances. Christ has our authoritative decree and direction and is the only head of the church not angels. Eternal life is longer than this life. We are from eternity and we will return to eternity. Seek those things above and not the things on the earth. Get rid of all idolatry. Sins like fornication and all uncleanness and anything else that you put before God.

Put off that old man. Put on Christ let the peace of Jesus Christ rule in your heart. Idolatry only brings the wrath of God. We are complete in Jesus Christ who rules over all principalities and power. Isaiah 43:13 says, "From eternity to eternity I am God." Man is part heaven and part earth. God breathed the breath of life into man and he became a living soul. God breathed part of himself into the dust that he formed man from it and he became a living soul.

God's breath or spirit made man and woman animated. This is where we get our physical motion from. If you doubt this just stop breathing. After death it will be too late to get it right. Do the congregations where you worship believe there is no hell? Why is hell not being preached? We must let the word dwell in us richly.

The parable in Luke 16 tells me all about activity that goes on after death. If it is alright to do or be whatever you want to; then what is the reason for going to church? You can go to hell without someone tricking you. Misery loves company. The enemy called the devil wants all God's creation to go to hell with him. You don't have to go to church to go to hell. The Church of Jesus Christ is to keep you from hell.

Thousands of sincere people have given their whole life listening to a manipulator that only care about money and his pockets. Ephesians 1:4 says "According as he hath chosen us in him before the foundation of the world, that we should "Be Holy" and without blame before him in love."

In Ephesians 1:18 wants you to know why Jesus came and that was so, "The eyes of your understanding being enlighten; that ye may know what is the hope of his calling, and what is the riches of the glory of his inheritance in the saints." Read Ephesians 1:16-23 to receive understanding of why Jesus Christ came. It is a shame how preachers can become rich in churches and the congregation don't even know who God is.

Examine yourself and see if you be Christs because we have one dance and one chance to be right. Five minutes after death will be too late. This is not a test. If you want to be right and you are sold out to God examine yourself and your leadership because saints we are being sold out. I was wondering how could God tell a person who has worshipped him 45 to 60 years of service in the Church this? "I never knew you; depart from me, you workers of lawlessness" Mathew 7:21-23.

CHAPTER 11

PLACEBO IN THE CHURCH

Placebo is a sham substance or treatment which is designed to not have any known therapeutic value. Common placebos include inert tablets, inert injection, or sham surgery. Inert tablets called inactive pills that do not contain any hormones. They are called placebo pills or sugar pills. There are many but the most common is the combination pill that contains synthetic forms of the hormones estrogen and progesterone (medically reviewed by Holly Ernst PA...by Nicole Galan who is a registered nurse specializing in women's health and infertility issues).

The Medical News Today reviews medical processes. This is how the Ministers of the church are supposed to review the Holy Scriptures to assure believers of their soul salvation. Ministers are to check the condition of the flock. Placebo can also help assist in keeping a sound mind. God says be fruitful and multiply and replenish the earth. Inert Injections are used for feed ingredients such as soybean protein concentrate, pectin. The same process is used for extracting CBD from cannabis. Because of this there have been many queries about injecting inert gas as a safety precaution."

Last of all, sham surgery serves as an analogous purpose to placebo drugs neutralizing biases such as the placebo effect. Placebo effects how a person will perceive their condition but have no impact on the disease itself. It encourages the bodies chemical processes for relieving pain and a few other symptoms. When preachers preach and don't preach against sin and disobedience that is the root of the sin disease. There are ethical concerns when the church is disguised not to represent the thoughts feelings and purposes of God's heart. Obedience and agreement to the word of God is the cure.

We are the salt of the earth. We have real salt and then we have substitute salt. We have Ministers and Shepherds then we have hirelings. A hireling is a person in charge as a leader of the church that departs when danger come upon the flock. Placebo and the Word of God are both medicines. Doctors treat symptoms. Treating the symptoms and not the cause is common in medicine. Sin and disobedience is the cause of the curse. If you are not addressing the sins of man they are on their way to hell. God wants obedience.

There is a world-wide marathon of false prophets that run to tear down the altar of God. Like counterfeit money that looks grand on the outside with serial numbers and everything but inside it has no worth. Serving in a false church pretending to be real can cost you your soul. False prophets are preying on the church with motivational speakers that wax fat because they don't speak out against sin. Placebo can be compared to homosexuality where two men or two women try to make up what we call the traditional family. God made male and female and told them to be fruitful and multiply. Two men or two women can't produce children so they adopt one. They try to get the desired result of a male and female traditional family.

The false prophet's message is sent by hell to make you feel good while you are all wrong. Satan makes you comfortable in your sins to keep you away from sound doctrine. The time has come when the order of the church is excepting disorder. Discouraging sinners want to enter in but they cannot see a difference between the holy and profane. The church is on its way to the Broad-way that leads to destruction. As you can see the lights are getting dimmer and dimmer getting ready for the church performances.

Mathew 7:14 KJV says, "Because strait is the gate, and narrow is the way, which leadeth unto life, and few there be that find it." For narrow is the way and there are few that walk in that way. We must choose whom we will serve. If you don't know what a real Rolex watch consist of you can spend your time and money believing that you have the real thing. Believers are saying their fake Rolex or their fake religion looks close enough because it looks like religion to them. There seems to be no consequences for their sins because of the grace of God. False prophets want you to be comfortable in your sins because they know you will not read the Bible.

You can also look at it as wolves among sheep. It can be compared to same-sex marriage when two people of the same-sex go thru a ceremony to get married that is not ordained by God. Another example could be a Family Church that looks like a church but all high positions are run by family members making it a family business. They both are not but they both get a desired result. There is true worship and false worship. Satan has an altar for Baal worshippers. If God be God then worship him, but if Baal be god then worship him.

John 4:23-24 states, "But the hour cometh, and now is, when the true worshippers shall worship the Father in spirit and in truth: for the Father seeketh such to worship him." (Vs.24), God is a spirit: and they that worship him must worship him in spirit and in truth."

It can be a business organization that hides behind the name of Jesus Christ but in heart they are not really His. It is only a money making Venture of set ups that only benefit family and friends. They know how to agree with sin and to dis-agree with God dressing up sin with a covering that add sin to sin. When you are out of God's word you become prey to the devil.

The world has medicine made of chemical compounds used to cure or prevent diseases and help diagnose illness. God gives his children the power to discern spirits. Try the spirit by the spirit of God in you. The Church has spiritual words or the power of God thru his word for healing. They both have the practice of bringing relief from pain and making you whole. The joy of the Lord is our strength because a merry heart doeth good like medicine. Jesus said, "It is not the healthy who need a doctor but the sick" Mathew 9:12.

Everything that God has the devil has a counterfeit. God's word is the same today, yesterday and forever more. It never changes but if you look at the church you see all kinds of changes from the Holy Scriptures made by man in the church to suit their organizations. They invent church titles that were never in the bible.

Check your bible and find the titles or name of your church if you can. They are not there and they are still trying to modify the traditions of men today. Our fore-fathers past down wrong teachings to this present generation of priest. The priests today are too proud and embarrassed to drop wrong teaching. They change the name of the church according to the flow of business even if they have to leave out Jesus Christ who is the head of the church. It is hard to catch a crook when he changes his name or identity a lot but during the process souls are being snatched into hell.

We must taste and see for ourselves the goodness of God. Study God's word or the bread of life that God gave us to live by. Desire the sincere milk of the word. Milk is for beginners. You can't give meat to babies. In the beginning was the word and God wants us to delight ourselves in his word. The Word of God must be the nucleus or the center of our being. Your spiritual house must be in covenant with God. Some food looks good before you put it in your mouth then the devil comes and take it away.

There is bread from heaven and there is polluted bread? Both are being served at church. Beware of the leaven of the Pharisees and Sadducees. Taste the Lord and see that he is good. There are two things on the table Bread from heaven and vomit. Things that don't agree with you come up because you have been eating something that you don't need. A wholesome word will make you throw-up sin that lay dormant deep in your heart. There were always more Baal prophets than those who represent Jehovah. We have to keep our feet on our enemy neck. Messengers of Baal do not worship the one God who made the heavens and the earth.

Vomiting is something that has irritated the gut. What cause you to vomit? Things like same-sex marriage, greed, and abortion causes me to vomit. When women prostitute themselves and upon pregnancy make the baby an occupational hazard makes me vomit. Vomiting is the body way of ridding itself of harmful substance from the stomach. Your body rejected it to relieve or unload it. It might have tasted good but it did not agree with your stomach. Showmanship in churches from the world point of view is vomit.

You throw up your food and now you are hungry again but don't go back and get the same thing. This time you will think twice. Lay aside every weight that so easily beset you. The Holy Bible says in Isaiah 28:8 "All tables are full of vomit and filthiness so there is no place clean." What is in your spiritual diet. When you change your diet you become spiritually unhealthy because a virus from past down wrong teaching will contaminate your soul results. Preachers are polluting God's thoughts from the pulpit by not explaining his sure and pure word.

Digesting what is not in the word of God will cause you to be sick and make you throw up. Meat need to be ground up so that a baby can eat it. We must take the word but people are looking for the preacher to grind it up for them every Sunday. They are not maturing. They want to be spoon fed baby food. They hear the word but don't take it or do the word because it is not broken down to the lowest denominator to them.

You must take God's word and eat it and act on it. I am talking to me. You are going to let me talk to me aren't you? Mankind won't even let God talk to himself when he said let us make man in our image.

Isaiah 40:13 says, "Who has known the mind of the Lord? Or who has been His counselor? "For who has known the mind of the Lord, so as to instruct Him?

People are still chewing on the word and have not swallowed it yet. They are spitting it out because there is no fear of God being taught. We must throw up all pass lies and teaching and false ways that are contrary to God's word. Your one and only soul is at stake. You have one dance and one chance to make it to heaven. This should be worth your investigation. What lies are you still chewing on? God gave the Church one menu. "Be ye holy, For I am holy." Find God's word and eat it. This does not mean you have a calling, gift and appointment to the pulpit. Our pulpit is wherever we stand for God.

Many are called but few are chosen. Samuel was called in the book of 1 Samuel 3:4-15, and Paul were called. Acts 6:3-15. Everybody is called to repentance but everyone is not called to the pulpit. Some that are called heard a voice. Jesus told the Apostles to follow him. They heard a voice. Men are told by God what ministry to fulfill according to their gift.

I am an author sharing the word of God because that is my delight to share. God called me three times, Steven, Steven, Steven with a voice that shook the whole house, but never told me where to go or what to do yet. There was a man dress in white with two angels that was small. There were two angels. There was one beside the front door whose body got large and then small again and one beside the feet of the man in white holding the Holy Scriptures.

It keeps me in the word of God. All the man in white holding the Bible said was take him. I was taken up in the spirit from my parent's home in south Memphis headed in a south east direction and the vision disappeared while I was in the air. There was no directions given me as of yet but I still tarry to hear and obey. The only thing that was said was take him. I like digesting scripture to stay away from occult influences, religiousness, Spiritism, false religious beliefs and all other evil and unclean spirits. God's word in Church is the center of our worship so we must keep holiness holy. Stay dedicated and consecrated to God for his purpose for our life.

There is a collision between Christians and their personal and professional life. Thousands of women are being loosed and every 2 minutes a woman is diagnosed with breast cancer. They are trying to redeem their time without the understanding of what the will of the Lord is. Over 1 million babies were aborted in the first 10 days of 2021.

They have inner debate, inner disharmony, and inner conflict about what is best for women in these given times. They concluded to throw their babies into the fire to be the answer. 1 Samuel 15:23, "For rebellion is as the sin of witchcraft, and stubbornness is as iniquity and idolatry. Because thou hast rejected the word of the Lord, he hath also rejected thee from being king." It is dangerous to rebel against the will and word of God and turn away from his path.

Rebellion always begins in the heart. This was humanities first sin in the Garden of Eden. Proverbs 17:11 says, "A rebellious person seeks only evil, "So a cruel messenger will be sent against him." In the Garden of Eden it was Satan and in our time it was Rhode Vs. Wade. On June 24th 2022 Rhode Vs. Wade was overturned and this made the devil real mad. Rebellious groups were out raged because the power of Satan had been diluted by the Truth about God's word.

God does not want his people two put children in the fire or abort them. Psalms 137:9 says, "Happy will he be who seizes your babies and smashes them against a rock! NCV. They will grab your babies and throw them against the rocks." Murdering the children of our nation is an outraged to drive to whatever state in the country that kill and allow women to murder their unborn child. God says, "Be fruitful and multiply and replenish the earth" is what he told man and woman to do.

Our government is creating a society opposite of the will of God. Satan's agenda made Jesus white for their own purpose. There are black religions that believe Jesus is black. These two agendas have God all wrong because God is spirit in John 4:24, God is Spirit and they that worship him must worship him in spirit and in truth."

In the book of Psalms 19:3 God hears all voices. "There is no speech nor language where their voice is not heard." God is spirit and those who worship him must worship him in spirit and in truth. In Revelations3:9 God says, "Behold, I will make them of the synagogue of Satan, which say they are Jews, and are not, but do lie; behold, I will make them to come and worship before thy feet, and to know that I have loved thee."

There are Legions of Satan worshippers that openly march in the streets of America past shame insisting on killing their unborn child. They are of their father the devil who only comes to steal, kill and to destroy. They are mad because they can't control the population with perversion. They Idol worship with their god Dildo that is a billion dollar a year business.

This practice is on the rise and the big giants of homosexuality and same-sex marriage will fall next because giants they do fall. The devil will try and test you if you are weak to try to introduce men to men and women to women because misery loves company.

Man, woman the devil can't touch you when you know who you are in Christ Jesus. Satan tries to discourage men from women and women from men by sending homosexuals spirits to them to try and deceive them. This is so the woman or man can say, I knew you were gay. This is deception to make you think you are something that you are not. So men you got to, "Hold Your Nuts Close These Days." The devil wants to turn the truth of God into a lie. Ladies stop the killing the babies and men stop killing each other over nothing. I never met people that want to go to hell so bad before.

Proverbs 11:21 declares, "Though hand join in hand, the wicked shall not be unpunished: but the seed of the righteous shall be delivered." It don't matter how tight the cooperation of all those who rebel against God's word, No matter how smart you maybe and no matter how clever you are and you are concealed, keeping in secret. No matter how high that your walls may be that you build. No matter the different techniques of hiding the truth. It's no matter. No matter where you meet up with your beloved group.

"Though hand join in hand," No sinner shall go unpunished. The wages of sin is death paid in sorrow. Any sin that is done in darkness will come to the light. Any sin you try to hide will eventually find you out and eventually bring you down. Sin is better than Perry Mason in finding you out when you try to cover it up. The Holy Scriptures says "Be sure that your sin will find you out" Numbers 32:23. No matter how you try to cover up your sin you must "Repent." Numbers 32:23 will haunt you down, "But if ye will not do so, behold, ye have sinned against the Lord: and be sure your sin will find you out."

There is imagery that is being used and it is called Satan worship. There are artificial images called image fusion. These images do not exist in nature. People used imagery or the picture of a white man on a cross to brand some thoughts in the mind to terrorize the whole races to make them bow down to them. Ephesians 5:29 reminds us that, "For no man ever yet hated his own flesh; but nourisheth and cherisheth it, even as the Lord the church."

Jesus Christ started the church and the devil also started churches. Everything that God created the devil made a counterfeit. Wherever God put a period in his word the devil put a question mark so man can rationalize what God said for you to make the wrong choice. God said it and it is final. Satan put a question mark to help support you so that you can keep the sin that you love so dearly and don't want to give up. Then the devil will connect you with a preacher that will condone that sin so that you will be comfortable in that sin.

A lot of women are forgetting that what they were made from they were made for. They want to denounce marriage and get on the internet and shake the nastiest part of their body in your face to make a living and make reservation to go to hell. Misery loves company. God only ordained marriage between a man and a woman. Two women or two men can never be married in God's eyes they are just dreaming and coveting that which God ordained. They would rather die with a Dildo in their hand than to be who God created them to be.

2 Timothy 3:1-7 talks about the last days and perilous times shall come. In Vs. 5 and 6 tells how Satan creeps into a woman's home by, ((Vs5), "Having a form of godliness, but denying the power thereof from such turn away." (Vs.6), reveals, "For of this sort are they which creep into houses, and lead captive silly women laden with sins, led away with divers lusts, They are in church every Sunday but they don't have self-control. (Vs.7) tells how they are, "Ever learning, and never able to come to the knowledge of the truth."

Everything that God made the devil has a counterfeit. It will either be heaven or hell for all humankind when we die. In Colossians 1:16 says, "For by him were all things created, that are in heaven, and that are in earth, visible and invisible, whether they be thrones, or dominions, or principalities, or powers: all things were created by him and for him." Jesus said, "I am the way, and the truth and the life."

Bad choices are being made which leads to a sacrifice for that sin. "Repent! This sacrifice can lead to abortion and that is the sacrifice of a child. It could lead to divorce by leaving their family. It could be the sacrifice of your job or a career move or even just running from God's plan for your life.

There are groups that seem necessary but with in-depth study they go against the will of God. Give yourself the opportunity to research every possible arguments side to these issues. Proverbs 14:14 tells us that, "The backslider in heart shall be filled with his own ways: and a good man shall be satisfied from himself." Your self can be your worst enemy. God wants to deliver you from yourself before you self-destruct.

People are submitting themselves to one another in different groups without understanding the will of God. It has become societies train wreck. 2 Corinthians 6:14 tells us to, "Be ye not unequally yoked together with unbelievers." Come out from among them and be ye separate. Placebo in churches can have you think you are saved. In churches all over the world people are being baptized wrong and think they are saved and are not.

They have three gods when there is only one. Jesus Christ is one Lord the only Lord and I shall love the Lord my God with all my mind, heart and soul and with my entire being, and with all my might. Jesus said when I do this I will live an active, blessed endless life in the kingdom of God. Therefore I will not worry or be anxious about what I am going to eat, drink, or put on.

Continue: My heavenly Father knows I have need of them all. Instead, I propose in my heart to seek for, aim at, strive after, first of all, your kingdom, your righteousness and your way of doing and being right and all these other things will be added unto me. Now thanks be unto you God, who always causes me to triumph through Christ Jesus Hallelujah!

Proverbs 14:15 tells us that, "The simple believeth every word: but the prudent man looketh well to his going." Ephesians 4:3- tells us that," Endeavoring to keep the unity of the Spirit in the bonds of peace. (Vs.4), "There is one body, and one Spirit, even as ye are called in one hope of your calling; (Vs.5), "One Lord, one faith, one baptism, (Vs.6), "One God and Father of all, who is above all, and through all, and in you all." The Lord has made all things for himself: yea, even the wicked for the day of judgement" Proverbs 16:4.

There is Placebo in medicine that can also be used to symbolize church. Placebo is a substance in medicine, a pill or other treatment that appears to be a medical intervention but isn't one. It is a clinical trial. Placebo can lead to the release of various small molecules like neurotransmitters and hormones. These can then interact with other parts of the body to cause changes. They are Satan's Merchandise.

In 1 Corinthians 12:28 "And God hath set some in the church, first apostles, secondly prophets, thirdly teachers after that miracles, then gifts of healing, helps, governments." God is the one who does the delivering in church but some men will make you think they do it. Study is still being done about specifics about these complex interactions. Placebo works on some symptoms such as pain and depression.

Placebo is not an active treatment and it should not have a significant effect on the condition. But in the church is there anything too hard for God? Of course not! For men things may seem impossible and life can get hard, but not for God. Researchers can compare the results from placebo to those from an actual drug. Placebo is used to make you think you have taken a drug to relieve you of your condition but it is not. It helps researchers determine if the new drug they are testing really works. Satan is working 24 hours a day while we sleep to make sure we die in our sins.

During trials in church ministers invite other ministers to see the effect it have on their members. Ministers of churches that were first Baptist then became Family Churches then Non-denominations and now Holiness. Do you see what the church went thru to get to the Truth and that is Holiness. God told us to be ye holy for I am holy in the Holy Scriptures.

Israel or the church has rose up to play. Aaron helped build the golden calf. Sin is magnifying itself because Moses or Jesus has not come back yet. Moses came back down and Israel was caught off guard in their sins along with Aaron the lying priest. Jesus will be coming back on a cloud like a thief in the night. No man knows the day or the hour. Noah warned the people and the world was caught off guard.

LET'S TAKE A HOLINESS BREAK

Exodus 19:6, "And ye shall be unto me a kingdom of priest, and an holy nation."

1Thessolonians 4:7, "For God has not called us unto uncleanness, but to holiness."

Leviticus 11:44 says, "For I am the Lord your God: ye shall therefore sanctify yourselves, and ye shall be holy; for I am holy: nether shall ye defy yourselves with any manner of creeping thing that creepeth upon the earth."

Leviticus 20:26 tells us, "And ye shall be holy unto me: for I the Lord am holy, and have served you from other people, that ye should be mine."

John 1:1-2, "In the beginning was the Word, and the Word was with God, and the Word was God. (Vs.2), "The same was in the beginning with God."

Leviticus 21:8, "Thou shalt sanctify him therefore; for he offereth the bread of thy God: he shall be holy unto thee: for I the Lord, which sanctify you am holy."

1Peter 1:15 "But as he which hath called you is holy, so be ye holy in all manner of conversation."

Luke 1:70, "As he spake by the mouth of his holy prophets, which have been since the world began."

2 Timothy 1:9 says, "Who hath saved us, and called us with a holy calling, not according to our works, but according to his own purpose and grace, which was given us in Christ Jesus before the world began,"

Titus 1:2-3 reminds us, "In hope of eternal life, which God, that cannot lie, promised before the world began; (Vs.3), "But hath in due time s manifested his word through preaching, which is committed unto me according to the commandment of God our Savior."

Jude1:20, "But ye, beloved building up yourselves on your most holy fath, praying in the Holy Ghost."

Remember Colossians 3:17, "And whatever you do in word or deed, do all in the name of the Lord Jesus, giving thanks to God and the Father by him."

Isaiah 62:12, "And they shall call them, "The holy people, "The redeemed of the Lord: and thou shalt be called, Sought Out, A city not forsaken."

Hebrews 12:14, Follow peace with all men, and holiness, without which no man shall see the Lord."

Isaiah 35:8 warns us, "And a highway shall be there, and a way, and it shall be called The way of holiness; the unclean shall not pass over it, but it shall be for those: wayfaring men, though fools shall not err therein."

All through the Holy Scriptures God wanted his children to be Holy because he is Holy. He wants us to hear him, and to obey him. All the other man made religions that man-made are nothing but quick sand, and the more you move around in them the deeper you sink. Churches today are still being led by men that are contrary to what God desires for us and that is Holiness. Jesus told Peter, "Upon his rock I build my church." If Jesus was in the flesh he would be tired from kicking over tables or the money changers in his church.

There are Fads that are forms of collective behavior that develops within culture, in this case the church. A Fad is a generation or social group in which a group of people enthusiastically follow an impulse for a short period. Fads are objects or behaviors that achieve and are short lived. Homosexuality is a learned behavior.

The Placebo effect is when you are given nothing and you begin to feel better because of that nothing. Your expectation from you taking this drug can make you think it was the drug. When God delivers you everybody can see your change. You take the drug because the doctor says take it as prescribed. The drug has no healing in it and it treats no symptoms. It is all in your mind.

Praise and worship in church services can do wonders for depression and pain. Healing in the churches comes from becoming filled or full of God and believing and confessions. ealing in Churches HHhHHHhhHHhhhResearchers try to determine if there is any improvement in an individual despite the individual has taken placebo as opposed to an active medical treatment. The doctors told me when I was paralyzed that we have done all that we can do for you and now it will have to be between you and the Lord. Doctors look at me today puzzled. God raised me up from paralysis and it has been me and the Lord ever since then. Thank You Lord!

There is a connection between the mind and the body where 1 out 3 received the placebo effect. There is no doubt when the blind see and the lame walk by touching Christ in spirit. In the world even though they were given placebo which is nothing makes them feel better because of their expectations. In our faith we have to have expectation when expect healing and in our finances.

You must be holy to stay saved. God said be ye holy for I am holy. He created everything so if he said that be holy for he is holy why would you want to be anything else. If you are not holy you won't be able to enter heaven. Hebrews 12:14 says "Follow peace with all men, and holiness, without which no man shall see the Lord." Without holiness we can't enter. We must have God's spirit to be his. Holiness was here before time existed even before the earth and the heavens were formed because God was here. He created the heavens and the earth with his Holy Words.

Placebo can resemble the church as the church walk according to the lies and course of this world, according to the prince of the power of the air, the spirit that now worketh in the children of disobedience. Church services are looking more and more like the world.

In the book of Acts 1:4-5 tells us "And being assembled together with them, commanded them that they should not depart from Jerusalem, but wait for the promise of the Father, which saith he, ye have heard of me. (Vs.5) "For John truly baptized with water; but ye shall be baptized with the Holy Ghost not many days hence." God said wait or tarry for the Holy Spirit. Tarry means to linger in expectation.

If you don't have God's spirit you are none of his. God knows those who are his. You may be his creation but you must have his spirit called the Holy Spirit inside you to be his. You must have the perfect plan for imperfect people in you. You are set apart for the glory of God and his purpose for your life.

So, "I hear the voice of the good shepherd, I hear my Father's voice, and the voice of a stranger I will not follow. I roll my works upon the Lord. I commit and trust them wholly to Him. He will cause my thought to become agreeable to His will, and so shall my plans be established and succeed" (John 10:27, Proverbs16:3).

After Satan finished using Judas who betrayed Jesus he received his reward of iniquity by suicide falling headlong bursting asunder in the midst and all his bowels gushed out. Judas was a true disciple who ended up being an agent in the fulfilment of God's plan because God knows all hearts.

Judas was a cross-out artist who as we see in crime today to give up information to save their own life and get paid in the process. He was a Snitch. The scripture says "that it must need be fulfilled." Judas went to his own place. Proverbs 28:13 reminds us that, "He that covereth his sins shall not prosper: but whoso confesseth and forsaketh them shall have mercy."

Satan wants to get you out of God's arm. Churches are sacrificing to Satan by not agreeing with the word of God gradually building an altar of Satan right in front of your face. Judas had the office of a Bishop or Bishopric in Acts1:20. The Judas of today says, you can wear your halo so tight that it will give you a headache. Holiness gets too hard for them and so they sin. They called it fun.

Preachers relieve themselves of that headache by getting all they can and canning all they can get. Then they muddy the waters and let the sheep drink. Some of them begin to hold the thoughts feeling and purposes of Satan that have evil spirits that call themselves one of the other Jesus, but that spirit is not the anointing of Jesus Christ.

Jehovah God is a spirit and those who worship him must worship him in spirit and truth. There are evil spirits that operate under the name Jesus. Witchcraft sends out prayers not inspired by the Holy Spirit with negative words coming out of people mouths. We should not think evil of any office that God has instituted because of the wickedness of any that is put in that office at Equal Opportunity Churches.

God's purpose will not be frustrated or any of his work to be undone because of any person entrusted in that office. Jehovah God is in full control. The unfit will just be replaced with someone who respects God in his position. Even in today's society of money loving preachers God's cause will never be lost for want of witnesses. Apostles were to attest to the world about Christ resurrection. They were ordained not to a secular dignity and dominion.

Souls are being snatched by Secular priesthood who practice things that have no religious or spiritual basis. But they are to preach Christ, and the power of the resurrection. Luke 21:19 says "In your patience possess ye your souls. "By your patient endurance, you will gain your souls. "By your patient endurance empowered by the Holy Spirit will gain your souls."

Keep watering your spirit and cultivating your mind. Being Christ like takes growth and development. What shall I do that I may inherit

Eternal Life? You must "Repent" and be born again. There was a man of the Pharisees named Nicodemus that ask Jesus in John 3:1 about being born again. Jesus Christ told him in vs.3 "Jesus answered and said unto him, Verily, verily, I say unto thee, "Except a man be born again, he cannot see the kingdom of God."

When you die Ecclesiastes 3:20-21 tells us, "All go unto one place; all are of the dust, and all turn to the dust again." (Vs.21), "Who knoweth the spirit of man that goeth upward, the spirit of the beast that goeth downward to the earth?" At death man will go to his long home in Ecclesiastes 12:7says, "Then shall the dust return to the earth as it was: and the spirit shall return unto God who gave it."

Genesis 2:7 says, "And the Lord God formed man from the dust of the ground, and breathed into his nostrils the breath of life; and man became a living soul." The spirit of God made man animated. God formed a man from clay called Adam out of the dust and then breathe life into him. (Vs.8), "And the Lord God planted a garden eastward in Eden; and there he put man whom he had formed."

You must go down in water and be baptized in the name of the Father, Son and the Holy Ghost and that name is Jesus Christ. Acts 2:38, "Then Peter said unto them, Repent, and be baptized every one of you in the name of Jesus Christ for the remission of sins, and ye shall receive the gift of the Holy Ghost." Acts 8:12 says, "But when they believed Phillip preaching the things concerning the kingdom of God, and the name of Jesus Christ, they were baptized, both men and women."

Hebrew 10:22 motivates us to, "Let us draw near with a true heart in full assurance of faith, having our hearts sprinkled from an evil conscience, and our bodies washed with pure water." We should not be sprinkled with water to be baptized. How can you be baptized in a bowl of water? Philip was guided by an angel to a eunuch who was his divine appointment. The eunuch had a strong desire to know God and Peter expounded the scriptures to him.

In Acts 8:36 the eunuch saw water as they went "and the eunuch said, See, here is water; what does hinder me to be baptized? In Vs.37, "And Philip said, If thou believest with all thine heart, thou mayest. "And he answered and said, I believe that Jesus Christ is the Son of God." We must go down in water because the next verse says, "And he commanded the chariot to stand still: and they went down both into water, both Philip and the eunuch; and he baptized him."

Christ suffered for our sins by trading places with us. It was the just for the unjust to bring us back to God. In 1Peter 3:20-21says, "Which sometimes were disobedient, when once the longsuffering of God waited in the days of Noah, while the ark was preparing, wherein few, that is, eight souls were saved by water."

Continue: Even in the days of Moses Christ was here in 1 Corinthians 10:1-4, "Moreover, brethren, I would not that ye should be ignorant, how that all our fathers were under the cloud, and all passed through the sea; (Vs.2), "And were all baptized unto Moses in the cloud and in the sea; (Vs.3), "And did all eat the same spiritual meat; (Vs.4), "And did all drink the same spiritual drink: for they drank of that spiritual Rock that followed them; and that Rock was Christ." Again I say, Christ or the anointing was in the wilderness with Moses.

1 Peter 3:21 brings us up to date, "The like figure whereunto even baptism doth also now save us (not the putting away of the filth of the flesh, but the answer of a good conscience toward God,) by the resurrection of Jesus Christ." 11 Peter 3:9 says, "The Lord is not slack concerning his promise, as some men count slackness; but is long suffering to us-ward, not willing that any should perish, but that all should come to repentance."

Humankind refuses to obey the laws of God. I don't know anyone that I want to go to hell with, or for. I don't want to burn in hell for something I can't take with me or for just a moment of pleasure for all eternity. That is a long time. Isaiah 1:16 says, Wash you, make you clean; put away the evil of your doing from before mine eyes; cease to do evil; (Vs.17), "Learn to do well; seek judgement, relieve the oppressed, judge the fatherless, plead for the widow."

Men and women are choosing hell for earthly pleasures for a moment over eternal life with God. Eternal life is always and never ending compared to this brief life we live here on earth. People find a church that does not preach against their sins so they can feel comfortable in their sins.

They are saying too each other, "Baby, I will go to hell and burn forever for you." This is where the phrase of the devil that says," I'll be with you in Hell or High-water" because high water reminds them of the flood in Noah's days. God says it's going to be fire next time. They are committed to go to hell together. Is that love or lust?

Mark 10:11 is where Jesus makes it plain about adultery as they tempted Jesus. In Vs. 11 explains "And he saith unto them, "Whosoever shall put away his wife, and marry another, committed adultery against her." If he or she is still living you are still married as long as he or she is still alive and you can't kill him or her to get another to get out of it.

The family is God's idea. God ordained marriage between man and woman and marrying the same sex can't get around adultery. There are preachers that honor these kinds of marriages to hide the truth about their second and third marriages. Their first wife or husband is still living.

Moses wrote a bill of divorcement for it was of the hardness of their heart where they took booty over bible. Read Mark 10:1-13 Paraphrase, Jesus said, "from the beginning it was not so it was from the hardness of their heart he (Moses) wrote the bill but the truth is in the beginning of creation it was not so. They devoiced and ran from one man or woman to another to satisfy their lust but the word of God will follow them to the grave. The truth will be still standing tall after all the lies have been told.

Jesus said in Vs.13 "And if a woman shall put away her husband, and be married to another, she committeth adultery." There are ministers that would rather please men rather than God because they were taught traditions of men and not God who will reveal his Son in them. They are building on things they should be destroying. They are building on the traditions of men and walking in the vanity of their minds because of the blindness of their hearts.

They begin to work all uncleanness with greediness. Ministers who have not learned who Christ is lacking the truth that is in Jesus Christ. They don't even know who God is. God has created us in and through Jesus Christ righteousness and true holiness. Don't leave God because the next person has sold out his soul to the enemy. You have been redeemed from the hand of the enemy. There is nothing in sin to go back for because Jesus Christ is the only one who has the words of life. There is not a man woman or group that I want to go to hell with.

CHAPTER 12

ARE YOU A MAN?

Men today are starting to overflow in churches. I am "calling those things that be not, as though they were." Men worshipped God before the woman was made. Men had been thinking that it was a woman's thing to go to church. Until man have a relationship with God he is still lacking as a man. God said let us make man in our image. He was speaking with himself.

God is working all things after the council of his will. God got into the man Jesus Christ to show mankind submission to the will of God. Jesus always gave God the credit not to himself. Man need to understand that without God he can do nothing. All men have to do is inhale and exhale and discover who breathe that breath into them and submit to the Father of Spirits and his doctrine. Any man that think different is proud and know nothing but they are men that are "Perverse disputing of men of corrupt minds, and destitute of the truth, supposing that gain is godliness, from such withdraw thyself " 1 Timothy 6:5.

In Proverbs 30:2-4 Agur having a man to man talk Ithiel and Ucal saying, "Surely I am more brutish than any man, and have not the understanding of a man. (Vs.3), I neither learned wisdom, nor have the knowledge of the holy." (Vs.4),"who hath ascended up into heaven, or descended? who hath gathered the wind in his fist? Who hath bound the waters in a garment? who hath established all the ends of the earth? what is his name, and what is his son's name, if thou canst tell?

Some men have the beast part right but to know who they are and whose they are they have no clue. God's knowledge is not in every man but God wish that all should be saved and come to repentance. God wish that all men would come into the knowledge of him says Ephesians 1:17-18, "That the God of our Lord Jesus Christ, the Father of glory, may give unto you the spirit off wisdom and the revelation in the knowledge of him: (Vs.18), "The eyes of your understanding being enlightening: that ye may know what is the hope of his calling, and what riches of the glory of his inheritance in the saints."

The more men know about God their creator the more they will learn about themselves. God's love for the church will open their understanding on how to treat their wives and raise their sons. Women are the nurturer of the family but the man is the nail and the glue that holds it tight together. There is a song that says, "Near the Cross. Men and women this could be your problem. You went near the cross but you never got on it with Jesus Christ.

Are you crucified with Christ, never the less I live but Christ that lives in me and the life you now live, you live by faith? Are your hands and feet nailed to the cross? Are your hands nailed when God says touch not taste not? Are your feet nailed to the cross to keep you from running to mischief? Galatians 2:20 states that, "I am crucified with Christ: nevertheless I live; yet not I, but Christ liveth in me: and the life which I now live in the flesh I live by the faith of the Son of God, who loved me, and gave himself for me."

Are you raised with Christ? If ye then be risen with Christ, seek those things which are above, where Christ sitteth on the right hand of God" (Vs.2), Set your affection on the things above, not on things on the earth." (Vs.3), "For ye are dead, and your life is hid with Christ in God" Colossians 3:1-3. When you get saved repent of your sins, and be baptized in the name of Jesus Christ asking God to receive his Holy Spirit you are becoming dead to sin and hid in Christ.

The death burial and resurrection symbolizes our salvation in Jesus Christ. There is no other name whereby we can be saved. The Holy Scriptures declares when Jesus said unto Thomas in verse six of John 14:6 that, "Jesus saith unto him, I am the way, the truth, and the life; no man cometh unto the Father, but by me."

CHAPTER 13

PRAYER

Men and women should ask God to open their understanding to His will for their life.

Pray Ephesians 1:16-23 with me, "I cease not to give thanks for you, making mention of you in my prayers; (Vs.17), "That the God of our Lord Jesus Christ, the Father of glory, may give unto you (Me) the spirit of wisdom and the revelation in the knowledge of him: (Vs.18), "The eyes of your (My) understanding being enlightened; that ye (I) may know what is the hope of his calling, and what is the riches of the glory of his inheritance in the saints, (Vs.19), "And what is the exceeding greatness of his power to us-ward who believe, according to the working of his mighty power, (Vs20), "Which he wrought in Christ when he raised him from the dead, and set him at his own right hand in the heavenly places, (Vs.21), "Far above all principality, and power, and might, and dominion, and every name that is named, not only in this world , but also in that which is to come: (Vs.22), "And hath put all things under his feet, and gave him to be the head over all things to the church, (Vs.23), "Which is his body, the fulness of him that filleth all and all."

CHAPTER 14

TRANS-HUMANISM WANTS YOUR SOUL

irst of all I am God's property and I ask that in Psalms 138:8, "The Lord will perfect that which concerns me: thy mercy, O Lord, endureth forever: forsake not the works of thine hands." When we think about the future of mankind we must keep Psalms 139:14 to heart because, "I will praise thee, for I am fearfully and wonderfully made: marvelous are thy works; and that my soul knoweth right well." God created man flesh and blood, but man is on quest to duplicate what God created using earthly materials. Thank God for advancement in the medical field but there are boundaries that humankind cannot cross.

The bionic man is coming into a reality. Prosthetic parts along with science and technology is coming for your mental individuality. Scientist are now making a connection with prosthetic parts connecting to your brain. The Transformer is now coming to pass. The target is to control of your mind. Your mind is the most important part of your soul that is your mind, will and emotions.

God said all souls are mine. The Apostle Paul tells us that in Romans 12:1-2, "I beseech you therefore, brethren, by the mercies of God, that ye present your bodies a living sacrifice, holy, acceptable unto God, which is you reasonable service. (Vs.2), "And be not conformed to this world; but be ye transformed by the renewing of your mind, that ye may prove what is that good, and acceptable, and perfect, will of God."

When we look at things from a human point of view or Afrofuturism point of view and not a spiritual point of view chasing things of flesh will conclude in losing your soul. Mathew 16:26 says "For what is a man profited if he shall gain the whole world and lose his own soul? or what shall a man give in exchange for his soul? This intersection of African diaspora culture with science and technology is putting your confidence in machines the things that God made other than in him who made all things..

This ideology with black identity steeped in the African culture and traditions that paints the future from the perspective of black people is not prevailing to reconstruct our blackness but it is a good reminder. Remember these are the last days. Without God we can do No-thing. Either we are together or we *are untogether. We still have evil people who will never change. We should keep our focus on the souls of men, women and children and let that be your posterity. One soul is worth all the silver and gold in the world.*

Meanwhile at the ranch; Women are abandoning their post. All kinds of evil abortions some by Odious women and black on black crime murders and sins of coveting that of another are still troubling black people. Everything is becoming instant for instance you can now go to a vending machine and buy bigger breast and buttocks with a shot of the needle. You can eat certain foods and lose weight while you sleep without exercise.

Proverbs 31:19 says, "Who can find a virtuous woman? For her price is far above rubies." Afrofuturism men are known in the city gates and the strength and honour of his woman are her clothing. She opens her mouth with wisdom.

Proverbs 31:28 reminds her, "Her children arise up, and call her blessed; her husband also, and he praiseth her." This wrath on unborn children and anger, rage by hot tempered individuals is an irritation to the growth of society as a whole. Proverbs 31:8 tells us to, "Open thy mouth for the dumb in the cause of all such as are appointed to destruction."

God do not have pleasure in wickedness: neither shall evil dwell with thee. There is none that can keep alive his or her soul. When you understand God you understand life and yourself. Transhumanism deals with the flesh and machines directed by the brain or a computer chip as your brain. We have chips in cell phones, TVs and credit cards that deal with the brain and its consciousness. When God created humankind he gave them a soul that consist of a mind, will and emotion. Our government wants to put your brain on file to pull up your memory.

Scientist are rallying those who have Alzheimer the disease that destroys memory and other important mental functions as a door to control your mind. Can scientist simulate the brain in a computer not knowing what to look for? Research is moving fast forward in the name of memory loss.

Humankind was made from the wisdom of God and man is invited to have the mind of Christ and hold the thoughts, feelings and purposes of his heart. Jesus Christ said in John16:12-14, "I have yet many things to say unto you, but ye cannot bear them now. (Vs.13), "Howbeit when he, the Spirit of truth, is come, he will guide you into all truth: for he shall not speak of himself; but whatsoever he shall hear, that shall he speak: and he shall shew things to come." (Vs.14), "He shall glorify me: for he shall receive of mine, and shall shew it unto you."

God sent us a helper and a guide. Anything contrary to the word of God and his spirit is a lie from the pits of hell. HumankindumankinH was not made for the multitude of Satan's merchandise to serve wickedly to sin. Are you free from mental kidnapping the skillful and seductive art of demonic enslavement? Our government is being governed by filty dreamers. They are unmindful of the one who created them. Deuteronomy 32:20 says, "And he said, I will hide my face from them,

I will see what their end shall be: for they are a very forward generation, children in whom is no faith."

Transhumanism is moving God to Jealousy as humankind put their faith in computers that only have a limited amount of knowledge that man put in them. Transhumanism is a combination of humanism and Technology. Yes, God is a jealous God when he sees you spending time on something man made other than the one who created all things. God gets jealous when his creation worships other gods and idols. Kids have become the ransom. If the government is building a new school a new private school in your city it is for research and it will be for experimental purposes. Our world is heading for what is called "The Great Reset."

This reset is an economic recovery plan drawn up by the World Economic Forum in response to Covid 19. God's fire is kindled in his anger to a people that are not his. Read Deuteronomy 32 starting at Vs. 20 thru. Like Ahab they have sold themselves. The whole head is sick. Our country is governed by opinions, not the word of God. The word of God is our balm for healing. Scientist are looking for insight in behavior studying to understand algorithm in the brain using artificial intelligence. War, famine and disease will take us into a new world of communication with each other because direct human contact or touching each other will be almost unheard of, or outdated.

The Holy Bible gives us insight into our behavior. Our world is headed into "Virtual Reality and this is a computer generated environment with scenes and objects that appear to be real, making the user feel they are immersed in their surrounding as though you are really there. You perceive this environment of virtual reality with headsets or digital helmets." This technology of the future is fiction or a figment of your imagination in other words it does not exist but it can take your mind into deeper areas of your sick imagination.

They have great expectation and a strong desire to be able to repair the brain. A I's have been putting micro- chips under the skin and this is their top priority. They want to control those who are angry and those who have a beast like behavior. In the beginning humankind fell into sin in the Garden of Eden and soon became as beast.

Trans-humanism is the mixture of the human body and machines. They want to transform our bodies to make us super human and upload our minds to computers to change the natural use of the body. They want to invent something that will be destined to get out of control by trial and error. Instead of receiving the power of God by praying in the spirit we put super on top of that natural as David by fellowshipping with God his creator. Men should look for the signs of the believer when they speak with new tongues and receive God's Holy Spirit.

Mad Scientist wants to restore the mind and download it to take the place of how the Almighty God made man to memorize. They dream of the body having no need for food as it will rejuvenate itself. God already made our body that heals itself and food for our daily use. Some of the rich feel limited in their normal body. They also want to put an end to worship to God and be their own god. Mad scientist wants us to resemble Frankenstein so we can become the monsters of their imaginations.

Some men who are twisted mentally say they are a women trapped in a man's body. And women say they are a man trapped in a woman's body because they played with the boys coming up in their youth. The excuses they give is no reason to go to hell. Women, it still don't change what you was made from, you were made for.

Some humans as we know them are unsatisfied with the natural way their creator made them. So science keep making mistakes to help science advance to change who Jehovah made them to be. This is an equal opportunity society. Everybody is given opportunity even by God to choose, but there are consequences that go with these choices. Practice makes perfect but there will never be a perfect homosexual or human.

When Jesus Christ returns we will all be like him for we shall see him as he is. WE know that Jesus was manifested to take away the law. Sin transgresses the law. Sin is separation from God. Homosexuals are not just sinning against the truth of God's word but they are an abomination against his will for man and woman whom he told to be fruitful and multiply and replenish the earth.

There will always be a counterfeit man or woman in their quest to be what they are not. The Socialist movement or the Left wants everybody to have a basic income by Cryptocurrency. It is no secret to me as I see what their brain is doing without going inside of their brain. I can see what you are thinking by the unthinkable words that come out your mouth and your actions wanting to be your own God.

I figured all that out without looking into your brain. Maybe I should look at your cell phone and get a digital blueprint of who you really are. The Holy Scriptures tells you who you are and where you came from and where you are going in Deuteronomy 28. The book of Genesis tells you where you came from.

The book of Deuteronomy tells you what to look forward to if you obey or disobey God. Choosing sex over God is another desire that humankind has chosen. The book of Leviticus clearly laid men and women laws down and there is no excuse. Isaiah 40:17 says, "All nations before him are as nothing; and they are counted to him less than nothing, and vanity."

Let us hear the conclusion of the whole matter. You are still a man or a woman. God made male and female no matter how many accessories you add on to your body. Mad scientist wants to make designer humans made to fit their imagination calling them other. You are either a man or woman or boy or girl. Scientist has even made it possible to place pig organs into humans to help prolong life. Thank God for creativity. Placing pig kidneys in humans is a new study that is happening as we speak.

People's minds are warped as they lay with animals. "Neither shalt thou lie with any beast to defile thyself therewith: neither shall any woman stand before a beast to lieth down thereto: it is confusion." They are cursed in Deuteronomy 27:21. This confusion goes along with a man that lieth with another man as he lieth with a woman. People are about to protest and hold signs to marry their pet.

Spousal abuse will be my dog bit me, arrest him, and spite and revenge will be, I am not going to bring you no dog biscuit to the dog pound. You never thought that you will be that stupid. The laws of this land need to be tightened up there are to many loop-holes in our government. Our world is slipping into darkness and the world is letting it happen with no opposition or complaints. The only thing the prince of this world wants to fight is truth.

Star Trek show episodes of human and animals mixed and this must be where society is headed with Bestiality. This is sexual relations between a human and a lower animal. Bestiality or animal cruelty in the Holy Bible is called confusion when sex is initiated with humankind and animals. Dogs, cats and horses are being confused and abused by their owner all over the world. This put a new twist on "Animal Lovers!"

Those who disbelieve the truth are commonly more credulous of errors and fancies. A guilty conscious needs no accuser or tormentor but itself. They know that God made woman from man for man. It is confusion to the animal to have sex with humans. A Spanish novelty once said, "If you lie down with dogs you will come up with fleas." When people live a life of sin they might as well be haunted by ghost and furies, as with the horrors of an accused conscience.

You must prove you have abandoned your sins by being honest first to yourself and God for deliverance. First you must admit that there is a problem. This is the first step into your deliverance. The truth will still be standing tall after all the lies have been told. There is nothing worth more than your soul and everlasting life.

Eternal life is never ending compared to our brief life here on earth. Heavenly treasures should be our goal because without God's spirit no man can enter heaven. Romans 3:10 "As it is written, There is none righteous, no, not one." There is no fear of God. Our whole world needs to plead guilty before God and Repent. Exodus 22:19-20 says, "whoever has sexual intercourse with an animal must be put to death."

Earthly riches will not get you there. We get there by the process of the transferring of the spirit of Jesus Christ that is in a believer after death. The spirit given to a believer when born again will return to God who gave it. Ecclesiastes 12:7says, "Then shall the dust return to the earth as it was: and the spirit shall return unto God who gave it."

Bad men and women have a conscience when they do evil to good men just like when Herod beheaded John the Baptist. Men of God must tell leaders of their faults. Just because a person has fame and more money than you don't mean that you look over their soul. They are the one who really need your spiritual support. The Holy Scriptures tells us to not be afraid of their faces in Jeremiah 1:8.

John told him plainly that it was not lawful for thee to have thy brother's wife. People who are just and holy have holiness toward God, and justice toward men. The wicked see you being a doer of the word and not just a hearer. There are also stony heart Christians that hear the word with joy and Satan comes immediately and take it away.

Even though he was king the Holy Scripture tells us not to be afraid of their faces. People will have you killed to stay in their sin like Herodias. People argue over the things that God said in his word and will go to hell over it. Those who pretend to honor prophesying are for smooth things only, and love good preaching if it keeps far enough from their beloved sin. Herodias must have the head of John the Baptist or the head of the Church now without delay as the ministers are granting it.

When Herod opened his mouth in front the nobles to give the daughter of Herodias half the kingdom they are beheading Jesus Christ who is head of the Church. The church is his body the fullness of him that filleth all and all. Preachers are being surprised into the moment like Herod when they repay faithfulness with this question, "Ask of me whatsoever thou wilt, and I will give it thee even if it goes against God's uncompromising, unadulterated, unchanging word.

Their own mouth condemns them. Like Herod they can't take it back and they will be exceedingly sorry. When men and women go against God and change their sex organs they will become exceedingly sorrowful. God already set the standard for the church but man is ignoring the scriptures that validate the church and are making their own rules.

Men and women's conscience will not let them sin easily but like Eve Satan finally prevailed. When Pastors go against God's word they must be mindful of their oath to Him. This sinful oath and act must be Repented of and not performed. Pastors need to stop people pleasing and obey God rather than pleasing men and women. Church is being filled with the latest technology and you can come to church by turning on your computer. God said forsake not the assembling of yourselves together as some do. Jesus said upon this rock I build my church in Mathew 16:18.

People are making themselves slaves to those who they respect putting their soul on the line. They are coveting by people pleasing. Like the Mafia they have bloody tyrants ready to obey their most cruel and unrighteous decrees. They do this in the name of the church when they cut the head off (Jesus Christ) and made it a present and hand it over on a platter to the damsel and her mother. Jesus told Peter upon this rock I build my church. False prophets in the church have cut off the head of Jesus Christ and they become head of their greedy organization. Jesus is the head of the church. Their church started out with Jesus as the head and the church ended just a worldly organization or business.

The Holy Spirit reveals to us things to come. Worldly things will disappear but God's word will last forever. When we believe in God's word it gives us power and authority over the enemy to cast out demons by commanding it. God gave us power to tread upon serpents and scorpions and over the power of the enemy in Luke 10:19. We need to fall on our knees and tell Jesus Christ to show us the path to walk on and to point out the right road for us to walk. Guide us clearly the path that he want us to follow.

We must remember that we are not just fighting God's war but we are fighting flesh and blood and everything and everybody that carry evil spirits that comes against us. They are putting people and things that distract, persuade, manipulate us from God's service and our God ordained destiny. Computers and electronics are getting us prepared for our future similar to the cartoon the Jetsons. Our new norm is the next step into that way of living, but scientist wants to inner-grate your body with robots. Remember they put their trust in Rosie the robot on the Jetson. They want to control your body by remote control.

The Holy Scripture says the body without the spirit is dead. Robots are dead to God because man is the only species that God our creator created to communicate with him because we were made in his image. Humankind is worshipping computers that have not the spirit of God in them.

Instead of asking and believing God they ask a machine. Romans 8:10-11"And if Christ be in you, the body is dead because of sin; but the Spirit is life because of righteousness." (Vs.11), "But if the Spirit of him that raised up Jesus from the dead dwell in you, he that raised up Christ from the dead shall also quicken your mortal bodies by his Spirit that dwelleth in you."

We are close to wearing the bubbles on our heads like the cartoon the Jetsons. This time it is Covid -19 and the Delta virus but the next time it could be radiation. There seem to be many versions of Covid 19 coming ahead. Omicron sounds as if it is from the movie Transformer. The clothing the Jetson's wore were the kind that Nano Tech is getting us prepared to wear. Don't worry about shopping as you see that this is already happening. The plastic bubble mask is already out.

Spaceships and rockets can't go where God is. God is in heaven above all the heavens. He is above the 3rd heaven. Deuteronomy 10:14 says,

"Behold, the heaven and the heaven of heavens is the Lord's thy God, the earth also, with all that therein is." Drones are flying and helping to fight crime and wars and drones will be making home deliveries. They are used also in space. Instead of wearing a hat you will be glad to wear a bubble just to stay alive from sickness and contamination. Plagues and radiation are destroying the freshness of the air, water and food. Satan only comes to steal, kill and to destroy. Like the Jetsons food is on its way to pill form.

The Holy Bible says dust thou art and dust thou shall return. In the cartoon the Jetson I did not see any ground. This must be why cremation is becoming popular. Flying cars are right around the corner and robots are about to blend in with the human population. Don't get lost with what the future holds but stay plugged in and rooted and grounded in the word of God who is the same yesterday, today and forever.

Humankind is always advancing even if it goes against its own common good into self-destruction. Our world is always looking for a quick fix. They would like computers to do all their thinking because we live in a lazy microwave society. Most people want to be served. Computers do not know what I want because my taste change all the time. Computer thinking for humankind does not sound like advancement. Instead of putting trust in God humankind wants to put their trust in machines that break down often.

Down loading my brain in a computer to receive everlasting life is competing with God. When your body is dead, and gone back to the dust your mind is in a recorder on record. After death the Holy Scriptures says man will give account of the things done in the body. People can see or hear that someone like you actually existed. Can you actually believe those in the future could believe that someone as silly as you existed at one time. They will be saying the world has really made progress. You will be like the stone age in their lifetime.

Programs in computers break down. Cities and companies are shut down because of computer break downs. There will be fewer people on earth as you witness how many people Covid 19 took out. Don't keep lying to yourself thinking you are going to live forever in the flesh. God hate every false way because deceit is falsehood. Man is a spirit who lives in a body and he has a soul. He has a soul a mind, will and emotions and a spirit that will go back to the one who gave it. Psalms 119:89, "For ever, O Lord, thy word is settled in heaven."

We are here for a moment and then we disappear. We are passing through this life on our journey back to where we came from. We are from Eternity and we will return to Eternity. Let me encourage you that if you are still breathing God's fresh air you still have a chance to receive Jesus Christ as Lord. Just Repent and be baptized in the name of Jesus Christ. Get the spirit of God in you so that you will have the proper spirit to return to him with.

Our nation was built on God's word. People want to do what they want to do. If this nation is not being built around the word of God it is being built around Satan. Our destiny will only be heaven or hell. There is no in between. Satan only comes to steal, kill and to destroy. This government has invited a Socialist form of government.

Who don't like something for nothing? Citizens want to be paid income and not work. The Holy Scriptures tells us that if you don't work you don't eat. Who want to depend on government handouts? A wise man once told me that you get what you pay for. America if you want to pay for nothing, you are going to get nothing. Nothing from nothing leaves nothing.

CHAPTER 15

SIMON SAYS

The New World government that is transpiring in front of our face and it will have its consequences. What we are seeing now is 2 Corinthians 4:4, "Satan who is the god of this world, has blinded the minds those who don't believe. They are unable to see the glorious light of the Good News. You are of your father the devil and the lust of your father you will do. People are making the wrong choice by choosing death and the curse rather than life and the blessing.

Simon in this chapter is Satan the prince of this world who is speaking loud to those who do not honor God. There is an empty place on the inside of them. Something is missing and that thing they are looking for is God. A relationship with God is what is missing from those committing crimes craving attention and wanting to be a movie star on camera while doing their crime on camera. Yes everybody is a star and what role are you playing in life?

Satan shows you the beginning but he never shows you the end. The end is death of some sort. Soul Snatching will snatch you into heaven or hell. They feel empty inside and do not know how to fill that void. The first place Satan attacks is your mind because where the mind goes the body will follow. In this case it will be heaven or hell. The Great Reset in our world is led by Satan who wants to serve its citizens and give them the royal treatment. He encourage his followers to steal, kill and to destroy.

God's enemy wants to reset the standards or the way that God planned for his creation. You don't have to work because government wants to play God and supply all your needs. People think that they are getting something for nothing because it is free. Where they do that at? You can't even die free because it cost to bury you. In return they want your obedience that belongs to Jehovah.

Like drug dealers control junkies that go out and lie, rob, steal, and kill for drugs. The government wants control of your soul. It wants your mind and body for the advancement of humankind. That's right they want to practice on you. They call it research. You know doctors always ask each other, "How is your practice?

Medical and Health care companies are programing Americans bit by bit by way of the Media to comfortably ease them into this transition. Before you know it you will be participating in that New World Government. Today our world systems remind me of the child game of "Simon Says" that is following after riches.

Movie stars and some of the music we listen to are the Simons. The news on television plus the Supreme Court are two of the Simons in our lives. Who are you listening to? Whatever drugs, movie star on TV, the government, or the devil tells you to do, you do it. When Satan dangles tempting self -seeking bait in the front of your face it looks good from the beginning. The enemy shows you the beginning but he never shows you the end.

He shows you fornication and adultery that brings death to your relationships and with God. Simon or Satan says turn your back on God because I got millions and trillions of dollars for you over here in the international monetary system. It is backed by international trade that is the exchange of capital, goods and services across international borders because there is a need or want for these goods and services.

Haggai 2:8 is where God screams out and says, "The silver is mine, and the gold is mine, saith the Lord of host." All the riches of the world are the Lords and all we have to do is be obedient to him. It is ours for the asking. We have to know what has been freely given unto us. When the storms of life hit you, your reply is, see you God I'll be right back.

Satan gives you dis-ease for your sin or moment of pleasure and most of the time you don't even get the whole moment. For disobedience God sends war, famine and disease to run you back to him and bring you to repentance. God left the world his word to govern his people by and now man wants to "Reset" what God has already established. God's word is settled in heaven and now we need to settle it in our heart.

God made woman for man and Satan reset woman for woman and man on man. God set marriage in order with male and female. He set adultery and divorce as enemies to that order of marriage, but Satan follower's is resetting divorce and it is becoming the new normal. The Truth has been "Reset" with a lie. They are the ones "Who changed the truth of God into a lie, and worshipped and served the creature more than the Creator who is blessed forever. Amen." Romans 1:25KJV

You don't have to work because the enemy shows you all the kingdoms of the world in Casinos and Lottery. He shows you how to covet that of another so that you want and desire the things that belong to another. Gambling can cause you to lose your home and family. Robbery and theft could lead you to death and prison. Disobedience to God brings the curse in the book of Deuteronomy 28 but Jesus Christ delivered us from the curse of the law being made a curse for us on the cross.

Walking contrary to the word of God makes you be controlled by the enemy that brings the curse. Romans 6:16 tells us that, "Know ye not, that to whom ye yield yourselves servant to obey, his servant ye are to whom you obey, whether of sin unto death, or of obedience unto righteousness." When you get saved God will deliver you from the curse of the Law so you can be led by the Spirit of God.

Men watch TV and television have stars with long hair and pony tails with bangs that belong to women hair styles. When we grew up in the fifties and sixties women wore pony tails and bangs. The Holy Scriptures tells us it is a shame for a man to wear long hair. Satan hates men because man was made in God's image and he hates God. What spirit are you being led by?

Go to the jail with your draws hanging down and it will look like an invitation to the homosexual spirit of another man unless you are a bad man. Women also have to fight that spirit physically and spiritually. God wants you sorry for your wrongs. If a man has 100 million dollars and put on a dress, panty-holes heels and a bra don't make him right. Men that are poor says, if that's how he got his millions I am going to do it too. You tell me money can make you compromise you manhood and make you start switching. Brothers you can keep the pony tails bangs, lipstick and earrings. Who taught you that?

Money can make you cut off your penis and make you want have a baby because your lustful thoughts told you to be a woman. Simon is talking to China because they are experimenting on how to make men pregnant. Thoughts like these come straight from the pits of hell. Women are out there lying to themselves like they are grabbing their penis that they have put away in their glove department in their car or bath room closet at home.

Simon talks to women who are raising boys to be girl and girls to be the one to bring home the groceries. Satan and Simon tell the boys to switch and the girls to strut. Women are putting pony tails and barrettes on boys. They are being led by Satan to help establish the lies of the wicked one. Satan even lied to himself when he told himself that he wanted to be like the Most High.

Men that are not rooted and grounded in the word of God will go for every lie the devil put out there. They become an object of cursing, an astonishment a great surprise, a curse and a cause or occasion of blame, discredit, or a disgrace. They become a puppet. They are the ones who love to go back to their Egypt or their sins. They choose to die in their sins.

Men and women worshipping Satan today are challenging Jehovah by saying, whose words shall stand mine or God. God's word will stand against them for their evil. God will give those who stand for evil into the hands of those who want to take them out. Satan comes to steal, kill and to destroy and he will be glad to do his job. God is looking for obedience from his creation.

God wants his sons and daughters to do, Deuteronomy 10:12, "And now, Israel, what doth the Lord thy God require of thee, but to fear the Lord thy God, to walk in all his ways, and to love him, and to serve the Lord thy God with all thine heart and with all thy soul."

When you try and get away from Satan or Simon is when the game Simon Says gets crazy. He tells you to do all kinds of crazy things that you would not normally do. The devil will come in your mind and tell you anything. He will tell you if he catch you alone to self-destruct. If you have anxiety he don't want you to be patient because you have jumped in front of God's plan for your life. You can be praying and the devil jump into your prayer and put naked pictures in your mind. Cast down these thoughts or imaginations and send them back down to the pit of hell where they belong in the mighty name of Jesus Christ.

Simon or Satan wants to control of your mind because he want to make you think that right is wrong and wrong is right. Simon gives you a twisted version of what life is all about. Satan or Simon knows what you like and this will be the bait that he will dangle in your face. The world is still making the choice to disobey God. God says choose you this day who you will serve. Wherever God put a period, Satan puts a question mark.

The Lord allows evil to control those who choose to do evil. Now the child game Simon says or our government is putting lies in children books to catch them in the 2nd 3rd grade to make grown-up decisions. The government wants to give the children the choice to choose to be male or female. We have choices all day long. When Covid 19 came your way you became horrified. Some people can't function alone and make bad decision when they are alone. When Covid came giving instructions the devil or Simon says stand six feet apart. Next, stay at home.

Then he says don't go to church and forsake the assembling of yourselves together. Simon says be afraid because you might be the next to die. All of these manipulating steps are preparing us for the New World Order. Simon or Satan was giving you these instructions assisting you through your fear of Coronavirus.

Our government is training a whole nation at one time to obey by putting on a mask or suffer the consequences. God corrects you by measure in Jeremiah 46:28. He will not leave you wholly unpunished. It is getting the world ready to get in line with this new norm called Socialism the New World Order.

Getting in soup lines became normal in 2020. Instead of God supplying all your needs the government says; don't work we are here for you. We got your back. They are fattening the frog for the snake. Our government is only giving us a preview showing you where we are headed closer to the appearance of Anti-Christ even though we have many in the world already. This is the time for you to get your God straight.

God wants his creation to humble them-selves and pray. He wants to forgive all sin when they are repented of. Repentance and Obedience takes away the curse. Saying evil is good can be called stout words against the Lord our God. If you think that God does not care is a lie from the pit of hell.

Married couples have become faithless to God first, then also to each other. They are violating the covenant of marriage by refusing to take care of and keep each other. They are going on their lustful way. They were put together to produce godly children from that marriage. From the married couple's heart are flowing the issues of life.

There are a lot of God's people coming out of the fire as dross. We are supposed to be a living sacrifice but we keep crawling off the altar.

They are losing faith in God because they are not staying close to him and they are not seeking him first. They begin to think what difference does it make to serve the Lord? Don't forget that with God delay does not mean denial.

Stop giving up and turning coward. God is still on the throne. If you are breathing you still have another opportunity to get it right. We will find out the difference in how God treats the good and the bad. We will find out how God treats those who love him and those who don't. Put on the mind of Christ and hold the thoughts feeling and purposes of his heart.

Proud men and women will burn from the rooter to the tooter. Repent! Men and women that get married need to put on one mind and heart. Add God into their marriage and that will be that three-fold cord that will be hard to break. Be believers and not doubters.

Hold fast to your confessions of faith. Decide to walk by faith and practice faith. Your faith comes by hearing the word of God. Your victory is assured through the shed blood of Jesus Christ. When you stay with the Lord God you already know in the end you are going to win. Jesus is the author and finisher of your faith. Let God finish developing you as you go thru the fires of life. We must pursue holiness, for without holiness you will not see the Lord.

Jesus was talking to the seventy when they returned with a praise report telling him about their experience on the spiritual battle field. They told Jesus (Luke 10:17-20LB), (Vs.17), "When the seventy disciples returned, they joyfully reported to him, Even the demons obey us when we use your name.

(Vs. 18), Yes, he told them, I saw Satan falling from heaven as a flash of lightning! (Vs.19), "And I have given you authority over all the power of the enemy, and to walk among serpents and scorpions and to crush them. Nothing shall injure you! (Vs.20), "However, the important thing is not that demons obey you, but that your names are registered as citizens of heaven."

CHAPTER 16

THE MERCHANDISE OF SATAN

If you are a child of God there are some things that you should be aware of when shopping for your spiritual diet. We should watch as well as pray not just for the coming of Jesus Christ but also watch and pray against the enemy of Jesus Christ. That is (Satan and his emissaries). Cursed be he that does the work of the Lord deceitfully. We all must stand before God. Even the devil and all the false prophets will have to stand before God.

Satan hates God and because you are a child of God he hates you too. Demons came from heaven but they did not come from God. These angels called fallen angels are in Jude 1:6, "And the angels which kept not their first estate, but left their own habitation, he hath reserved in everlasting chains under darkness unto the judgement of the great day." God have them locked down. Malachi 3:6, "For I am the Lord, I change not; therefore ye sons of Jacob are not consumed." Division is Satan's battle plan.

Brothers we should all speak the same thing not giving Satan a place in us because either we are together or we are untogether. 1 John 1:5-7 says, "This then is the message which we have heard of him, and declare unto you, that God is light and in him is no darkness at all." (Vs.6), "If we say that we have fellowship with him, and walk in darkness, we lie and do not the truth: (Vs.7), "But if we walk in the light, as he is in the light, we have fellowship one with another, and the blood of Jesus Christ his Son cleanseth us from all sin."

Christ is the wisdom of God and the anointing power of God. God's wisdom is his word. Satan is using past truth to become a present lie and we need live coals to burn that which is not like God off our mouth. Gays did not use to have gay parades in Jerusalem and that use to be unheard of but that is a past truth, but today they have them. Now we must wait on that New Jerusalem because abominations are marching down the main streets of Jerusalem.

Homosexuality in the past was a sickness of the thoughts of the brain that need counseling and has now become part of the New Normal. This is past truth becoming a present lie. Giving birth was God's plan for women but certain groups of women say that's a lie while they still bleed every month. Even China is trying to make men become pregnant and you know that is a lie from the pits of hell.

The baptism of John became a past truth when Jesus came. After John's baptism we kept the repentance and added in the name of Jesus Christ to our baptism. Satan has nothing but lies, false concepts and false hope that come from his merchandise.

Anything whether thoughts or feeling that are contrary to God's will and intended to change God's truth is the merchandise of Satan. The left or those who believe in the devils lies are coming after the children asking the child at an early age what sex they want be. They are giving children the ability to decide if they want breast or a penis. They are coming in the schools letting kids decide what sex they want to be and they are not old enough to make that type of decision that last the rest of their lives.

One spirit encourage a third of heaven to rebel against God. (Genesis 1:1-2), "In the beginning God created the heaven and the earth". (Vs.2),

"And the earth was without form, and void and darkness was upon the face of the deep. God did not come from darkness because 1John 1:5 says "This then is the message which we have heard of him, and declare unto you, that God is light, and in him is no darkness at all." Some preach God was created from darkness but God created darkness and separated darkness from the light and called it day.

God separated darkness from the light. God is Spirit. "And the spirit of God moved upon the face of the waters". Then God revealed himself in Jesus Christ in Ephesians 3:9-10 KJV) "And to make all men see what is the fellowship of the mystery, which from the beginning of the world hath been hid in God, who created all things by Jesus Christ." God did not come from darkness and this is a twisted lie from Satan that loves darkness.

Ephesians 3:10 says, "To the intent that now unto the principalities and powers in heavenly places might be known by the church the manifold wisdom of God". (John 1:1-5 LB) says, 'Before anything else existed, there was Christ, with God. He has always been alive and is himself God. (Vs.3), He created everything there is – nothing exist that he didn't make. (Vs.4), Eternal life is in him, and this life gives light to all mankind. (Vs5) His life is the light that shines through the darkness and the darkness can never extinguish it."

This is Lucifer before he was transformed into Satan on earth. God spoke to Satan in the book of (Ezekiel 28:14-19 KJV), "Thou art the anointed cherub that covereth; and I have set thee so: thou was upon the holy mountain of God; thou hast walked up and down in the midst of the stones of fire." This is Lucifer before he was transformed and called the devil hear on earth.

Continue: (Vs. 15), "Thou wast perfect in thy ways from the day that thou wast created, till iniquity was found in thee." (Vs.16), "By the multitude of thy merchandise they have filled the midst of thee with violence, and thou hast sinned; therefore I will cast thee as profane out of the mountain of God: and I will destroy thee, O covering cherub, from the midst of the stones of fire."

Satan's character is in his merchandise. His followers became children of no understanding. Ezekiel 28:17-19, "Thine heart was lifted up because of thy beauty, thou hast corrupted thy wisdom by reason of thy brightness: I will cast thee to the ground, I will lay thee before kings, that they may behold thee." (Vs.18), "Thou hast defiled thy sanctuaries by the multitude of thine iniquities, by the iniquity of thy traffic; therefore I will bring forth a fire from the midst of thee, it shall devour thee, and I will bring thee to ashes upon the earth in the sight of all them that behold thee." (Vs.19), "All they that know thee among the people shall be astonished at thee: thou shalt be a terror, and never shalt thou be any more."

According to the Spirit of Holiness and the Holy Scriptures homosexuality is a fallen spirit in man or woman. Satan fell from heaven with his merchandise. Their mind became violent angels in heaven over Satan's merchandise in heaven and God was not having it. When Jesus Christ cast the demons out of Legion and the got into the pigs and ran violently over the cliff. Satan gets violent when he is about to be cast out.

For us to understand darkness you must understand morning. Morning starts in darkness. Lucifer was the son of the morning. You were born or developed in darkness of the mother's womb. Light and darkness represent the state of two minds. There is a lesser light and greater light. The sun is greater light and it is called day. The moon is lesser light and it is called night. Satan is called son of the morning because morning begin in darkness and don't get it wrong thinking that it is light.

Satan transforms into an angel of light. A man is transformed into a woman but he is not a woman. He knows he can't say he is a woman so he takes on the name or title Trans--- gender or other. The heavens became dirty or unclean with Satan's merchandise. Satan introduces thoughts and feeling you never had and makes wrong right and good evil. Children are being taught evil is good. Transformation starts in the mind. Anything that the mind can conceive can be done and everything that we do begins with a thought.

Everything God has Satan has a counterfeit. The Holy Scriptures want believers to be transformed by the renewing of the mind in Romans 12:2. "And be not conformed to this world: but be ye transformed by the renewing of your mind, that ye may prove what is that good, and acceptable, and perfect, will of God. We must have the mind of Christ and hold the thoughts, feelings and purposes of his heart.

In order to plant a good seed in a believer's heart first you have to dig up that carnal mind and get all the dead roots of your past out. Get all the rocks and uproot the weeds out of that hard heart. The enemy comes to take away the word of God before it can reach or settle in your heart. The word is where God's power, love and sound mind lay. Our world is looking for the answer to its mental problems. What they are looking for is in Jehovah whom they are rejecting. Hosea 4:6 says, "My people ae destroyed for lack of knowledge, I reject you from being a priest to me. And since you have forgotten the law of your God, I also will forget your children."

Satan is always ready to rob you of the word of God. When the word is sown we must be more ready to hear God's word without distraction. Take heed how you hear when the word is preached. When the word is being preached is when Satan comes for the word to take it away.

Sometimes realty will only sink in when death come upon those who are evil. Trans-gender teachers are spreading the spirit of Homosexuality. Growing up in school as a youngster we first prayed to God in the morning or pledge allegiance to the flag. Now the first thing children see is an abomination in front of them to train their brain that it is alright to go to hell. You need to take time and go in the school in the morning to see who you are dropping your child off with.

Satan is trying to exalt his throne over that of God. Satan's speech changed in heaven when his heart was lifted up. God heard the change in his lifted up voice. It was like when a parent tells a child; don't you raise your voice at me! Satan and his followers became high minded with corrupted wisdom. TV commercials are merchandising Satan's agenda. Men are bumping mustaches on TV commercials women are bumping each other's bellies.

The Old Serpent wanted to be like the Most High coming from being created to wanting to rule like God the creator of all things. Doctors who practice to be a transformer can change men and women sex organs but God know who they are and they will burn in hell. The death angel knows exactly who you are no matter how many times you change your identity.

If you were born a man named Tom and you have a sex change and become a fake woman Chiquita that will not fool the death angel. When God calls Tom home at his death there will not be any mistakes because the death angel will be snatching off wig, false eye lashes, high heels, and dress off Tom because it is your time man. The same with the lesbians the death angel know exactly who you are.

Romans 1:18says, "For the wrath of God is revealed from heaven against all ungodliness and unrighteousness of men, who hold the truth in unrighteousness." When the death angel comes for you there will be no place to hide under any other name or sexuality. You can hide, but the angels of the Lord know exactly who you are and they are coming to get who you were born to be if you were born male or female.

On the street you can hide your name from humankind calling your -self big man or a woman calling herself big booty Suzie but you can't hide from God. You can change you sexuality to a drag queen but the death angel knows who you are. Man and woman are the only creation that God created who does not know who they are but the death angel won't miss and they will be without excuse.

Since the Left does not want to retain God in their knowledge. They became desperate like Satan. God gave them over to a reprobate mind to do things inconvenient. A reprobate mind has no convictions.

In Romans 1:24-32 Paraphrase is the multitude of Satan's Merchandise. God gave them up unto the lust of their own hearts as they changed the truth of God into a lie. God gave them up to vile affections where men and women's mind changed from their natural use and working the unseemly not wanting to retain God in their knowledge.

Continue: They became filled with all unrighteousness backbiters and haters of God without natural affections without understanding. (Vs. 32), "Who knowing the judgement of God, that they which commit such things are worthy of death, not only do the same, but have pleasure in them that do them." Romans 2:2 says, "But we are sure that the judgment of God is according to truth against them which commit such things." There is not a man, woman or group that I want to go to hell with!

John 17:17 says sanctify them through thy truth, thy word is truth." Romans 2:8-9, "But unto them that are contentious, and do not obey the truth, but obey unrighteousness, indignation and wrath, "Tribulation and anguish, upon every soul of man that doeth evil, of the Jew first, and also to the Gentile." Romans 2:11 tells us, "For there is no respecter of persons with God." Acts 2:38 says, "Then Peter said unto them, "Repent, and be baptized every-one of you in the name of Jesus Christ for the remission of sins, and receive the gift of the Holy Ghost."

Satan wanted to have God's power and war broke out in heaven. Satan was devising, plotting and scheming in heaven causing spiritual adultery. There was conflict in heaven. Satan had designs to change God's truth. God put his chief angel Michael to work and fought the dragon. The dragon fought back because when some-body wants what you got bad enough to fight for it, look out. Angels or messengers of God who were given the power to bind on earth and loose in heaven is the same power that Jesus Christ gave the Apostles in Mathew 16:19.

John 1:10 LB says, "But although he made the world, the world didn't recognize him when he came." Those who believe that God is only the God of their race need to hear this. In John 8:42, 44 KJV,

"Jesus said unto them, If God were your Father, ye would love me: for I proceeded forth and came from God; neither came I of myself, but he sent me." (Vs. 44), "Ye are of your father the devil, and the lust of your father ye will do. He was a murderer from the beginning, and abode not in truth, because there is no truth in him."

Continue: "When he speaketh a lie, he speaketh of his own: for he is a liar, and the father of it." (Vs.14 LB), in the book of John 1st chapter states that, "And Christ became a human being and lived here on earth among us and was full of loving forgiveness and truth." In the King James Version it says, "And the word was made flesh, and dwelt among us". Luke 3:34 is where Jesus was born from the descendants of Abraham and Ephesians 2:11-22, is where we are all one in Christ.

Christ the anointing got in the body of the man Jesus. God's spirit was upon Jesus Christ without measure or limit. He came into the world to save all nations. He did not just come for Israel or the KKK, but for all nations. He also came for the Gentiles. God gave his promise of salvation before Israel existed. In Genesis 12:2-3 that Abrams offspring would bring salvation to all nations. "In thee shall all families of the earth be blessed."

In Romans 1:18-32 KJV Paraphrased tells us how God wrath is revealed from heaven against those who hold the truth in unrighteousness. "They that keep holiness holy, shall be judged holy" Wisdom of Solomon 6:10. Do this and the second death will have no power over you. All sinners and even homosexuals know the truth but they hold the truth in unrighteousness. They know right from wrong.

Churches with first ladies have overflowed into the wicked first man. This is a new virus of the Church waddling in filth. There are Churches with homosexual Pastors. God don't trust churches to go across the street. God said "Behold he putteth no trust in his saints; yea the heavens are not clean in his sight" Job 15:15. God ejected Satan from heaven above all heavens to rule the skies in our heavens being called the prince of the air. Psalm 113:4 reveals, "The Lord is high above all nations, And his glory above all heavens." God outshines everything that you can see in the skies.

God has already manifested in them the truth by giving them male and female organs and showed them in his word. God has already shewed it unto them between their legs. Sin still pays the same wages. Jesus condemned sin in the flesh. From the beginning made God male and female and it is clearly seen and understood by Satan.

Adam and Eve's choice help bring sin into the Garden and they knew God's eternal power and God head. Satan and his followers are determined to turn the Truth of God's word into a lie but we must stand firm in God's truth and his Spirit and keep Holiness, holy. We must be centering in on the Gospel's work.

They glorified him not as God and it became open rebellion. Eve became vain in her imagination and her foolish heart was darken and gave her husband some. Those against God thought they were wise and became fools by changing the glory of God making it look corruptible. Men kissing men and two women bumping bellies make God's Glory look corruptible. God threw up his hands and gave them over to lust and uncleanness of their own hearts to dishonor their own bodies between themselves. They changed a truth into a lie and began to worship the beast in them instead of God who created them.

So God gave them up to vile affections and some women as we see today have changed the natural use into that against nature. Some men have also turned against the natural use of the woman lusting after other men. They leave God out of their knowledge and God gave them over to a reprobate mind to do those things that they were not created for.

They became haters of God being filled with all unrighteousness and are proud and wicked. Jesus Christ came that we may have life but those who are openly rebelling against God at abortion clinics put their pride and selfishness before him. Then war broke out against those with God and those with the devil who represent death and destruction.

They know the judgement of God when they commit such things and they loved to see others do them. "Righteousness exalteth a Nation: but sin is a reproach to any people." Misery loves company. The fool has said in his heart there is no God. Wisdom says, in Proverbs 8:36 "But he that sinneth against me wrongeth his own soul: all they that hate me love death." (Proverbs 14:12) reveals that, "There is a way which seems right unto a man, but the end thereof are the ways of death."

CHAPTER 17

GRACE

You woke-up this morning, and it is a new day, and it is up to you where it goes from here. God's grace is God giving you what you don't deserve, another opportunity to get it right. Today is the day that the Lord has made and I will rejoice and be glad in it. God is saying "Come and get it. I agree that it is time to come and receive God's grace. "Acts 2:21gives an invitation to all God's creation saying, "And it shall come to pass, that whosoever shall call on the name of the Lord (Jesus Christ) shall be saved."

We must appreciate and exalt God's word every day as we still breathe his fresh air. In order to know God you must dig into his wisdom of the word like we are digging for hidden treasure. Let his word become first in your life. Then make your schedule around his word and let God's word have final authority over all questions that concerns you. Then your heart will be fixed and established on a solid foundation, and that foundation will be the Living Word of God.

God has the blueprint for your life and he prepared it before the earth was formed. Proverbs 3:13-14 states that, "Happy is the man that findeth wisdom, and the man that getteth understanding." (Vs.14), "For the merchandise of it is better than the merchandise of silver and the gain thereof than fine gold". So, "Let us therefore come boldly unto the throne of grace that we may obtain mercy, and find grace to help in time of need" Hebrews 4:16. Wisdom says, "I was set up from everlasting, from the beginning, or ever the earth was" Proverb 8:23.

Grace is God giving us what we don't deserve. "Grace is God's call to mercy." Grace is God's overwhelming desire to treat me as if sin never existed! "Grace is God's access to Jesus cleansing from all sin." "Grace is God's declaration of "no condemnation" for me. "Grace is God's strength in the face of my weakness." "Grace is God's power in my life to do his will. "God's marvelous grace has saved me healed me, delivered me to be the victor-always!"

Jesus said in the book of John 5:24 LB that, "I say emphatically that anyone who listens to my message and believes in God who sent me has eternal life, and will never be damned for his sins, but has already passed out of death into life." Spend your energy seeking eternal life. God's will is His word and we have to believe in Jesus Christ the one that he sent.

Jesus Christ is the true Bread from heaven the Bread of Life that gives life to the world. All who eat worldly bread will die, but the Bread from heaven gives eternal life to everyone who eats it. Eat the Bread of the flesh of Jesus that was sent to redeem humanity and live forever. God told Ezekiel Paraphrase in chapter 3:1 to eat this roll and go and give the message to the people of Israel. God said eat this roll, not part of it. Eat the whole roll. Obedience is what God wants. We must trust his word because in Psalms 19:7 tells us that, "The law of the Lord is perfect, converting the soul: the testimony of the Lord is sure, making wise the simple."

Today man is looking for the fountain of youth and wants to live forever. Simon Peter is telling humankind in John 6:68 saying, "Simon Peter replied, Master, to whom shall we go? You alone have the words of eternal life." Humankind is headed to self-destruction. God want his creation to Hosea 10:12, "Sow to yourselves according to righteousness. Reap according to mercy. Break up your fallow ground. For it is time to seek the Lord till he come and rain righteousness upon you."

God said in Hosea 10:9 LB, "O Israel ever since that awful night in Gibeah, there has been only sin, sin, sin! You have made no progress whatever. Was it not right that the men of Gibeah were wiped out for acting out a lie? Covid 19 has chased us inside and we are on our way to live in a bubble like the cartoon the Jetsons. Humankind has not made any progress from Noah to Christ and Trump to Biden and there is still only sin, sin, sin. Stop taking God's grace for granted.

CHAPTER 18

CHOSEN

God is giving all humankind an invitation to step into a new life with him. "Take words with you, And return to the Lord. Say to Him, "O Lord, take away our sins; be gracious to us and receive us, and we will offer you the sacrifice of praise" Hosea 14:2LB. (Hosea 14:9) tells us, "Whoever is wise, let him understand these things. "Whoever is intelligent let him listen. "For the paths of the Lord are true and right, and the good walk along them." "But sinners trying it will fail." When we return to the Lord our God he will be gracious and merciful. God is not quick to get mad because he is full of mercy and kindness and really does not want to punish you. God's will is to bless you, not curse you.

There are some who will never get the message regardless of what God does in their lives. God is capable to break all your defenses for not serving him. God likes to see us flooding in to help one another and doing good to one another. He likes to see us loving one another as we love ourselves. God is telling many of us to go and tell the world about its wickedness like Jonah.

Many are afraid and run and hide from the Lord. Some will have to be at near deaths door before they respond. God covers those whom he calls in their wild living. 1Peter 2:9, "But ye are a chosen generation, a royal priesthood, a holy nation, a peculiar people; that ye should shew forth the praises of him who hath called you out of darkness into his marvelous light."

God helps you through your storms of life even though he calls you and you rebel. Those who live in sin don't understand why he is so good giving them what they don't deserve by his grace. God snatches your soul from the jaws of death and this makes you glad to do what he asked. When Jonah was locked out of life confined in the belly of the fish, God was merciful. People confined to the bed with sickness and disease when all hope is gone God shows his mercy. When God snatched Jonah's soul from death he was more than glad to do God's will.

We have to remember like David the same God that delivered me in the past will be the same God who will bring me out of this mess too. Ephesians 1:3-4, reminds us "Blessed be the God and Father of our Lord Jesus Christ, who has blessed us with all spiritual blessings in heavenly places in Christ." (Vs.4), "According as he hath chosen us in him before the foundation of the world, that we should be holy and without blame before him in love." God know those that are his and he knew you before you were formed in the belly. He knew you before you were formed in your mother's womb even before the earth was formed he knew you. If God be lifted up he draws us back to himself through Jesus Christ by his own will.

Whether we worship God in the church building or in our homes, it will be how we worship. We are temples of God and wherever we worship it is spiritual and real? We should worship in spirit and in truth with help from the Holy Spirit. There are evil spirits but we need the Spirit of God to assist us so we can worship as we should.

We should never lose our confidence in God because in Joshua 1:8-9 says, "This book of the law shall not depart out of thy law; but thou shalt meditate therein day and night, that thou mayest observe to do according to all that is written therein: for then thou shalt make thy way prosperous, and then thou shalt have good success. (Vs.9),

"Have I not commanded thee? Be strong and of a good courage be not afraid, neither be thou dismayed: for the Lord thy God is with thee withersoever thou goest."

Jeremiah 1:5 reminds us that "Before I formed thee in the belly I knew thee; and before thou camest forth out of the womb I sanctified thee, and I ordained thee a prophet unto the nations." Ask God to show you the path to walk in, and to point out to you the right road for you to walk and to guide you clearly the path that he wants you to follow in the mighty name of Jesus Christ. Yeah, God knows our path but we must choose to hear and obey his voice. We must set our affections on things above and not the things that are on the earth.

We must realize where our help comes from. When you are close to death you realize that you are no more than dust and worms. When I was paralyzed the first thing I did was to remove all sin out of my life. Then I drew closer and closer to God who was my help, my healer and my redeemer. My old job was like a used car salesman and I twisted the truth to make sales. My first move was to get rid of my old master so I quit and walk off my job of sin. I stop my lies. I got a brand new conversation called the "The Truth." I walked away from sin; not my job.

Satan is the father of lies and he only comes to steal, kill and to destroy. So I fired Satan and grabbed the truth in John 17:17 that says, "Sanctify them through thy truth thy word is truth." Millions of people die in spiritual darkness and I was glad to have another opportunity to get it right. I repented and turned and went the opposite way than where I was headed.

Some people let money pull them away from trusting in God and they start to trust in casinos. Casinos can be a trap that is snap shut when stepped in. The glitter and glamor baits you in by showing you all the kingdoms of the world that could be yours until you lose everything you have. They bait you in by setting new cars in the entrance of doorway. Satan plays on your wants and needs. You forget that casinos are in business to make money and not to give it away. When gambling you win once but lose twice. We should trust God with our finances where there will be nothing but a win, win situation.

Keep God's promises on the front burner because God always causes us to triumph through Christ Jesus. "It's God good pleasure to give us the kingdom." "It's the blessings of the Lord that maketh rich and addeth no sorrow with it." You can become rich but if you get them the wrong way it can bring to you many sorrows. "For it is he (God) who gives you power to get wealth." Many rich sinners have sorrow with their riche. "The Lord is my shepherd I shall not want." "But my God shall supply all your needs according to his riches in glory by10 Christ Jesus." God blesses you so you can be a blessing as he did Abraham in Genesis12. 2 Corinthians 2:14, Luke12:32, Proverbs10:22, Deuteronomy8:18, Psalms23:1, Philippians4:19

God gives you all sufficiency in all things so that you may abound in every good work and charitable donation. Fast money can make you rich but there could be sorrow that comes with it. Trust the Lord with all thine heart and lean not to thy own understanding. Psalms 37:4 says, "Delight thyself also in the Lord and he shall give thee the desires of thine heart." When we cry out to God he hears us and always responds. He may not respond in the way we want him to, but he responds nonetheless.

Deuteronomy 14:2 says, for thou art a holy people unto the Lord thy God, and the Lord hath chosen thee to be a peculiar people unto himself, above all the nations that are upon the earth." Humankind would lay around content in their sin thinking that God will leave them along. They see days of pestilence like Covid 19 that brings terrible distress and anguish because of the sins committed against the Lord will allow these things to happen. Money is no use to you in the day of the Lord's wrath. In your trouble you can't buy your way out of it. At death you cannot buy another second, minute, hour or day.

Repentance and obedience to the Lord will be the only ransom that you will be able to pay. We should ask God daily to let your perfect will be done in our life here on earth even as it is in heaven. His will is his Word. The only way to evade God's wrath will be to hear, obey and to show humility to God who made the heavens and the earth. Isaiah 43:10, "Ye are my witnesses, saith the Lord, and my servant whom I have chosen: that ye may know and believe me, and understand that I am he: before me there was no God formed, neither shall there be after me."

Why would you want to transgress the commandments of the Lord? Who wants to receive the wages of their pride? Pride comes before destruction and a hearty spirit before a fall. Pride is false security thinking of yourselves more highly than you ought too. In just a moment of time you will see how helpless you really are. Proud people will not listen to the voice of God. When you are in your pride no one can tell you anything. Not seeking God or trusting in him who is the only one that can help you will be your ruin.

When people cater to the world they will lie to get gain. They become their own god and their temple is defiled when caught because they are living in the curse. The wicked says, Ain't no shame in my game, and die a terrible death. Evil men do not see or hear the warning that our streets are becoming empty and silent and deserted.

Cameras on every corner as criminals get their chance to play the role of the world's dumbest criminals. Evil continues like it is business as usual. Please be advised that God is going to move all pride and arrogance off the set so that his children can live a quiet and peaceable life. Jehovah keeps his children under his wing and in the palm of His hand. He sets them on a cleft so they cannot be reached.

God wants to restore our fortunes. He wants to be the arbitrary force that affects our human life. God wants to be my fortune and choice naturally. Just because your family member is rich in God does not make you rich in God. Holiness does not just rub off on you and every man and woman must die for their own sins. John 3:16 says, "For God so loved the world, that he gave his only begotten Son, that whosoever believeth in him should not perish, but have everlasting life."

The new normal is a new curse in disguise because it is giving sin slavery a different look. It is the sin of a proud government that is receiving sickness, disease, plagues from homosexuality to abortions with same-sex marriage that is opposing God's purpose for humankind. Sometimes God will allow curses on the disobedient. These solemn utterances intended to invoke a supernatural power to inflict harm or punishment on the disobedient. "All the ways of a man are clean in his own eyes; but the Lord weighest the spirits" Proverbs16:2.

God even allowed a lying spirit against those in power. God used a lying spirit to deceive Ahab because King Ahab rejected God's rebukes and warnings all through his life and the cup of God's wrath was full. God was giving him time to Repent. 1Kings 22:20 a spirit or angel/ became a lying spirit. God don't lie, but the angel or messenger suggested to God to become a lying spirit in the mouth of the prophets. He said I will be a lying spirit in the mouth of the prophets.

Hebrews 4;13 states that, "Neither is there any creature that is not manifest in his sight, but all things are naked and open unto the eyes of him with whom we have to do." God gave the spirit permission to succeed and Ahab received the message he desired. We should not be afraid of the words that we hear from those leaders that blasphemy the Lord.

We need a King like Josiah in 11Kings who open the book of the Lord and did all which was written in it. He was a leader that turned to the Lord with all his heart and with all his soul, and with all his might. This is how we should respond to our troubles and afflictions by trusting in the Lord with all our heart and lean not to our own understanding.

You can read all over the Holy Bible where God warns his children not to participate in the sins of the heathens. In the Old Testament

God kept Israel from mingling with sin period. When disaster strikes we pretend to act like we don't know why. The world is constantly trying to get God's people to conform to the sins of the flesh. Never, Never, Never! When I see how floods, fires, earthquakes, diseases and mudslides are destroying cities and homes and people hearts are so hard they still want fear God. If death and destruction do not turn you to God with fear and trembling, the only thing left is God's Judgement for your disobedience.

Sin and judgement is not new. "The Lord hath made all things for himself: yea, even the wicked for the day of evil" Proverbs 16:4. Jehovah does not want his people looking for knowledge in tea leaves. God wants you to seek after him and not seek after what's in your own heart and what you see from your own eyes.

There are so many different groups being formed that are contrary to the will of God. No matter how many evil hands join together with their proud hearts they shall not go unpunished. 1 John 1:9 reminds us "If we confess our sins, he is faithful and just to forgive us our sins, and to cleanse us from all unrighteousness."

All man can think of is wine, women and songs that take their mind away from God. God wants to lead you to your green pastures and to lead you into his righteousness to a blessed place. The Lord wants you to stop pretending you love him and do what he says. Some of his children sin so much their heart becomes hard against him.

They have an adulteress spirit and a spirit of fornication that makes them afraid to come into his presence. These two spirits of the flesh are against God and they also commit them with Idols. This keeps them from knowing him. God is a holy God and he wants you to be holy. How can you know someone for yourself without spending time with them?

When you run from God you run from your help and cure. You run because you do not want to be held accountable for your sins but as soon as trouble comes like clock-work you run right back to God just like you never left. You take God's kindness for weakness. You take his kindness for granted because you know he will take your lying, hardheaded, rebellious, disobedient self- back. When you "Repent" with a sincere heart and turn from your sin God forgives you.

This lack of love for God brings his judgement on you because you have broken the contract and covenant by refusing his love. All he wants to do is bless you. God see you in your sin but thank God for Jesus Christ who died for our sin. What shall we say then? Shall we continue to sin, that grace may abound? No! Romans 6:15 says, "What then? Shall we sin, because we are not under the law, but under grace? God forbid. (Vs.16, Know ye not, that to whom ye yield yourselves servants to obey, his servant ye are to whom ye obey; whether of sin unto death, or obedience unto righteousness? We are now dead to sin and we don't live at that address any longer.

Your sin catches up with you and your sins find you out showing your nakedness with no excuse to hide behind from lusting constantly! When God's people mingle with the world and it's heathens they pick up some of their ways and spirits through association that brings about assimilation. They become guilty by association. Friendship with the world is an enemy of God. You lay down with dogs you are going to get fleas. God wants his people to choose none of their ways. Spiritual wickedness in high places makes and pushes us to build up ourselves on our most Holy faith, praying in the Holy Ghost to war against sin, not to agree with it.

It is an abomination for Kings to commit wickedness. God put men on the throne for righteousness. They tell an outward lie with an inward devil. The wrath of a King is a messenger of death. Proverb 16:18 says "Pride goeth before destruction, and an haughty spirit before a fall." Some of our leaders remind me of the Kings in the Old Testament that did that which was evil in the sight of the Lord and their reign was short. Isaiah 45:7 where God said, "I am the Lord, and there is none else I formed the light and created darkness: I make peace, and created evil: I the Lord do all these things." When you choose evil ways you become good for nothing in God's eyes. You cannot witness for him resembling sin.

You will be like Samson when he did not even know that he had lost his power and strength from God. All you know is that you were not witnessing to others because the Holy Spirit in you has left or lying dormant inside you. God gives man power from on high until men let Delilah vex their spirit and even Eve gave her husband some and God's glory left them. Sin is separation from God. The weight of sin in the world is showing hatred towards God's people. In return God gives the world war, famine and disease. Pharaoh told the people to "Go to Joseph; what he saith to you, do" in Genesis 41:55. There was a famine in the land. When the wine ran out at the wedding feast at Cana Mary told the people; whatever Jesus tells you to, do it.

God desires obedience. When people do not regard the word of God's counsel they will be made to hear his words of reproof. They think they are smarter than God and want to tell him what they think is good for him. Isaiah 40:13-14 says, "Who hath directed the spirit of the Lord, or being his counsellor hath taught him? (Vs.14),"With whom took he counsel, and who instructed him, and taught him in the path of judgement, and taught him knowledge, and shewed to him the way of understanding?

They will not be exempt of punishment because of their sin. It is necessary that God should vindicate his own honor by making it appear that he hate sin and hates it most when it is done by those close to him. If there is no friendship how can there be fellowship. A lion roars only when he is about to pounce upon his prey.

"Friendship with the world is an enemy of God." God wants you to give-up and surrender all to him. If you are breathing God's fresh air you were created and formed for his glory. There was no god formed before him and none after him and besides me there is no savior" Isaiah 43;10-11 Paraphrase. God said in (Vs.13) of Isaiah 43, "Yea, before the day was I am he; and none can deliver out of my hand: I will work, and who shall let it?"

If we are God's witnesses then Vs.8 in Isaiah 44 tells us to, "Fear ye not, neither be afraid: have not I told thee from that time, and declared it? Ye are even my witnesses. Is there a God beside me? yea, there is no God; I know not any." God said in Isaiah 45:23 "I sworn by myself, the word is gone out of my mouth in righteousness, and shall not return, That unto me every knee shall bow, every tongue shall swear." God declares the end from the beginning.

There is no comparison when it comes to God. "To whom will ye liken me, and make me equal, and compare me, that we may be like?" Isaiah 46:5. God wants people from all the ends of the earth to look upon him to be saved. There is no other name whereby men can be saved. Jesus said I am the way the truth and the life. He said the only way to get to the Father is to come by him. With God, warning comes before destruction. God interfere and take part intervening without invitation or necessity.

God keeps us out of the traps and snares of the enemy. Repentance is the only thing that can bring you out of entanglement of a trap or snare. If you are going the wrong way God will send trouble your way to deter you. Warning comes before destruction. Warnings come from pastors, parents and those who have experience with God. God uses similitude with whomever and whatever he chooses. He comes in different forms and fashions to get his message through.

In the book of Amos 3:6-8 Paraphrase Prophets cannot but make known to the people what God has made known to them. When God speaks his word who can but prophecy? In the book of Numbers 22:41 "And it came to pass on the morrow, that Balak took Balaam, and brought him up into the high places of Baal, that thence he might see the utmost parts of the people. Balak tried to get Balaam to curse Israel three times.

This puts us in remembrance of how Satan came unto Jesus to tempt him three times and all he said was it is written, or what God said. Balaam chose to only say what God said. God is looking for obedience in the earth to use vessels of honor to bless his name. Balaam said "All that the Lord speaketh, that I must do. Balak sounded like Satan when tempting Jesus by wanting to give Jesus all the kingdoms of the world when the world belonged to Jesus Christ who had God's spirit in him. Balak wanted to promote Balaam but the man of God was obedient as Jesus Christ was all the way to the Cross. That is what God wants from us and that is for us to hear and obey.

Those who hear the word of God and know the knowledge of his will must be obedient and stop selling out. Balaam told Balak, "If Balak would give me his house full of silver and gold, I cannot go beyond the commandment of the Lord, to do either good or bad of mine own mind; but what the Lord saith, that will I speak." We must know when a prophet is speaking in the name of the Lord because if it don't come to pass; the Lord did not speak it. They are presumptuous words. "The heart of the wise teacheth his mouth, and addeth learning to his lips."

The world needs to confess their sins of wickedness because God's plan is that they will return to Him their creator. Humankind must put away the guilt of innocent blood from among them. The wicked need to hear God's warning and live paying attention to his word and be taught. Some have no intention whatsoever of doing what God says because their mind is set on being free from his restraints.

This is when God will turn his back on them and won't hear them when they call for help. God's desire is the same and that is for you to turn from your evil road of wickedness that you are traveling on. God wants to meet you where you are. When God busted Adam when he sinned in the garden by asking him; "Where art thou? He was running from God and afraid. Not, In what place? In jail! But, in what condition? I am looking at the death penalty. God is asking sinners, is this all you got for being your own god by dis-obeying me?

God and his goodness is still in a gracious pursuit in being kind to you to bring you out of your troubles. When sinners are in trouble with their backs up against the wall they will have no rest until they come to God. Some be in court lying to the judge afraid and will not own his guilt, but yet confesses it in fear and shame by pleading no contest. These offenders are found guilty by their own confession and yet endeavoring to the fulfillment of their obligation of responsibility or an obligation by employment or to improve their quality of life in the inner city. They are excused and extenuate the cause an offence to seem less serious, their own fault.

God ask Adam, Who told thee thou was naked? Instead of aggravating the sin and taking shame to themselves, they excuse the sin and play the blame game and put the shame on others. Caught dead in their sin act they put the blame on someone else. Adam put the blame on his wife. He not only lays the blame on his wife but put God into the lie by saying, that woman you gave me. Adam said, God gave him the woman and she gave him the fruit, but he chose to take it.

There are a lot people that will say in a heartbeat I am tempted of God. Abusing God's gifts will not excuse us of violating God's laws. They make God an accessory. Eve lays the blame on the serpent. "The serpent beguiled me." Sin is a brat that no one is willing to own. Sin is a scandalous thing. Satan's temptations to humankind are all beguiling, his arguments are all fallacies, his allurements are all cheats.

Sin is charming or enchanting, often in a deceptive way. Sin deceives us, and by deceiving cheats us. It is the deceitfulness of sin that makes the heart hardened. Jeremiah 17:9 reveals to us that, "The heart is deceitfully above all things, and desperately wicked: who can know it."

See Romans 7:11 and Hebrews 3:13. Satan's subtlety will not justify us in sin. Though he is the tempter we are the one who sin. It is but every man is drawn away of his own lust and enticed James 1:14. We have to be more like God not to condemn the person, but the spirit within that person.

In the Garden of Eden God began his sentences first where the sin began, the serpent. God knew he started that mess in heaven. The devils instruments or his merchandise in those who agree with sin must repent or share in the devils punishment. Satan enticed Eve to eat that which she should not and God sentenced him to the same. Satan was cursed above all cattle. He is now looked at as a vile despicable creature. "Dust thou shalt eat was his sentence. He is a noxious creature and a proper object of hatred and detestation.

The woman and Serpent had just been familiar and friendly in discourse about the forbidden fruit. They came to a wonderful agreement together. God made Satan and women points of view so different from each other that they cannot be made compatible. Sinfull friendships make enemies. Those who unite in wickedness don't be together long. Most women can't stand a lie.

Satan uses you for his sinful purpose and dispose of you. Satan the pimp will use you up and throw you away and go to the next person. Next! He used me and I thought he was my partner only to find out what a friend we have in Jesus. The spirit of the devil only used the serpent as his vehicle to sin but he himself was the principle agent. Satan uses so many different vehicles, lust in men, women and things today but he is the principle agent. God detest a disobedient and sinful nation.

In return God gives them war, famine and disease. He sends the sword using the enemy to spank you to bring you to repentance. God used Nebuchadnezzar in Jeremiah 43 to spank Israel when they ran back to their Egypt. There are a lot of people that run, duck and hide from God instead of running to him. They will not give up their sin that is causing all the problems in their life. "There is a way that seemeth right unto a man, but the end thereof are the ways of death" Proverbs 16:25.

Yes, God spanks his creation only enough to correct them. We don't understand until our dance is turned into sorrow or death. Our only hope is for Jehovah to bring us back into his care. When the sin cup becomes full and God allows the nether world or death, then people have a tendency to despise God. All the world events are under God's control.

He is the God that gives us the breath of life and controls our destiny. Trying to change God's laws and demoralizing his servants, still will not be able to stand against God (the Ancient of days). We must walk in the light while it is still time. Consecrate yourselves for growth in truth and holiness. The world cannot heal its wounds by saying and acting as though the wounds are not there.

God said in Deuteronomy 22:5 "The woman shall not wear that which pertaineth unto a man, neither shall a man put on a woman's garment: for all that do so are abomination unto the Lord thy God." Men and women are putting on abominations on a daily basis. Even to wear makeup from aborted babies and dead animal making their face look like plastic. They are putting on their Jezebel rebellious uniform. Jezebel's heart and rebellious look got everyone in her family killed. "He that justifieth the wicked, and he that condemneth the just, even the both are abomination to the Lord" Proverb 17:15. Our government has become abomination to the Lord.

God told Israel to choose none of the ways of the people whose land they go to war with because of their abominations. America allows all their enemies the freedom to worship their god after they are defeated and invited into this country. God brings evil upon those who will not listen. It is the fruit of their own sin. It seems that no matter what God allows people still continue in the wickedness of their ways.

God will get their attention for a moment and like a child they go right back doing what he says not to do. There are new idol gods called electronics that is being worship unknowingly. The New World Order is materializing right in front of our face. The process will be over when the masks come off. We are being beat down into submission.

There is also human trafficking where the Holy Bible declares is wrong. Although human trafficking started in Africa the Holy Scripture says, "If any man be found stealing any of his brethren of the children of Israel, and maketh merchandise of him, or selleth him; then that thief shall die; and thou shall put evil away from among you" Deuteronomy 24:7.

With these devices it has become hard to get people's attention when they bury their minds into these devices. You never know what a person is thinking, planning or watching using these devices. Technology has swept the nation at a fast past and who knows where we will go from here. God knows the end from the beginning. It seem like we have went backwards instead of forward.

The more technology share information the less people want to be taught as they keep living in the mystery of iniquity. There are a lot of people that sin and don't seem to care if they are going down the wrong road even though they are being warned. People get on the internet and expose their wickedness. In Ezekiel vision in chapter 8, "The image of jealousy is being set up in God's church as worship. Ezekiel saw the statue of deity situated at the entrance that arrested the attention of all worshippers as they entered. Since man is born in sin learning the mystery of Godliness is an up-hill climb.

There is competition against God that made the heaven and the earth as with the worship of the queen of heaven called idolatry. God is a jealous God who will not give his honor to another having no god before him. People are displaying themselves offering their bodies for sale worshipping reverencing and idolizing their bodies. God told Ezekiel in chapter 8 to dig into the wall and told him to go in the door and behold the wicked abominations that they do here.

They say, "The Lord seeth us not; the Lord hath forsaken the earth." Today they do greater abominations than these. Technology allows people to share their abominations on the Internet to the world with no shame. Women and men share their nakedness as in old times on every high hill. Some still serve the Queen of Heaven in their lasciviousness. Some hide them in their closets. Ezekiel 14:3 says, "Son of man, these men have set up their idols in their heart, and put the stumbling-block of iniquity before their face: should I be inquired of at all by them?" When you repent and turn God answers by himself those polluted by the multitudes of their idols.

Our nation has made wrong right and our government is not listening to those who say, this is a mistake. They are saying God who made the heavens and the earth made a mistake in them. God's laws are being tailor made by the enemy to support its wicked intentions. Our world is trying to improve the lies they are telling us by telling people that all is well when it is not well At ALL. Your God has chosen you out of all the people of the face of the earth.

The Lord is choosing you to be his most valuable possession. The wicked plan seems to lie to themselves first and then convince the world to believe it. God has a four sore judgement that he sends on the disobedient in Ezekiel 15:21, "For thus saith the Lord God; How much more when I send my four sore judgements upon Jerusalem, the sword, and the famine, and the noisome beast, and the pestilence, to cut off from it man and beast."

CHAPTER 19

THIS COULD BE YOUR LAST CHANCE

When you try to explain to a child that you have adopted them and how you had pity and had compassion on them expresses how you feel from the heart. The more you blessed them the more ungrateful they became. God was explaining to Ezekiel what to say to Jerusalem in chapter 16 Paraphrase about Canaan. He talks about their ungratefulness.

He tells them when they were born no one cared for them enough to wash the blood off them or even cut their naval cord. No one had pity on you but you were thrown out in the field to make it after you were born. Example; in today's news show a woman throwing her new born baby in the trash. One woman put her child in the oven and burnt it up. After God has pick you up, turned you around and placed your feet on solid ground he desires obedience and appreciation from you.

God was saying to Jerusalem when they were in their sins he came by and had compassion on them. Remember the men who were dumpster diving and found the little baby the woman had discarded into the dumpster. This symbolizes, that God came by when you was in your sin or blood and said, Live. God nourished you and clothed you when you were naked and bare in his love. He covered your sins and made a marriage covenant with you.

He made a contract with you and washed away thoroughly the blood with his word and anointed you. He dressed you with jewels and put a crown on your head. God turned your ashes into beauty and made you prosper. Now you are on the internet naked trusting in your own beauty that he allowed you to be.

Now you are pouring your fornication out all over the internet on anyone that passed by having sex in every high place and hill. You are playing the harlot. Now you have taken the gold and silver that God gave you and made images of men (Dildo). Ezekiel 16:17 says "Thou hast also taken thy fair jewels of my gold and of my silver, which I had given thee, and madest to thyself images of men, and didst commit whoredom with them." You have taken the sons and daughters that God gave you and sent them to the fire of abortion. Children are a blessing from the Lord. Psalms 127:3, "Lo, children are an inheritance of the Lord: and the fruit of the womb is his reward."

It was over 1 million abortions in the first 10 days of January 2021. After all these murders that you are doing you don't even remember when you were naked and bare kicked to the curve polluted in your blood. God says woe unto you because you shew your wicked nakedness on every site on the internet. You have multiplied your whoredom and your beauty has turned to ugliness. You are marching in the streets defying God in open rebellion to kill you inheritance and that is the fruit of the womb. You are delivered into the hand of every nation and still can't get satisfaction.

God says, "How weak is your heart? You are as a wife that committed adultery preferring a stranger instead of your husband! All the gifts you receive you give to your lovers and hirest them making them a bigger whore. Now you are surrounded by whores contrary to God. "Wherefore O' harlot hear the word of the Lord." Since you pour out filtiness showing your nakedness through whoredoms with idols called Dildos, that make you kill the innocent blood of children with abortion.

God said in Ezekiel 16:38, "And I will judge thee, as women that break wedlock, and shed blood are judged; and I will give thee blood in fury and jealousy." God will allow you to be robbed and stripped naked and left bare and burn thy house to stop your whoredom then God's jealousy will leave you. All these things will happen to you when you forget where you came from and who brought you out.

Leviticus 19:29 KJV, "Do not prostitute your daughter to cause her to be a whore, lest the land fall to whoredom, and the land become full of wickedness." This will be the Proverb that people will say against thee, saying "As is the mother so is her daughters." Return to God your former estate and if you don't know God it is time to get with him. All those who are trying to outdo Sodom and Gomorrah it is time to repent and renew or get back in covenant with God.

Look at and remember your ways and be ashamed. Go ahead and sign and renew your contract with God. Ezekiel 16:63 says, "That thou mayest remember, and be confounded, and never open thy mouth anymore because of thy shame, when I am pacified toward thee for all that thou hast done, saith the Lord God."

The heavens and the earth are reserved unto fire because the day of the Lord will come. Do you want Jesus Christ in a jug? The best gift any man or woman can receive is to have the spirit of God in him. Ecclesiastes 9:10 says "Whatsoever thy hand findeth to do, do it with thy might; for there is no work, nor device, nor knowledge, nor wisdom, in the grave, wither thou goest."

Solomon said after all his knowledge and riches that the race was not given to the swift or to the strong but time and chance happeneth to them all. (Vs.12), "For man also knoweth not his time: as the fishes that are taken in an evil net, and as the birds that are caught in the snare; so are the sons of men snared in an evil time, when he falleth suddenly upon them."

Men and women are not understanding how the Holy Spirit being inside them. When Jesus return he will be looking for a sanctified people set apart from sin. He will be looking for a Holy people because he is holy. A wise man heart is at his right hand but a fool is at his left. The Left is now running our government. Only a fool would reject the word of God. We must be blessed and holy to make the first resurrection because he is holy. The Left who run this country heart is hardened against God. We have men competing with a woman for a wife is a lie from Satan but God's wisdom is better than Satan's strength.

God did not give us free will to lust and drink iniquity like water. Job 15:16, "How much more abominable and filty is man, which drinketh iniquity like water". God said, don't eat the blood but witchcraft, sorcery and lesbianism is doing the opposite. The Holy Bible says "Whoso findeth a wife findeth a good thing, and obtaineth favor of the Lord."

Women are having a fatal attraction by men and women who eat the blood from the flowing of a woman's menstrual. This is not holy. It is a dungeon of sin that need to be washed and scrubbed with the unadulterated, uncompromising, unchanging word of the Living God. God is coming back for a sanctified people.

What these lustful people do causes the deeper curiosity of women to go against what God said about being unclean. The life of the flesh is in the blood. Some men and the lesbians eat the blood. Their mind is warped to do anything as a device in their heart to do that which is contrary to what God says don't do. Deuteronomy 12:23 tells us to eat not the blood.

This is one of the multitudes of Satan's merchandise. Open rebellion against God will only bring the fire that he has reserved for all sin. Amos 5:18, "Woe unto you that desire the day of the Lord! "to what end is it for you? "the day of the Lord is darkness and not light." People say all the time I can't wait for the Lord's return. No more pain. No more troubles and no more sorrow. This is to all those who are still living in sin, What end is it for you? Why are you in a hurry to go to hell where devil and the false prophet are.

I was walking with one of my neighbors when she spotted a group of women who looked like construction workers and she became frighten. She knew that even the thought of foolishness is sin. She said there go those Lesbians and dikes and I am not going pass them. This is when I realized what women have to go through in our new norm. We have to endure hardness. 1Peter 2:21 show us, "For even hereunto were ye called: because Christ also suffered for us, leaving us an example, that ye should follow his steps.

Proverb 20:12 KJV, "The hearing ear, and the seeing eyes, the Lord hath made even both of them." Jude 8:10 "Likewise also these filty dreamers defile the flesh, despise dominion, and speak evil of dignities." We even have to repent even for having sex in our dreams and cast down that imagination and send it back down to the pits of hell where it belongs..

Ezekiel 33:25 says,, "Wherefore say unto them, Thus saith the Lord God; Ye eat with the blood, and lift up your eyes towards your idols, and shed blood: and shall ye possess the land?" Evil men and women do vile and foul things as they obey their idols in their closet. They are obnoxious or contemptible people typically used of women. They are filty dreamers.

Proverbs 21:2 "Every way of a man is right in his own eyes: but the Lord pondereth the hearts." Their hearts have turned away from the Lord our God. They have a root that beareth gall and wormwood. They are not showing any shame but are marrying one another men on men and women on women. They can't even do wrong, right. They have peace in the imagination of their heart and add drunkenness to thirst, over the counter drugs and cocaine to it.

Proverbs 20:1 states that, "Wine is a mocker, strong drink is raging: and whosoever is deceived thereby is not wise." God separates them unto evil and a reprobate mind. Satan is raising and catching children early with his agents in the school system. This is being done so that the generation to come of your children that shall rise up after you will be perverted.

Our government who are led by the so called Left is training your kids at an early age through children's books to except two mommies or two daddies as a normal couple. They are hiding the truth by not telling them all people are born from a man and a woman. The question that the child should ask is which one of you two women is my daddy and which one of you two men is my mummy?

Proverb 21:27, "The sacrifice of the wicked is abomination: how much more, when he bringeth it with a wicked mind." The Left wants to undermine the Lord. God is righteous. Married people even believe they can leave their wife or husband and marry another while their spouse is still alive. The Holy Scriptures says you commit adultery.

They find a church that will agree with their sins so they can feel comfortable in their sin. Romans 6:1-3 warns us, "What shall we say then? Shall we continue in sin, that grace may abound? (Vs.2), "God forbid, "How shall we, that are dead to sin, live any longer therein? (Vs.3), "Know ye not, that so many of us as were baptized into Jesus Christ were baptized into his death?

Deuteronomy 29:29 says, "The secret things belong unto the Lord our God: but those things which are revealed belong unto us and to our children forever, that we may do all the words of the law." God is calling these things to mind so we will return to the Lord thy God. God wants to turn you from your captivity and lead you out of whatever has you in bondage. "He that saith unto the wicked, Thou art righteous; him shall the people curse, nations shall abhor him" Proverbs 24:24. You must return and obey the voice of the Lord this day.

"There is no wisdom, nor understanding, nor counsel against the Lord." Just turn to God with all thine heart and thy soul. God's goodness is not hidden from you neither is it far away from you. It is so close to you that all you have to do is speak it with your mouth and believe it with your heart. God has said in Deuteronomy 30:15 KJV, "See, I have set before thee this day life and good, death and evil."

Isaiah 35:7-8 says, "And the parched ground shall become a pool, and the thirsty land springs of water: in the habitation of dragons, where each lay, shall be grass with reeds and rushes. (Vs.8), "And an highway shall be there, and a way, and it shall be called The way of holiness; the unclean shall not pass over it; but it shall be for those: the wayfaring men, though fools, shall not err therein." God says even fools can't go wrong in holiness. Jesus said, "I am the way the truth and the light, no man cometh to the Father but by me." Jesus Christ came to give us an example of how to live holy.

The unclean will not be able to pass over into God's kingdom. God will give them over to a reprobate mind and no one will be able to save you no matter who pray for you. Repent if you are being filled with unrighteousness, fornicators, haters of God, proud, boastful, inventors of evil things trying to make men into women and women into men. Fake finger nails with rhine stones and clothes that show nakedness these are inventors of evil things.

Romans 1:30-32 warns us about those who are, "Backbiters, haters of God, despiteful, proud, boasters, inventers of evil things, disobedient to parents, (Vs.31), "Without understanding, covenant-breakers, without natural affection, implacable, unmerciful: (Vs.32 "Who knowing the judgement of God, that they which do such things are worthy of death, not only do the same, but have pleasure in them that do them." God saw you coming before you were born even your great, great, great, great grandparents were born. God knows the end from the beginning and he wrote this warn the people through his word.

Our Lord God does not want you to turn away from him and be drawn away. So he says in Deuteronomy 30:19 "I call heaven and earth to record this day against you, that I have set before you, life and death, blessing and cursing: It is a multiple choice question and it gives you the answer it says, "therefore choose life, that both thou and thy seed may live." Men, women and children, and thy stranger need to hear and learn the fear of the Lord, especially those who have not known anything about Jehovah need to hear and learn to fear God.

Learning to fear God is a process as you receive the knowledge of God. There is so much evil that humankind thinks God is not among us. We must teach the children and put God in their mouths and hearts. We need to do this so when it shall come to pass and many evils and trouble come upon them your teaching will testify against them as a witness. Plant the seed of God in them when they are young before their imaginations take over.

Young homosexual rappers are advertising and planting seeds for the devil and the children have a desire to be like them. The kids want to sing what they sing and wear what they wear. Children follow celebrities. If celebrities say wrong is right children is going to believe them.

Jesus said I am the way." Not we are the way. Mathew 19:4 says, "And he answered and said unto them, "Have ye not read, that he which made them at the beginning made them male and female." God made male and female, not homosexuals. Roman 1:18-19 says, "For the wrath of God is revealed from heaven against all ungodliness and unrighteousness of men, who hold the truth in unrighteousness: (Vs.19), "Because that which may be known of God is manifest in them; for God hath shewed it unto them."

Man was made in God's image formed from the dust of the ground. Then God breathe part of himself into man and He became a living soul. Where did the life of homosexual come from? We know that a woman came from the rib of man after God put him to sleep. This is what I call the first surgery. Homosexuals came from heaven but did not come from God. The mindset the emotions the heart came from heaven. It came from Lucifer who rebelled against God in heaven.

The devil is the author of confusion. You often hear homosexuals say, I'm confused. Are you in the church that Jesus Christ started? We are victims of man made religion. Go to your bible and see if the name of your church is in the bible. Ask God. Mathew 16:18 tells you about his church. Jesus told Peter, "And I say unto thee, Thou art Peter; and upon this rock I build my church; and the gates of hell shall not prevail against it."

Jesus Christ did not come to build these denominations that divide God's people. Apostle Paul spoke clearly in 1Corinthians 1:10 that states, "Now I beseech you, brethren, by the name of our Lord Jesus Christ, that ye all speak the same thing, and that there be no division among you; but that ye be perfectly joined together in the same mind and in the same judgement. How can men and women feel justified when everybody has a different song and doctrine.1 Corinthians 14:26 pleads, "How is it then, brethren? When ye come together, every one of you hath a psalm, hath a doctrine, hath a tongue, hath a revelation, hath a interpretation. Let all things be done unto edifying."

Man's wisdom is foolishness to God. Luke 16 says, "for that which is highly esteemed among men is abomination in the sight of God." 1Corinthians 2:13, "Which things also we speak, not in words which man's wisdom teacheth, but which the Holy Ghost teacheth; comparing spiritual things with spiritual. We have hand me down religion that has never been in the bible. Don't go over the edge with the herd of swine because of your confusion.

There is too much religion being taught by shade tree preachers. When you take your car to a mechanic and he gives your car back to you the part that he fixed had five screws on it when you gave it to him. When he gave it back to you it only had two screws. The Holy Scriptures has everything we need that pertains to life. He took the other 3 and threw them over his shoulder and said you don't need those. I fixed it for you. I want everything thing in the word of God that was meant for my learning. Ministers are taking scriptures tearing pages out saying, this does not pertain to me.

Look at Colossians 2:8 that says, "Beware lest any man spoil you through philosophy and vain deceit, after the traditions of men, after the rudiments of the world and not after Christ." We got to do a Holy Ghost investigation. Celebrating Christmas knowing there is no fat white man coming down your chimney, especially in that wicked neighborhood where you live. Soul Snatching is going on when you celebrate these heathen holidays not holy days. Friendship with the world is an enemy of God. You tell me you are going to hell guilty by association.

The Passover is not about Easter bunnies. Why are you allowing men and women to play with your mind and keep you "Mentally Kidnapped? Why are you playing with yourself still jacking off time with these festivals trying to make them holy. These are heathen holidays not holy days. Satan knows the value of the word of God. We need to have the helmet of salvation and the sword of the spirit at work. Men and women ought to always pray.

No man knows the day or the hour when Jesus will return. The Church is like a runaway child running wild from God. I have not seen any man or woman that I want to go to hell with or for. There are men who will deliberately lie on God and play with your soul just for money sake. It is God's way or no way. Either you are with him or against him. It is heaven or hell. Who's on the Lord's side. The Holy Scriptures contradicts wrong teaching and man's wisdom. This is why you must stay read up. There are traditions of men being passed down and even some preachers don't know that it is wrong.

1 Corinthians 10:15-16, "I speak as to wise men; judge ye what I say. (Vs.16), "The cup of the blessing which we bless, is it not the communion of the blood of Christ? "The bread which we break, is it not the communion of the body of Christ. There is a cup of the Lord and a cup of devils. God is not the author of confusion. Transgender always say they are confused because they are of their father the devil who is the author of confusion. Confusion was put out of heaven. Romans 1:18 says, "For the wrath of God is revealed from heaven

against all ungodliness and unrighteousness of men, who hold the truth in unrighteousness." Evil had a beginning. Ezekiel 28:14-15 this was Satan before he sinned.

Lucifer was in heaven then became Satan and the devil on earth. There was a great transformation in Lucifer to Satan's character by way of his merchandise. Satan distributes his character in rebellious merchandise. Merchandise are goods to be bought or sold. Satan likes to advertise his goods. Look how hard gay men and women work to advertise the lie they are projecting to the public. Men begin to sell their soul. You are of your father the devil. They are children of no understanding.

Children are teaching parents instead of parents teaching the kids. Children singing rap songs that they hear on radio saying I want to be a whore. Little 5 year old girls running around the house telling their moms I want to be a whore mummy! Leviticus 19:29 says, "Do not prostitute thy daughter to cause them to be a whore; lest they fall to whoredom, and the land become full of wickedness." HBO is called the Hell Box Observation. We must be strong and very courageous. Tell them that God is truth and he is their rock to stand on. Satan's devices are in clothing. Some music and TV shows are programing Satan's merchandise.

Ministers need to speak all the words of this life to God's creation and make known the thoughts of their evil hearts with the wisdom of God's word. Satan wanted to change heaven by the multitude of his merchandise. The carnal mind, sin thoughts or feeling designed to change God's truth was put out of heaven. Satan tried to change the truth of God into a lie in heaven and was kicked out like a lightning bolt.

Jesus Christ and same sex marriage don't have nothing in common. With their mouth they shew much love, but their heart goeth after their covetousness. Any merchandise used to change God's truth is the merchandise of Satan. God's word is preached to the wicked and it beats upon them but beat nothing into them.

They are almost ripe for their own ruin. They make jest of the word of God and have made a covenant with death. The wages of sin is death.

Satan is playing hard ball and he is coming to snatch your soul in hell with him where the beast and the false prophet will be. Homosexuals took the rainbow as their mascot symbol that God made as a promise that he would no longer destroy the earth by flood. It will be by fire next time. That's how much they defy God.

Satan made all the heavens unclean. They were dirty in Gods sight. Romans 1:24-25 changed truth of God into lie. Lesbians are in a fallen state. Gay men are in a fallen state. Another spirit takes them over. Even rape and murder is Lucifer's merchandise. When people are down deep in their dungeon of sin their mind and hearts are rearranged.

All unrighteousness was put out of heaven. Lucifer fought for his merchandise. Satan fought here on earth in the Garden of Eden and manipulated mankind and won the right for sin to be excepted and now with help from the Supreme Court and Barack Obama sin is advancing. There was war in heaven. Isaiah 14:12 "How art thou fallen from heaven O Lucifer, son of the morning, Satan is a form of light but his light is not brighter than Gods light. Jehovah is the God whose air you breathe and is the reason why you inhale and exhale.

Satan transforms, or transgender. Satan's spirit is transformed into men and women but not a real man or woman. The word trans is not their real identity and gender because it does not correspond to their birth sex. The change occurred in their mind. He transforms into an angel of light. It is not real light. Satan is the prince of darkness but transforms into an angel of light. Your sins and iniquities have separated between you and your God, and your sins hide God's face from you and he will not hear. Read Isaiah 59:1-21 to see how God feels about sin.

"In 1 John 1:5-6, "This then is the message which we have heard of him, and declare unto you, that God is light, and in him is no darkness at all." God is the true light. Homosexuals say with their mouth and believe in their heart. They believe they are homosexuals. When we confess Jesus Christ as Lord and Savior with our mouth and believe in our heart that God raised Jesus Christ from the dead we are saved.

Everything God has the devil has a counterfeit. Life and death are in the power of the tongue and so is the blessing and the curse.

Satan was called son of the morning. Morning starts with darkness. You start with darkness in the mother's womb. There are those who love darkness because there deeds are evil. John 3:19, "And this is the condemnation, that light has come into the world, and men loved darkness rather that light, because their deeds were evil. Satan comes to steal, kill and to destroy. Satan coveted the rainbow and made a symbol of homosexuality out of it. When Satan fell vain imagination was introduced. Isaiah 5:20 states, "Woe unto them that call evil good, and good evil: that put darkness for light, and light for darkness; that put bitter for sweet, and sweet for bitter."

We must seek the soul of the wicked because God still wish that all should be saved and come to repentance. Isaiah 14:9 is telling us that, "Hell from beneath is moved for thee to meet thee at thy coming: up it stirreth up the dead for thee, even all the chief ones of the earth; it hath raised up from their thrones all the kings of the nations." When the wicked rise a man is hidden because he hides himself from God's law and man's law and that is the police. God also hides himself using your body or temple to hide his spirit in you to work through you.

The wicked love darkness rather than light. They mix God's spirit with all these other spirits. Some suck on cigarettes and whisky bottles and suck on crack pipes and suck on blunts and joints of weed and then men and women suck on each other. We can talk can't we? Shirako is a Japanese delicacy from fish sperm and it is the male equivalent of caviar. All the unknowns that travel in sperm cells that help reproduce could have viruses because not knowing where the person has been and with whom. The mouth is one of the nastiest parts of our body because of the meat that we eat from dead animals.

The Holy Scriptures also talks about our tongue in speech. Who can tame the tongue? James 3:8 says, "But the tongue can no man tame; it is an unruly evil, full of deadly poison." (Vs.9), "Therewith bless we

God, even the Father; and therewith curse we men, which are made after the similitude of God."

Evil communication corrupts good manner. The first place Satan attacks is your mind and he uses his agents to seduce your mind. We must monitor the condition of our heart. (Vs.14), of James 3 says, "But if ye have bitter envying and strife in your hearts, glory not, and lie not against the truth." (Vs.15), "This wisdom descendeth not from above, but is earthly, sensual, devilish." There is nothing more deceitful than your heart.

They don't ask was the cup clean or where was it before you put it in your mouth and who else has been using it? The series Survivor shows where people try to survive by self-consumption like a person in the wilderness with no other food would deteriorate rapidly. People are still worshipping these gods of fertility. They call it sex and the only thing that sex will produce is babies. Taking sex for granted will produce disease like breast cancer.

Our government allowed over 1 million abortions in the 1st ten days of January 2021 throwing babies in the fire. I recommend Sun Flower seeds and vitamins A thru E and then these perverts will stop swallowing the seed of man that God meant for man and woman to be fruitful and multiply and replenish the earth with.

There are many that are not trusting in the Lord but they are trusting in their own heart. They need to know who made them and whose air they are breathing before their abominations provoke him to anger. They do abominations that sacrifice unto devils who does not give you air to breath. Isaiah 2:12 warns us, "For the day of the Lord of host shall be upon every one that is proud and lofty, and upon every one that is lifted up; and he shall be brought low."

Our country has forgot God. Have you forgotten the God that formed you in your mother's womb? Deuteronomy 32:28 "They are a nation void of counsel, neither is there any understanding in them." This is the vine of Sodom poison of dragons and venom of asps. "The man who wandereth out of the way of understanding shall remain in the congregation of the dead" Proverbs 21:16

God is crying out to the world in Deuteronomy 32:39 declaring that, "See now that I, even I, am he, and there is no god with me I kill, and I make alive; I wound, and I heal: neither is there any that can deliver out of my hand." I am not just talking, but I am talking about your life.

Be a strong child of God and fear the Lord, The Lord will rise up and shake and terrify the earth. For the fear of the Lord is coming to all those who has breath in his or her nostrils. Those who declare the sin of Sodom openly gets the reward of evil for their souls. "Therefore hell hath enlarged herself, and opened her mouth without measure; and their glory, and their multitude, and their pomp, and he that rejoiceth, shall descend into it" Isaiah 5:14. All those who are lofty or elevated in character shall be humbled.

Isaiah 5:20 says, "Woe unto them that call evil good, and good evil; that put darkness for light, and light for darkness; that put bitter for sweet, and sweet for bitter! I am not afraid of the new world order neither do I fear their fear. I sanctify the Lord of host himself; and I let him be my fear and my dread. I don't look to the dead or familiar spirits instead I look to a living God. Those who are called wizards and witches, that peep and mutter communicating with the dead but they have no light of God in them.

Hosea 10:12 reminds us to, "Sow to yourselves in righteousness, reap in mercy; break-up your fallow ground: for it is time to seek the Lord, till he come and rain righteousness upon you." You have trusted the lies of your leaders and received the fruit of their lies of drugs, same-sex marriage and abortion. Sin + sin equal sin and more souls burning in hell. Hell has enlarged itself because of wickedness. Let the Lord of Host be your memorial and become sinless.

CHAPTER 20

SATAN'S CLOUD

E vil has exalted itself in the world today and God is offended. Hosea 13:2 says, "And now they sin more and more, and have made them molten images of their silver, and idols according to their own understanding, all of it the work of craftsmen: they say of them, Let the men that sacrifice kiss the calves." (Vs.3), "Therefore they shall be as the morning cloud, and as the early dew that passeth away, as chaff that is driven with the whirlwind out of the floor, and as the smoke out of the chimney."

Our world as we know it is coming into fruition. Sinning yet more and more we see those destined to self-destruct and on their way to hell without Jesus Christ as Lord and Savior. They ignore God and his Word and think there are no consequences after death. They run to the grave at a young age unprepared for Eternal life. This is the life that will be always, never ending and it is longer than this short time that we live on this earth.

Jesus said "Search the scriptures. "Jesus answered and said unto them, "Ye do err, not knowing the scriptures, nor the power of God." There are two churches. There is God's church in Mathew 16:18 and the synagogue of Satan found in Revelation 2:9. Satan is connected with the internal disputes on how one is faithful to Israelites or God's people and how they should live.

People are more dedicated and loyal to a religious organization more than they are to Jehovah our God and His word. Man-made traditions and heathen practices are celebrating heathen holidays and not God's Holy days. Satan twisted the word of God to accomplish his plan in the church. He took God's church and made most them his churches. We must endure hardness to be Christ-like and we must fight with our thoughts and stop compromising with the enemy.

I am speaking about the compromise with Rome or the world. Some churches do not obey the voice of the Lord God and walk in his way but walk in the counsel and the imagination of their evil heart, and are going backwards and not forward in the things of God. The soul business is on the back burner and they are compromising their salvation and are dying going to hell. Jehovah is the God that delivers us and there is no god but him, and there is no Saviour beside him. There is no middle ground but it is either heaven or hell. We only get one shot to live for God and woest me if my soul be wrong after death.

Those who do compromise were not fit to be called God's people because you can't eat from the Lord's and Satan's table too. Joel 3:14 says, "Multitudes, multitudes in the valley of decision: for the day of the Lord is near in the valley of decision." Some get filled with pride and their heart became exalted having an exaggerated opinion of their own importance.

Jeremiah 7:8-10 says, "Behold, ye trust in lying words, that cannot profit, (Vs.9),"Will ye steal, murder, and commit adultery, swear falsely, and burn incense unto Ba-al, and walk after other gods whom ye know not; (Vs.10), "And come and stand before me in this house, which is called by my name, and say, we are delivered to do all these abominations?" Strangers or sinners will not be allowed on God's holy mountain without holiness. God said, "Be ye holy for I am holy." We must first water the earth with the holiness of God's word across the whole earth.

Jesus said he did not come to bring peace but a sword. He said come out from among them and be ye separate. Their Synagogue on the other hand argued that peaceful coexistence with the world or Rome, could it be possible? Two men marrying and two women marrying allowing open rebellion against God is not Jehovah's church. God and homosexuality has nothing in common.

What church are you attending? People want to serve the devil unmolested. "Ye do err, not knowing the scriptures, nor the power of God" Mathew 22:29. God told Jeremiah in chapter 7:28, "But thou shalt say unto them, "This is a nation that obeyeth not the voice of the Lord their God, nor receiveth correction: truth is perished, and is cut off from their mouth."

The children of Judah had set abominations in God's house polluting it and they were committing fornication under every green tree. There was also over 1 million babies aborted in the first ten days of 2021 world-wide and God commanded them not and neither came into his heart. No, the women's movement that goes from country to country pushing same-sex marriage and abortion are not doing God a service. God wanted Adam and Eve to be fruitful and multiply and replenish the earth by spreading Eden across the earth. The final result from having sex is pregnancy and same-sex cannot produce that result.

Everything that God has Satan has a counterfeit. Again I say he has already kidnapped God's grace for all mankind the rainbow and made a flag to represent his aggressive evil force. Churches that wave that flag represent Satan's agenda because Jesus Christ and homosexuality has nothing in common unless they repent and turn from their sins. Christians are the righteousness of God through Christ Jesus, not the Left of God through Christ Jesus.

Some people are begging for the Lord Jesus to return but are they really ready for his return. If we are still breathing God's fresh air we have another opportunity to get it right. I know that I am not without spot or wrinkle. What about you? Our world in its condition plagued by sin is not ready. God is coming back for a church without spot or wrinkle.

Amos 5:18 warns us, "Woe unto you that desire the day of the Lord! to what end is it for you? The day of the Lord is darkness, and not light." If you are disobedient why are you in a hurry for Jesus Christ return and his judgement? God is giving transgressors time or grace to get it right to keep them from that dark day. All the laws being passed by the Supreme Court seem to be exalting itself above the commands of God.

Satan's agents are out in full force and the pride of their heart has deceived them. Pride makes a man or woman exalt themselves therefore I will bring thee down saith the Lord. Satan is proud and he was brought down or abased from heaven to earth. Isaiah 14:13-15 says, "For thou hast said in thine heart, I will ascend into heaven, I will exalt my throne above the stars of God: I will sit also upon the mount of the congregation, in the sides of the north: (Vs.14), I will ascend above the heights of the clouds; I will be like the Most High. (Vs.15), "Yet thou shall be brought down to hell, to the sides of the pit." Therefore God says in Amos 5:24, ""But let judgement run down as waters, and righteousness as a mighty stream."

There is earth where we live and there is heaven where God lives in purity. In the heavenlies is distinct from heaven. God does not need the heaven to exist. He is self-existent and infinite. Heaven is the physical reality beyond the earth and the spiritual reality in which God lives is the heaven above all heavens.

God is the Most High and he is spirit and lives in the heaven above all heavens. John 3:31tells us that, "He that cometh from above is above all: he that is of the earth is earthly, and speaketh of the earth; he that cometh from heaven is above all." Ephesians 4:10 that says, "He that descended is the same also that ascended up far above all heavens, that he might fill all things."

Flesh and blood cannot inherit the kingdom of God. There was a place where Lucifer and his angels were cast when they sinned against God and were thrown out of heaven. Ephesians 2:2 talks about this place. "Wherein in the past ye walked according to the course of this world, according to the prince of the power of the air, the spirit that now worketh in the children of disobedience." Ephesians 6:12, "For we wrestle not against flesh and blood, but against principalities, against powers, against the rulers, against the powers, against the rulers of darkness of this world, against spiritual wickedness in high places."

two miracle workers. God work miracles and so does the devil. Pharaoh also called his wicked sorcerers, and wise men and magicians of Egypt who were not of God and they did the same wonder. They did a lying wonder because Aaron's snake swallowed up all their snakes.

So we can't be impressed when we see miracles with signs and wonders. There aWe should ask ourselves by what power was it done? When Moses and Aaron take the rod and stretch forth thine hand upon the waters, streams, ponds and rivers and it turned to blood, but the workers of iniquity did the same thing. The magicians of Egypt and those who use enchantments today do lying wonders with no fear of God. The anti- Christ will be doing miracles through the activity of Satan who attended with great power all kinds of counterfeit miracles in 2Thessalonians 2:9. The people in authority, millionaires, soothsayers and magicians all workers of iniquity will have to face God at death. God wants obedience and he will tell these miracle workers plainly, I never knew you, depart from me all you workers of iniquity.

Anything that you put before god is Idolatry. It is Idolatry when you worship the good things in life before God. Lust of the flesh and the pride of life come from wealth that seems important giving you

Satan the ruler of this realm is what we refer to as the prince of the power of the air. He is also called the god of this world. Remember he tried to offer Jesus Christ all the kingdoms of this world if he would bow and worship him. He said it has been given to me. Adam and Eve sold out by disobeying God. Today his agents have cloud computers. "Cloud computers storage and computing power without direct active management by the user" (Google Cloud Computers). It is the on demand availability of computer system resources especially data Computers."

"Large clouds often have functions distributed over multiple locations where each location being a data center. Cloud computing relies on sharing of resources to achieve coherence and economy of scales. Pedophiles have also been located using the cloud for their personal use."

When you google "Cloud Computers" it will reveal how "Cloud Providers typically use a pay as you go model which can help in reducing capital expenses, but it may also lead to unexpected operating expenses for unaware users. Paid subscribers can now automatically receive a cloud recording. When you record a meeting and choose "Record" to the cloud, the video, audio, and chat text are recorded in the zoom cloud."

"The recording files can be downloaded to a computer or stream forms a browser. Cloud recording takes more time to make connections, It takes at least 72 hours during the Covid19 pandemic because of high volume" (Google Cloud Computers). Our world determination is to have a quick microwave lifestyle where everything you want and need is at your fingertips. There have been threats recently about destroying the Library of Congress because of these new files.

"The past 25 yrs. research shows that brain processes in music perception, music cognition, and music production can engage and shape non-musical perceptual, cognitive language, and motor functions to effectively restrain the injured brain in neuro-habilitation and neurodevelopment" (Understanding music perception).

Our world has become the valley of slaughter from murders, abortions and confusion in the minds of women and men not knowing why they were born. They now go to their music like Saul when evil spirits entered into him and David played for him. "Understanding music as therapy is a new practice that fire neurons in the brain to help scientist defeat loss of memory."

They still overlook God's word as medicine. Praying in the Holy Spirit brings back to our remembrance. When Joshua was in his seventies and eighties he was strong in the mind ready to go out and lead for war. Staying close to God and putting on the mind of Christ and holding the thoughts feeling and purposes of his heart keeps our mind in focus. Isaiah 55:8-9 says, "For my thoughts are not your thoughts, neither are your ways my ways, saith the Lord." (Vs.9),"For as the heavens are higher than the earth, so are my ways higher than your ways and my thoughts than you your thoughts."

"People with chronic pain sometimes report impaired cognitive function including a deficit of attention, memory, executive planning, and information processing. "There is an adaptive parameter modulation of deep brain stimulation based on improved supervisory algorithm. Supervised learning is the machine learning task of learning a function that maps an input to an output based on example input-output pairs"(Google Cloud Computers). The algorithm of saints should be the great commission." "Repent and be baptized every one of you in the name of Jesus Christ and receive the gift of the Holy Spirit. Keep your mind fixed on the word of God.

Future technology is taking us into controlled studies of the brain. Photo-bio-modulation is the study improving bioenergetics of brain health with red to near infrared light stimulation in the process called photo-bio-modulation. This is a low level laser therapy that is a form of medicine that applies low level lasers or light emitting diodes to the surface of the body. The devil gives us evil thoughts, ideas and suggestions but God know the thoughts of humankind.

The scientist should be interested in finding out why men and women are not a shame or fear God when they commit abominations against him. Scientist should want to find a cure for sin rather than to control ones thoughts. We need to stick to finding a cure for humankind's sins by executing true judgment and shewing mercy and compassion to every man and woman. If not this, then, their plan is an accident just waiting to happen.

God has already given our bodies everything it needed to sustain itself. God has already sent his laws from his spirit in his Word. Sin is bacteria and pollution to your health. Obedience is life and health. We have probiotics that are a combination of living beneficial bacteria and or yeast that naturally live in your body. "Bacteria is generally viewed in a negative light as something that makes you sick. We have two kinds of bacteria in or on us—good bacteria and bad bacteria" (Google Probiotics).

"According to NCBI Probiotics are made of good bacteria that helps keep your body healthy and working well. It fights off bad bacteria when you have too much of it helping you to feel better. We have microbiome or microbes that consist of bacteria, fungi including yeast, virus." Disobedience is when humankind hardens their heart against Jehovah our God. Sin is bacteria that separates us from God and throws us off course from our God ordained destiny.

"When you are sick bad bacteria enters the body and increases in number will knock it out of balance." Sin knocks us out of balances and separates us from God. We fight off evil by binding evil and loosing God's goodness in our lives. Read Mathew 16:19 and Mathew 18:18 for binding and loosing. Good bacteria will fight off the bad and makes you feel better. God's goodness will fight off evil to bring you into a peaceful state of mind.

"Good bacteria supports your immune functions and control inflammation." "Good bacteria help you digest food. "It keeps bad bacteria from getting out of control and making you sick. "They create vitamins and help support the cells that line your gut to prevent bad bacteria that you may consume through food and drink from entering the blood. "Finally it breaks down and absorbs medications. Staying in the presence of God keeps us in safety. Reading, praying in communion in God's presence is the safest place to be.

Things are naturally happening in your body. We are fearfully and wonderfully made. Good bacteria is naturally part of your body when you eat a well-balanced meal or a diet with fiber gives you the right amount of good bacteria the body need to fight off bad bacteria as the word of God helps you fight off sin.

God says in Psalms 107:18-20, "Their soul abhorreth all manner of meat; and they draw near unto the gates of death." (Vs.19), "Then they cry unto the Lord in their troubles, and he saveth them out of their distresses." (Vs.20), "He sent his word, and healed them, and delivered them from their destructions."

Living under Satan's cloud leads to all hurt, harm and danger. We have become guinea pigs to our nation for research and churches are on the money quest. Science is looking for long life but God said in Psalms

91:16 that, "With long life will I satisfy him, and shew my salvation." "Length of days are in his right hand and riches and honor are in his left" Proverb 3:16.

Ephesians 6:3 tell children to "Honor thy father and mother; which is the first commandment with promise; (Vs.3), "That it may be well with thee, and thou mayest live long on the earth." God's wisdom is, "For the merchandise of it is better than the merchandise of silver, and the gain thereof than fine gold." Wisdom extends to you long life in one hand and wealth and promotion in the other. God promised a savior. His name is Jesus Christ.

The anger of the Lord will fall on all those who reject him. You are going to meet him. You are going to meet him as Savoir or you are going to meet him as Judge. One thing for certain and two things for sure and that is you are going to meet him (Jesus Christ). God want to bring you out of your Egypt or sins and knock Satan who is the father of lies off the throne in your life. God said, "And I will strengthen them in the Lord; and they shall walk up and down in his name, saith the Lord" Zechariah 10:12. Go d wish that all should be saved and come to repentance. He wants you to be baptized in the name of Jesus Christ and to ask and tarry for his Holy Spirit.

The Holy Spirit will be your helper when you are in the parenthesis of his grace and mercy. The Holy Spirit will lead and guide you into all truth and where your treasures are when you obey God. You must be willing and obedient. God repented that he had made man and woman with our lying, hardheaded, rebellious, disobedient self.

Well brother Treadwell I don't lie. Look at you. You just lied then. He that is without sin is a lie and is calling God a lie. 1 John 1:10 reveals, "If we say that we have not sinned, we make him a liar, and his word is not in us." We must be grateful and appreciate God's mercy and that is God not giving us what we do deserve. God's grace is God giving us what we don't deserve. We surely don't want God's judgement and that is God giving us what we do deserve.

ABOUT THE AUTHOR

Steven Treadwell is a noted author and a man chosen by God to encourage, uplift and motivate those I came in contact with the unadulterated, uncompromising, unchanging word of God. He was born in Memphis Tenn. Where he graduated from George Washington Carver High. He started to serve God at an early age being baptized at the age of 10. He sung in the choir at church and Jr high school, high school and on to college. He studied Sociology and song the college choir under Omar Robinson the mastro of music for a year and a half at Shelby State now called Southwest Tenn. College. He transferred from Shelby State to Philander Smith in Little Rock Arkansas studying Sociology and singing with choir. Steven Treadwell's mission has always been the motivator the one that provides a reason to do something., always motivating the people. He is the encourager of the brethren sharing courage and confidence. This is when he moved to Los Angeles Ca. and I begin to study the teaching of Fredrick K Price at Crenshaw Christian Center where my revelation to the word of God began. I began to walk by faith and not by sight. I was not afraid of what I saw or heard. I became conscience about what I said. I studied real estate briefly at West Los Angeles in Culver City Ca. I was in the city of angels with a devil's heart and don't take that likely. While working across from CBS on Beverly Blvd and Fairfax, I rubbed shoulders with the stars that gave me a larger than life picture of myself. This florist driver had a great job that kept me on the scene in L A Ca. I left California and moved to Atlanta attending a small business college called Rutledge. I used my outreach to try and save a struggling school, but it was too late. I returned to Memphis after sharing my teaching that I acquired from Crenshaw Christian Center to Atlanta now to Memphis. I studied more and evangelized at Northwest College South haven Mississippi. University of Phoenix, Strayer University and the University of Memphis. I am now writing my second book still providing a reason to do something with courage and confidence.